Riyadh 1/9-81

To Bob and Tania,
with the best of love
for our mutual interest in
this corner of the world,
for happy evenings in the past,
(and the future)?,
and of course the
lovely Red sea around
the "bend"

Yours Gunnar Bennet

RED SEA CORAL REEFS

RED SEA
CORAL REEFS

GUNNAR BEMERT
RUPERT ORMOND

Kegan Paul International
London and Boston

First published in 1981
by Kegan Paul International Ltd
39 Store Street,
London WC1E 7DD and
9 Park Street,
Boston, Mass., 02108, USA

Design by Logos Design

Set in Monophoto Ehrhardt
and printed in Great Britain by
Westerham Press Ltd, Kent

British Library Cataloguing in Publication Data

Bemert, Gunnar

Red Sea coral reefs.
1. Coral reef fauna – Red Sea
I. Title   II. Ormond, Rupert
591.9'2'733   QL137

ISBN 0-7103-0007-7

Contents

TO HELEN,
MAY AND MARGARETA,
AND IN MEMORY OF
SUZANNAH BRONWYN

Preface

THE RED SEA is a distinctive and unique tropical sea, and the only enclosed coral sea in the world.

Since 1975 I have been a professional diver and photographer working on the east coast of the Red Sea. In this book I will share with you some of my impressions obtained during those exciting and fantastic times in Saudi Arabia. For me, diving in the Red Sea, to enjoy its beauty, its colours, its life and struggle, the strange and the well known, the symmetry and harmony, has become part of my life and way of living. Still, after hundreds and hundreds of hours under water, after all I know and all I have seen and experienced, the Red Sea remains an unparalleled source of surprises, entertainment, and beauty.

These are my impressions and images. This is my Red Sea.

GUNNAR BEMERT

Acknowledgments

I would like to acknowledge the help I have received over the years from my various friends. A particularly warm 'thank you' is due to Inge Lennmark for being my teacher and master: my interest in underwater photography started with you. Also to Nils Nordkvist and Hans Pettersson, who instructed me in diving; to Torbjörn Gahmberg for diving with me day and night in the first years; to Anders Hådell for being a continuous source of technical knowledge; to Lars-Gunnar Westfeldt who introduced me to the beauty of the Red Sea and shared many dives there; to Issam and Doreen Sharabati for all the hours of joy and adventure we shared together in the Red Sea; to Bud Reichel, Magnus Hagelstam, Bob Richardson, Tore Dahm, Allan Falk, Brynn Bruijn, Jim and Dolores Ciardelli, Tom Blackerby – all fellow divers.

One cannot miss this opportunity of acknowledging the help received by H.E. Dr Adulaziz H. Al-Sowayyegh, the assistant Deputy Minister of Information, in the Kingdom of Saudi Arabia, whose encouragement added a great deal to accomplish this work.

Additional gratitude goes to Michael Moore and Leslie Lott for their advice, to John Mulholland and Guy Pharaon for their support and kindness, to Cynthia Fetterolf for her encouragement and especially for drafting the first chapter of this book, and to May Loring: without you this book would have been that much more difficult to start and complete.

All the pictures were taken with Nikon cameras and Nikon lenses. Oceanic Products, in California, USA, manufactured the underwater housing for the Nikon camera and four of the underwater strobes. All pictures were taken on Kodachrome and Ektachrome films from Kodak Eastman in Rochester, New York, USA. Poseidon diving equipment of Sweden, was used exclusively throughout all the dives.

GUNNAR BEMERT

During over ten years of diving and scientific research in the Red Sea a great number of people have helped and been of assistance to me. I would like to thank them all, but would particularly like to mention Chris Roads, who introduced me to the wonders of the Red Sea, and my colleagues Andrew Campbell, Rick Moore, Adrian Sanders and Pete Vine, who have been partners in the field and been stimulating co-workers. I should like to acknowledge the financial assistance of the Royal Society, the Overseas Development Administration, the International Union for the Conservation of Nature and the Arab League Educational Cultural and Scientific Organisation. Also I would particularly like to thank the many people of the countries around the Red Sea who have shown me such hospitality during these years, particularly my many friends in the Sudan. I also thank those scientists who from time to time have helped with the identification of Red Sea species, especially Jack Randall, and Michael Mastaller, Greg Brown and Dr L. B. Holthuis. And I should like to thank Margaret Messer for helping with the manuscript, and especially my wife Katie and my family for tolerating my long absences in the Red Sea, or at my desk.

RUPERT ORMOND

Author's note

The photographs are by Gunnar Bemert. Rupert Ormond is responsible for the text. Chapter 1 was written with Cynthia Fetterolf and chapters 8 and 9 with Gunnar Bemert.

1 The Red Sea

RIGHT: 2 The Red Sea, red in the light of the setting sun. By day the fiery sun renders the surrounding lands harsh and inhospitable; but it also warms the sea and provides the light energy in which coral reefs thrive.

The Red Sea runs, a narrow strip of deepest blue, for 1,500 miles between Africa and Arabia. At its head lie the twin gulfs of Suez and Aqaba, while its southern end joins through Bab-el-Mandab, the gate of tears, with the Indian Ocean. On either side lie arid lands, desert and semi-desert, where few animals appear to flourish; but framing the Red Sea, basking in its shallow waters, spread thousands of untouched coral reefs, oases of teeming life, close to the dry and thirsty land. This book is about these reefs, and this chapter about the sea in which they grow.

The Red Sea is of course not really red, but rather many magnificent shades of blue. The name is the same not only in different European languages, but also in Arabic – *El Bahar Ahmer*. But how the Red Sea came to be known as such has long been forgotten. There are various theories: that dust carried out to sea by sandstorms might make the sea look red – but dust quickly sinks; that the name comes from the rosy sunsets – although in fact the sunsets are frequently less spectacular than those in more cloudy parts of the world. It has been suggested the name might arise from the not uncommon occasions when so-called 'red tides' occur. Red tides are phenomena which have been observed throughout most of the tropics. The surface of the sea is scattered with large patches or windrows of a dense orange-red scum; this is usually due to a sudden bloom or outbreak of one of a few species of phytoplankton (microscopic planktonic plants) which contain a reddish pigment. In the Red Sea local or more extensive outbreaks of a planktonic plant called *Oscillatoria erythraeum* may occur for a week or two every few years. However, perhaps the best clue to the most likely explanation for the name of the Red Sea comes from the Arabic name for the neighbouring Mediterranean, which is *El Bahar Abiad*, the White Sea. There are no white tides or white sunsets here, but the coastline from afar often does appear white because of the limestone cliffs along the shore. Similarly, in light scattered through the dust and sand of desert and semi-desert, the coastline of the Red Sea appears cloaked in vermilion and orange.

GEOGRAPHY AND OCEANOGRAPHY

The Red Sea is a spear-shaped body of water reaching a maximum depth of 2,359 metres. It extends for 1,932 kilometres north and south, and at the widest point the distance east and west across its waters is only 306 kilometres. On either side, beyond the shoreline, are desert and semi-desert. In the central and southern parts this forms a well-defined coastal plain, twenty to forty kilometres wide, and known for example in Saudi Arabia as the *tihama*. Beyond this rise rugged and barren mountains, which become higher to the south with massive peaks of over 3,000 metres in both Yemen and Ethiopia.

The sea itself has a narrow coastal shelf zone with a depth of 100–500 metres. Beyond this the sea bed falls rapidly to a main trough at a depth of 600–1,000 metres or more. Within this again is a deeper central or axial trough which is more than twenty kilometres wide, but which reaches depths of 2,000 metres or more. The deepest parts form a series of fairly well-defined hollows or deeps, the best known of which are the Atlantis II deep (2,167 metres) and the Discovery deep (2,190 metres). These deeps have recently aroused considerable interest because the water within them is very warm (up to 55°C), very salty (up to eight times that of normal sea water), and contains very high concentrates of various metals, especially iron and manganese.

The axial trough reappears within the Gulf of Aqaba, which, despite its narrow dimensions, reaches depths of over 1,800 metres. By contrast the Gulf of Suez nowhere exceeds 90 metres in depth. The Red Sea and Gulf of Aqaba are in fact part of a large rift system in the earth's crust which extends north to include the Jordan Valley and the Dead Sea, and south into the East African Rift Valley. The whole rift is now understood to have been formed by the movement apart of two major tectonic plates, those which constitute the African and Arabian continents.

This movement, which is still continuing, is believed to have originated about 70 million years ago. The new basin at first became connected with the Mediterranean, a link which was broken and re-established several times during geological history. Subsequently, about 10 million years ago, the Red Sea became connected with both the Mediterranean and the Indian Ocean. But later, probably during the lowering of sea-level during the ice ages, half a million years ago, the Red Sea became completely isolated again. The Red Sea finally became linked to the Indian Ocean only about 300,000 years ago, and even now this link is not a very secure one, since the water over the sill at Bab-el-Mandab, the southern entrance to

BELOW: 3 The coral gardens of the Red Sea, second to none for colour of coral growth and density of fish life.

the sea, is little more than a hundred metres deep. It seems that during this last isolation of the Red Sea it must have dried up sufficently for the previous fauna to have been destroyed, for the present animals are all of Indian Ocean origin.

The main oceanographical feature of the Red Sea is its high salinity – up to 41 parts per thousand at the north end, compared to 35 parts per thousand in the open oceans. This higher salinity is a consequence both of the hot climate and the absence of any river adding fresh water to the sea. The surface sea temperatures range, according to the time of year, from approximately 20° to 26°C in the northern part, and from 25° to 31°C in the central and southern parts. The temperature gradually falls with increasing depth to about 700 metres, beyond which it is remarkably constant at about 21.5°C; by comparison in other seas the temperature falls to only a few degrees centigrade.

The normal tides are small and occur on a semi-diurnal (twice a day) basis, with the whole sea oscillating around a nodal point approximately at the latitude of Port Sudan. The peak tides, at the northern and southern ends, are of about half a metre, while in the centre there is virtually no daily tide. There are, however, throughout the Red Sea, seasonal variations in water level over a longer period, so that in summer the mean water level in the centre of the Red Sea is nearly a metre lower than it is in winter. In addition the water level at the northern end of the Red Sea is over half a metre lower than it is at the entrance.

These seasonal tides, and the pattern of prevailing winds and currents, are all influenced by the change between summer and winter monsoons in the Indian Ocean. During the summer northerly winds prevail through the whole Red Sea, the main surface current generated by these winds is to the south, and water is driven out of the Red Sea, thus lowering its level. During winter the prevailing winds are still northerly in the northern half, but in the southern part are from the south, and these winds generate a northerly current, thus bringing water back into the Red Sea again. The essential pattern of circulation within the Red Sea is completed by a deeper countercurrent moving in the opposite direction to the surface waters. The seasonal pattern of winds has also had, as we shall see, some impact on the area's history.

HISTORY

The geography of the Red Sea has always been the main feature forcing much of a fateful past upon the peoples whose lands lie along its coasts. For the Red Sea forms both wedge and link between *Jazirat al Arab*, the Arabian Peninsula, and the great African continent whose western shoreline is divided amongst the nations of Egypt, Sudan, Ethiopia, Djibouti and Somalia.

This strategic geographical position has assured the Red Sea of a continuing role in the fortunes and misfortunes of the Middle East, an area which has itself always been both land bridge and barrier between Europe and the Far East. Perhaps no area of earth has been so long or so hotly contested, either in the name of religion, or for a claim to its booty or for control over its trade routes.

In olden days the sailing ships from India and China used to ride the north-eastern monsoons across the Arabian Sea each February, passing via Aden to unload at Jeddah, the designated port of the Holy City of Mecca, and, in even earlier days, at Yanbu, port city of Medina. On the west side of the sea also cargoes from the Orient were unloaded at such ancient ports as Suakin. The almost constant northerly winds at higher latitudes made it difficult for such ships to press closer to the centres of population around the Mediterranean. Then, on a regular schedule, these ships would return to the Indian Ocean in August or September, as weather permitted, often laden with a cargo of Arabian horses or African ivory. The transhipment of goods from the Far East continued by land to the eastern Mediterranean countries or via the Nile to Egypt, and beyond, by sea again, to Europe. The caravans made their arduous overland journeys plagued by bandits, accidents, disease and thirst until the coming of steamships and the building of the Suez Canal dispensed with the need for this kind of travel.

Along with frankincense, myrrh, silk and pepper travelled the books and the lighter baggage of ideas. Travellers brought their science, philosophy, medicine, languages, political and religious thought with them. Even in the pre-Islamic 'Age of Ignorance' the merchants and rulers of the area remained informed of events and innovations in the rest of the world by way of the gossip exchanged in the bazaars and around the campfires of the caravans. The famed hospitality of Arab homes attracted many a weary wanderer with tales to tell for his supper.

Thus it was perhaps no mere chance that at this crossroads of ideas and beliefs the religion of Islam was revealed to and proclaimed by the Prophet Mohamed. Mohamed was born in Mecca, early in the seventh century, and while still an orphaned boy he found work on the caravans, as did many of the Hedjazis in his day. The Meccan idol worshippers, rich and comfortable through their trade and pagan pilgrimages, were not amused when the now forty-year-old Mohamed began to preach, in the name of Allah, the Oneness of God. Thus, in AD 628, he was forced to flee the persecution of his fellow Meccans, and he made his way to Medina: an event which marks the start of the Anno Hegira and the Islamic calendar. At the same time the Prophet sent some of his followers across the Red Sea to seek refuge in the Christian Kingdom of Ethiopia, where other 'People of the Book' received them. In Medina the Prophet built Islam's first mosque, and it was there that God's revelations were collected and organised to become the Holy Book, the Koran.

The first pilgrimage took place in AD 629 when Mohamed and the faithful returned to Mecca and gathered to pray at the Ka'ba, towards which all Muslims turn to say their prescribed prayers. By the time the Prophet died, Islam had become a militant state as well as an established religion, and the succeeding Caliphs carried its banner onwards.

The early Muslim conquests included Byzantium, Persia, Egypt, Iraq and Syria. Naval victories for the Arabs included the occupation of Cyprus in 655. Within a hundred years of the death of the Prophet, the Islamic Empire stretched from Gibraltar to India. Absorbing peoples, cultures and languages, the Muslims translated Greek texts, refined medicine, advanced alchemy, astronomy, mathematics, geography, architecture, law and literature.

After the initial peak of the Arabian-based empire came Crusaders, Mongols and Turkish Ottomans, battling to secure the caravan routes and the Red Sea ports through which passed the trade to the Orient. The fortunes of the Red Sea ports fluctuated with accidents of history. When in 1453 Constantinople first fell to the Turks, this closed the alternative overland route to China, thus handing a monopoly to the Arabs and Egyptians controlling the Red Sea. But within a century the Ottomans had conquered Egypt and the Arabian coast and were themselves promoting the area. Thus, by 1560, half a million pounds of spices were reaching Alexandria via the Red Sea each year.

In the 1600s, however, the development by the Dutch and English of Vasco da Gama's route around the African cape to the Far East spelt disaster for the Red Sea trade. The increasing development in Europe of superior ships and technology initiated the expansion of European control and influence, which brought European galleons to the Red Sea, and eventually colonialism to the African shore. But just as Red Sea trade had so swiftly declined, so it was revived, at a stroke, by the opening, in 1869, of the Suez Canal.

While the political power of the Islamic empire fluctuated and became divided, the spread of Islam seems scarcely to have been checked. The Red Sea, which divides Arabia from Africa, also joins them, and by this route, up until the present day, numerous Arab tribes have migrated to the African continent in search of greener pastures, carrying language and religion with them, and spreading both among the African peoples. Today there are approximately 750 million Muslims spread over the globe. And as once the Red Sea stimulated the birth and spread of Islam, so in later years her waters carried millions of pilgrims on the return journey to the Islamic motherland.

In ages past Western needs were for silk, spices, incense and coffee, and the political and military means necessary to assure a steady supply of these goods. Today the need is for oil, as energy-hungry Western nations look east once more. Huge superships now make the journey to and from Arabia itself, replacing the wooden ships and camel caravans that once plied this

RIGHT: 4 A sand dune encroaching on the semi-desert coastal plain, the *tihama*, of Saudi Arabia.

route with different cargoes. And as the powerful nations manoeuvre for control of this new trade, the Red Sea may find itself still to be of the greatest strategic importance.

RESEARCH AND EXPLORATION

Only at a late stage in its history, of course, did the scientific study of the Red Sea begin, and only now is the knowledge gained being applied to man's benefit. The first attempt at a systematic investigation of the Red Sea's marine life was that of the Danish expedition of 1761–67, led by the extraordinary Peter Forsskål, a pupil of the great biologist Linnaeus. A large part of the fauna of the Red Sea, and thus incidentally of the Indian and Pacific Oceans, was first described and named by Forsskål. But of the six scientists who set out on the expedition, five of them, including Forsskål, died *en route* in Saudi Arabia or Yemen. Thus work in the area was fraught with difficulty, and in the next two hundred years perhaps thirty or so major expeditions or independent explorers carried out serious work here. But in more recent years the development of the surrounding countries and the ease of travel has meant not only that many scientists, from those countries themselves as well as from elsewhere, have been active in research, but also that an increasing number of visitors has been able to experience the pleasures of the Red Sea.

The natural resources of the Red Sea that might have been exploited by man have turned out to be perhaps a little less important than had been hoped. There is within the Red Sea no huge stock of fishes comparable to those which support the major fisheries of the Atlantic or Pacific. There are however moderate numbers of a great variety of fish which in part are already being exploited by local fisherman using traditional gear. The development of this industry depends on the establishment of the necessary infrastructure – roads, refrigerated boats and trucks, and freezer plants – and projects of this type are under way in most of the coastal countries.

The Red Sea also appears to offer significant mineral wealth, for within the deep pools of the central trough the hot salty brines and muds contain huge amounts of extractable concentrates, not only of iron and manganese, but of a range of other metals including zinc, silver, copper and gold. Mining trials have already been undertaken, but unfortunately extraction on an economic scale would lead to the release into the sea of large amounts of sediment and toxic heavy metals, such as cadmium and mercury, and these could well affect the marine life of the area.

But perhaps the main resource of the Red Sea should be seen as the coral reefs themselves. Not only are they proving the most valuable natural laboratory in which to further our understanding of life on earth, but they promise to be a source of great beauty and pleasure for generations to come. Well cared for they may continue to provide such value for thousands of years after the mineral wealth has long been gone.

THE THREAT TO THE REEFS

That such coral reefs as those found in the Red Sea should be conserved goes perhaps without saying. They are places of such beauty and interest, providing such pleasure to those who visit them, that they demand protection in their own right, as might a work of art or a rare jewel. More routinely the value of coral reefs and associated habitats may be listed. They provide an important recreational and touristic resource – even along the parts of the Red Sea where tourism is unlikely to develop it seems certain that in the future, as local living standards rise, large numbers of local people will become interested in snorkelling and diving on the reef, as one of the limited number of recreational facilities available in this area. In addition, coral-reef environments have considerable educational and scientific value. They provide a situation in which much basic biology can readily be illustrated and taught, and they provide a living laboratory in which important insights can be gained into many of the principles which govern life on earth. Also coral reefs and the associated ecosystems, sand-bed, mangrove and sea-grass communities, play a critical role in potential fisheries, particularly as nursery and feeding grounds for open-water fish.

As yet the degradation and destruction of coral reefs and coastal marine habitats has not proceeded to the situation reached in many other parts of the world where thriving coral communities have been vandalised, and inshore fisheries worth billions of dollars, year after year, completely lost. Nevertheless, there are developing threats to the Red Sea's reefs, and it is very much to be hoped that all individuals as well as the relevant authorities will do all they can to minimise many harmful effects.

As yet the impact of industrial pollution and other commercial activities has been comparatively localised, but as development proceeds rapidly, especially along the coast of Saudi Arabia, this threat could become very significant. Reef deterioration from such causes has been most marked near the head of the Gulf of Aqaba where there is considerable pressure to utilise the available coastline. Regular minor spills of oil from one of the ports in the Gulf of Aqaba have effectively invalidated the nearby marine reserve; it seems that the oil reduces the rate of reproduction of the coral and hinders the settlement of new coral colonies. Also, pollution has occurred where mineral phosphates mined inland are loaded on to ships, and a proportion of the phosphates escapes as dust into the sea. The phosphate in the sea acts as a fertiliser as it would on land, and promotes the development of algae which tend to overgrow the coral, for coral reefs are essentially communities adapted to low nutrient conditions.

The disposal of municipal and domestic waste and sewage has a wide impact on reefs in the Red Sea. Many of the towns and villages of the Red Sea have been increasing rapidly in size, and often the waste is piped or dumped directly into the sea. Especially where polluting materials are added directly to the lagoon behind a fringing reef, the semi-enclosed position of the lagoon results in the rapid accumulation of noxious agents there so that the fringing reef may soon be killed. The rapid expansion of residential areas and holiday chalets along the shoreline for many kilometres from the large cities poses a particularly important threat since the problems of sewage disposal into the sea are rarely considered.

In many areas, however, the damage done by visitors, coming to admire the beauty of the reef, is as great as that due to any other factor. Coral collection, spearfishing and shell collection all do considerable harm to the reef community when indulged in by more than the very rare visitor, but now, with various areas being visited by an ever increasing number of people, obvious deterioration is apparent. In some parts of the Red Sea legislation has already been enacted to prohibit these activities, either within marine reserves, or else more generally, and it is hoped that such controls will be introduced throughout most of the region before too long. But, in the end, protection from this sort of menace must depend on the individual self-restraint of visitors. There seems little excuse under present conditions, for example, for the shell collector who avidly collects more than one or two specimens of a particular type of shell. The coral-reef system depends on an efficient recycling of nutrients and materials within it, and removal of more than a limited proportion of this material results in a run-down of the system. Moreover, many of the reef animals, especially the corals, take many years to grow and are not easily replaced; the production of new generations may occur only spasmodically and depend on the presence of a sufficient population of adults. In any case it certainly seems reasonable that where small numbers of corals or shells are taken to be available as souvenirs this should be done by local fishermen, who may thus derive an income, rather than by the temporary visitor who has little stake in the long-term future of the reef. We would urge the visitor seeking some memento of his trip to pursue the more exacting and challenging task of capturing photographs of the living animal.

2 The Coral Gardens

7 The endless and colourful variety of reef life. Here from front to back, a brilliant red sponge, an alga (*Halimeda*), a soft coral (*Xenia*) and the purple branching coral *Pocillopora danae*.

A great variety of animals and plants play key roles in establishing and maintaining the reef community. Besides the corals themselves, the simple plants called algae, the sponges, and a great variety of other invertebrates, as well as fish, are of critical importance (see Plate 7). Without the corals, however, such a diverse habitat could probably not exist at all. The corals and their associated organisms generate much of the food on which the variety of other reef animals depend, and the corals by means of their varied and complex forms provide the wealth of hiding places essential for the sustained survival of most of the other animals. But above all the corals actually build up the reefs and their environment. How they achieve this, and the distribution and detailed form of the reefs thus created, will be the subject of this first chapter of our account of the coral reefs of the Red Sea.

Coral reefs are widely scattered in warm tropical seas around the globe. Their distribution is limited by a number of factors. Corals cannot tolerate a water temperature in winter lower than $18\frac{1}{2}°C$, and on a map of the world all the thriving coral reefs are nicely contained within a line indicating where water temperatures reach this critical point. Also corals are unable to withstand more than minimal amounts of sedimentation; silt and sediment carried in the water and settling on the sea bed clog the mouths and tentacles of the coral and prevent its feeding and breathing. Thus corals do not thrive in shallow sandy seas or where rivers bring much particulate matter into the ocean. Nor are corals able to tolerate much dilution of the sea water in which they live, dilution which occurs near coasts where rivers add large amounts of fresh water to the coastal seas.

In all these respects the Red Sea provides an ideal environment for coral. The sun beats down in the cloudless desert sky warming the sea to a temperature distinctly above that which might normally be expected at such latitudes. In fact the reefs at the north end of the Red Sea are the most northerly fully developed reefs in the world. Despite its narrow shape, the Red Sea is surprisingly deep; thus the amount of sediment derived from the sea bed and suspended in the water is kept to a minimum. And while the almost rainless conditions produce an arid environment on land there is almost no fresh water to run off into the sea, and, save at the actual point where occasional *khors* and *wadis* cross the beach, the sea waters remain undiluted even near the shore.

The suitability of different parts of the tropical seas for coral-reef growth varies considerably. The main coral-reef areas of the world, in addition to the Red Sea, are those lying north-east of Australia and the adjacent islands, the islands of the West Pacific, the East Indies, East Africa and the islands of the Indian Ocean, and the Caribbean.

In comparing the Red Sea coral reefs with those of the other main reef areas a first point that should be made is that there is an important distinction between the coral reefs of the Atlantic and Caribbean, and those occurring in the other areas. Because the tropical waters of the Red Sea, Indian Ocean and Pacific Ocean are continuous with each other, many of the species typical of one of these areas are to be found in the others. This large area which has many species of animals and plants in common is referred to as the Indo-Pacific. By contrast, there is no warm water connection between the Indo-Pacific and the Atlantic, so that there are very few tropical marine organisms which occur in both areas. There are, for example, no corals which occur both in the Caribbean and in the Indo-Pacific, although by contrast there are many species of coral which are to be found both in the Red Sea and on the islands of the Western Pacific Ocean. In addition to this major difference in the species occurring in the two areas, the coral reefs of the Caribbean differ in that many fewer species of coral occur in the Atlantic, and the whole nature of coral-reef areas there is slightly different.

In comparing the Red Sea reefs with those of the other areas of the Indo-Pacific perhaps the most important point to make is that although they do share many species with the reefs of the Indian Ocean, and to a lesser extent with those of the Pacific, each area within the Indo-Pacific does have some species which are unique (technically described as endemic) to that area. However, the tendency to produce endemic or unique species has been particularly great within the Red Sea, no doubt because of its almost enclosed situation, nearly isolated from the rest of the Indian Ocean, and to some extent because of the slightly different environmental conditions of warmer waters and slightly increased salinity which occur there. Thus within the different major groups of animals it has variously been estimated that the proportion of species occurring in the Red Sea which are endemic or unique to that sea ranges between ten and twenty per cent. At the same time, within

particular smaller groups which are either more liable to form new species, or for which scientists have been more inclined to separate off different species, the proportion of endemics may rise as high as fifty per cent. Thus for example among shellfish the well-known cowries (Cypraeidae) and among fishes the butterfly fishes (Chaetodontidae) have both been considered to have over forty per cent of species endemic to the Red Sea and the adjacent part of the Indian Ocean.

At the same time there are in fact somewhat fewer species from most coral-reef-associated animal groups to be found in the Red Sea than in the main areas of the Indo-Pacific. It seems that in general the greatest number of species are to be found in the area of the East Indies, and that moving away from this area there is a tendency to find fewer different species. The reason for this is thought to be primarily geological and evolutionary. Thus, considering the Red Sea in particular, this sea is much younger than is the main part of the Indo-Pacific, ocean water, as mentioned earlier, having had continuous access to the Red Sea basin since only recently in geological time.

This slightly smaller variety of plants and animals occurring within the Red Sea is however in no way apparent as a decrease in the amount of life to be found on the Red Sea's coral reefs. Rather, many of the species which do occur there, occur in much greater abundance, and the view of those who know the Red Sea's coral reefs well is that in terms of the density of life, the thick cover of the reefs with thriving corals and the huge numbers of fish which live above and among them, the coral reefs of the Red Sea may be considered as second to none.

FORMS OF CORAL REEF

Coral reefs vary considerably in the exact form which they may take, both when, as it were, considered in cross-section, and also when viewed in plan from above. The different forms vary in the types of location in which they may be typically found. Charles Darwin, the founder of modern evolutionary biology, was with his ever active mind amongst the first to consider the nature of coral reefs, and he recognised three main classes of reef; *fringing reefs, barrier reefs* and *atolls*. To these three classic types we may perhaps add a fourth, the *patch reef*, in order to provide a very simple classification of the different types of reef.

Fringing reefs occur as elongated structures, fringing a shoreline. They lie parallel with the shore, perhaps as

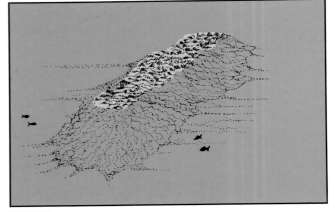

FIGURE 1

little as fifty metres or as much as a kilometre away from the water's edge, and they may extend almost unbroken along many kilometres of coast. In the Red Sea area the fringing reef is the most immediately obvious type of reef to be seen from land (see Plate 9), for fringing reefs extend along most of the Red Sea coastline, except where the coast is interrupted by creeks or bays. *Barrier reefs* are similarly elongated structures, extending more or less parallel with the shore, but lying much further away, from a couple to ten or more kilometres from land. Barrier reefs and their associated complexes are often broken into a series of disjointed sections off particular parts of the coast (see Plate 11). *Atolls* are reefs arising from very deep water, often at great distance from land, and which when viewed from above have a more or less ring-like form; they may be some kilometres across or much smaller. And the term *patch reef* may be used to cover a variety of smallish reefs having the general form of a flat-topped hill. They may be somewhat elongated, and perhaps as much as a kilo-

metre or more across in the greatest direction, but they retain a fairly simple form with all sides sloping away into slightly deeper water. Patch reefs tend to occur where they are extended areas of comparatively shallow sea bed, either close to the coast, or further out to sea.

These four types of reef may serve to enable the non-specialist to impose some classification upon most of the reefs which he may come across, but in fact coral reefs do occur in an almost continuous variety of forms which in reality constitute a multi-dimensional spectrum. The four reef types that we have mentioned may be regarded as the most common forms within this spectrum, but many other forms also occur.

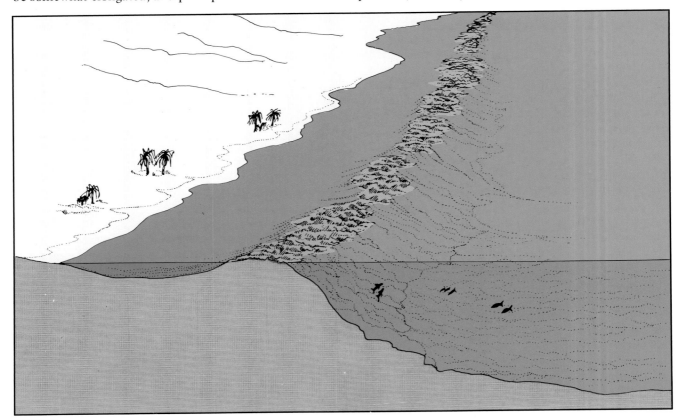

FIGURE 2

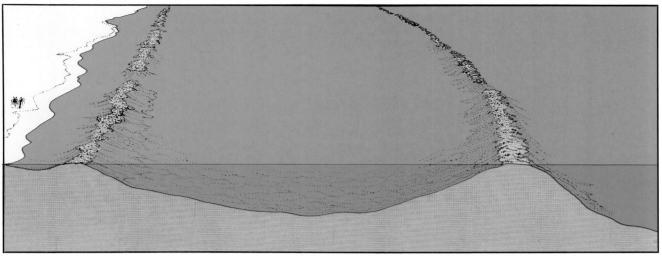

FIGURE 3

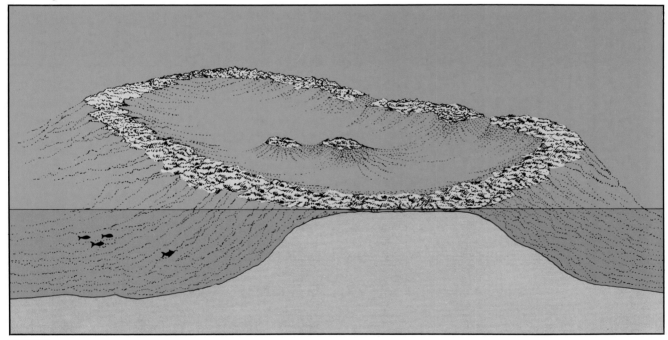

FIGURE 4

THE ORIGIN OF REEFS

Having simply categorised these four most conspicuous reef types, we can now consider in more detail the way in which they develop. It is easiest to begin by considering the development of patch reefs. The development of any new reef can only occur where the sea bed is sufficiently shallow, no more than approximately seventy metres in depth. This is because the reef-building corals, that is those corals with well-developed calcareous skeletons, can only grow in water to which sunlight penetrates, and even in clearest ocean water less than one per cent of light remains unabsorbed by the time depths of about a hundred metres are reached.

Thus let us imagine an extended area of sea bed at a suitable depth of say fifty metres. Provided that the conditions are otherwise appropriate and, for example, that the bottom is not too sandy, corals will gradually colonise the area, settling on exposed areas of rock, or even in time on the open sand. Soon in some places new coral colonies will begin growing on the skeletons of earlier corals, and as this process is continued underwater mounds will be built of the aggregated skeletons of numerous corals.

Here it is useful to distinguish between two general shapes of coral. Some corals form large rounded colonies with solid skeletons – these are termed *massive*

corals. By contrast many other corals develop much more fragile colonies, often with a branching or *arborescent* form. These contrasting forms are well shown among the corals illustrated in Plate 8. Basically it is the massive corals which by growing on top of each other are able to build up the reef, whereas the fragile forms occur as secondary growths upon the reef and their skeletons are subsequently broken down to contribute to the sand.

After the skeleton of a *massive* coral has been deposited, its crystalline form changes and eventually it comes more and more to resemble a type of limestone. Immediately after a coral dies the detailed structure of the skeleton takes the form of the rock of which, on looking under water, the coral reef appears to be built. This rock we may call coral rock.

Where conditions are appropriate the mounds of coral on our underwater scene will continue to grow until they begin to resemble the characteristic patch reef. Clearly when the tip of the mound reaches the water's surface the mound will no longer continue or need to grow upwards, because coral cannot grow out of water and is killed by more than a few hours' exposure to air. The height that a reef will reach is thus limited by the lowest water level occurring for more than a few hours during any sea-level fluctuation, such as may be due to daily tides or to longer-term movements of water. However, while the newly formed reef will not increase in height, the mound will continue to grow outwards, its base gradually expanding over the sea floor, and the area of the top lying near the surface of the water also

gradually increasing. Thus we arrive at the simple form of a flat-topped hill, characteristic of simple patch reefs.

Fringing reefs as explained above extend parallel with and just off the shore along much of the coast of Saudi Arabia and other parts of the Red Sea. As shown in Figure 5, on the seaward side of the fringing reef the reef structure generally drops rapidly away to the sea bed; the top of the fringing reef comes very close to the surface of the water, but between the top of the reef and the shore is an area between fifty and several hundred metres wide where the reef is deeper again and the sea bed often consists of fairly deep sand. This gap between the fringing reef and the shore is known as the *lagoon*. Typically the lagoon is a metre or two deep, but it may be much deeper at its centre or else, as with much of the fringing reef near Jeddah, it may be comparatively shallow.

We can imagine the process by which the fringing reef is formed much as we imagined the development of a patch reef, for while there may be areas of sufficiently shallow sea bed out from the coast, there is always of course such an area stretching down from the shoreline; thus reefs tend to develop parallel to the coast. Accumulation of coral skeletons will proceed at first much as was the case with the development of our patch reef on an underwater plateau. The coral will naturally first reach the surface of the sea comparatively close to the shoreline; but as growth continues, as shown in Figure 5, the reef will grow further and further out to sea until eventually the base of the reef reaches the critical level below which reef-building corals cannot

LEFT: 8 Reef corals may be delicately branched or solid and massive. The massive corals develop to form the bulk of the reef on which branched and other corals may in turn grow. The main corals here are: far upper left and far lower right, the fire coral *Millepora dichotoma*; middle left and middle right, bushes of *Acropora* spp.; centre, three rounded colonies of *Goniastrea pectinata*.

FIGURE 5 Development of a fringing reef. Sequential stages are shown in cross section from top to bottom.

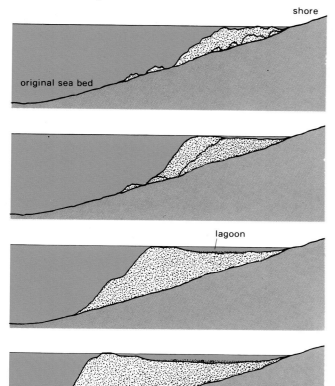

FIGURE 6 Development of a barrier reef. The barrier reef shown in the lower diagram develops from the old fringing reef shown in the upper diagram.

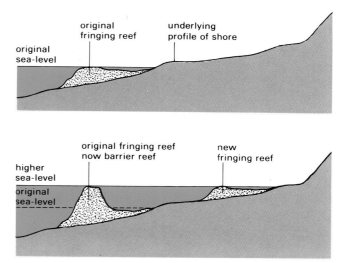

grow. As the base of the reef extends outwards into deeper water, so the top of the reef will also extend outwards, but this has the consequence that the corals nearer the shore will gradually be cut off from the supplies of fresh water which they need in order to thrive. As a result, some way back behind the edge of the reef the corals will tend to die and the coral rock will get broken down to form sand, and in this way we get the development of the lagoon.

In many places, especially where the original sea bed continues to fall gently away, reef growth eventually leads to the development of a very steep outer face. The top edge of the reef will continue to grow upwards until, as it approaches the vertical, or extends outwards beyond the vertical, the rate at which the outgrowing coral is broken off and falls away limits the extension of the reef edge. In other areas, however,

where the conditions for coral growth are not so favourable, and especially where the sea bed slopes only very gradually away from the shore, such cliff-like reefs are not formed. The outer side of the reef may slope only gradually to a comparatively shallow bottom, or the process of reef formation may not even proceed as far as the development of an outer reef edge. In such cases corals may colonise the sea bed sloping away below the shoreline, and may build up a little, but do not give rise to a proper reef. This situation has been called a *coral fringe* (see Plate 9), rather than a fringing reef, and it is the typical situation to be found within the creeks (known locally as *sharm* or *mersa*) which occur regularly along the coastline on both sides of the Red Sea.

The development of barrier reefs and of atolls as originally proposed by Darwin depends on the possibility that after the initial formation of a reef, the levels of the original sea bed and of the surface of the sea might change with respect to each other. Darwin originally proposed that changes in the level of the sea bed were principally involved, but changes in sea-level have also been important in effecting current reef form. Originally the idea that either the level of the sea or of land might change significantly was treated with considerable scepticism, but now there is considerable evidence both that the global level of the sea has altered considerably over geological time, a main factor being the fluctuation in

the size of the ice-caps during the ice ages, and that huge tectonic movements of continents and sea-bed have occurred. Evidence for changes in sea-level can in fact be seen directly in the Red Sea. Along much of the coastline of the Red Sea, from a few metres to a few hundred metres inland, may be found a small cliff or bank where the level of the land rises quickly before extending further from the shore across the relatively flat coastal plain. The top of this cliff or bank lies between five and ten metres above present sea-level, and examination of the front edge of this bank will show that it contains numerous old skeletons of coral intermixed with very old worn and semi-fossilised shells and the remains of other organisms. These banks are in fact the remains of extensive fringing reefs which stretched along the coast, as do the fringing reefs today, but at a time when the sea-level was higher, about 80,000 years ago.

Darwin envisaged the formation of barrier reefs and of atolls as follows. Let us imagine a coastline on which, at a previous geological time, the level of the sea was rather lower than it is today. Along the coastline is a well-developed fringing reef. Let us now imagine that the level of land gradually sinks over some thousands of years to a new level. If the terrain bordering the sea slopes only gently upwards this will mean that, with a new higher sea-level, the coastline is much further inland than was previously the case. However, if the relative change in level occurred sufficiently slowly, new coral growth will have occurred on top of the old fringing reef at a sufficient rate to keep pace with the inundating water. Eventually therefore we would find an elongated reef, parallel with the coast, but at quite some distance from land and growing on top of the old fringing reef. The position of the reef would now correspond to that of a barrier reef, while on the new coastline the development of a new fringing reef could take place, as illustrated in Figure 6.

By considering how change in sea-level might affect the coral reef around an island, rather than those along the coast of a continent, we can see how Darwin envisaged that atoll formation might take place. Given a comparatively round volcanic mountainous island, perhaps a few kilometres across, one might well imagine that a fringing reef would develop around it. If the sea-bed with the island then subsided to a small extent this fringing reef might then give rise to a barrier reef as

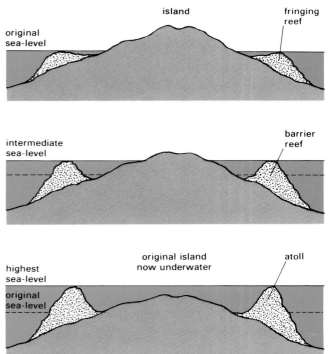

FIGURE 7 Darwin's proposal for the development of an atoll.

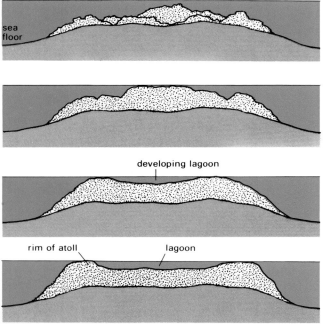

FIGURE 8 An alternative way in which some atolls may have developed. Successive stages are shown from top to bottom.

described above. However, if a tectonic subsidence was sufficiently great, the island itself might be completely covered by water and there would remain only a circular reef, grown up on the foundation of the old fringing reef. Thus arises the classical form of the atoll, with a circle of reef surrounding a deeper centre which is again termed the lagoon (see Figure 7).

Darwin's theory for the development of barrier reefs and atolls generated considerable debate, and even when real evidence began to appear much of it was contradictory. Today, given the benefits of comparatively sophisticated technology, the picture seems somewhat clearer. To cut a comparatively long story short, it should be emphasised that it now seems that while some barrier reefs and some atolls have indeed been formed as the result of processes like those envisaged by Darwin, other barrier reefs and atolls have been formed in different ways.

How then might the typical barrier reef develop without the disappearance of a shoreline behind it, or the typical ring-like atoll form appear without the drowning of an island in the centre? One factor may well be the way in which active reef growth up-current alters the conditions down-current and makes them less favourable for coral growth. Thus large patch reefs often tend to develop sandy areas in their centre where conditions are no longer favourable for much coral growth. It can be seen that on an extended area of shallow sea bed lying well off shore such a reef could expand to a considerable size. Open seawater, approaching the reef from all sides, would maintain active coral growth in a ring around the outside of the reef, whereas within this ring a sandy lagoon would be formed. Thus the reef would have developed into an atoll. Perhaps also, in a somewhat similar way, where water just shallow enough to allow coral growth extends for some way off shore before the sea bed falls more rapidly away into the deep ocean, as for example happens where the edge of the continental shelf stretches out for some way beyond the edge of the land, a barrier-like reef system may develop.

In fact, each of a number of different factors contribute to a greater or lesser extent to the development of the form of any particular reef; the pre-existing topography of the sea bed, changes in sea-level, the presence of fossil or old coral reefs, the direction of prevailing currents, the exposure of the reef to erosion, and the change in the suitability of conditions for coral growth produced by the development of the reef, all affect the pattern of coral reefs present in an area.

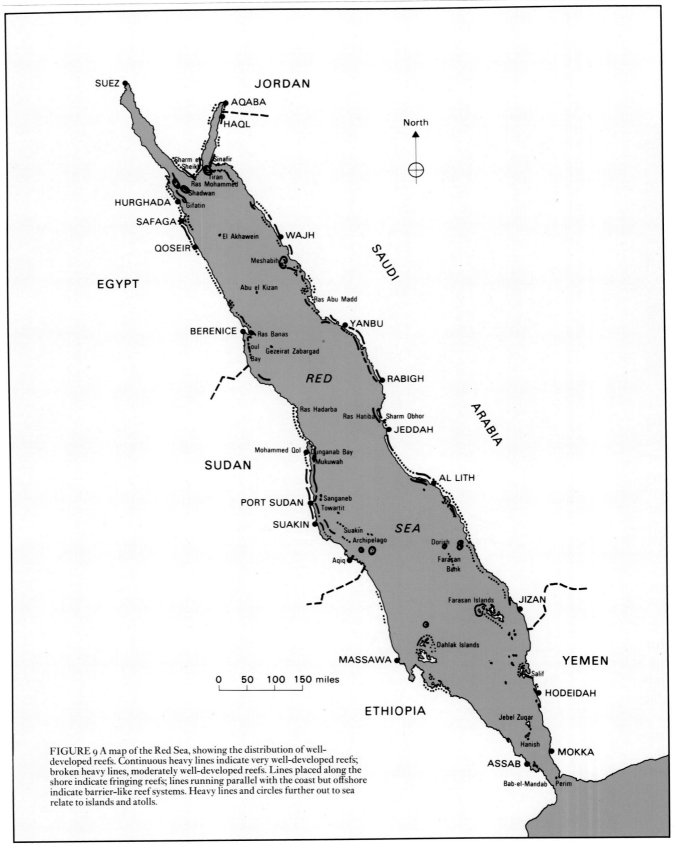

FIGURE 9 A map of the Red Sea, showing the distribution of well-developed reefs. Continuous heavy lines indicate very well-developed reefs; broken heavy lines, moderately well-developed reefs. Lines placed along the shore indicate fringing reefs; lines running parallel with the coast but offshore indicate barrier-like reef systems. Heavy lines and circles further out to sea relate to islands and atolls.

TOP RIGHT: 10 The dense cover of coral typical of the reef edge or reef crest; strong currents bring plenty of food but here the corals are not too exposed to strong wave action. In the foreground, the blue form of *Acropora hemprichi*, and the white *Acropora variabilis*.

CENTRE: 11 Swarms of small, dazzling plankton-feeding fish hover around coral knolls along the reef crest, but dash for crevices among the coral when threatened. Further away, to the left, small green and grey damselfishes, *Chromis caeruleus* and *Chromis ternatensis*. Below the red *Anthias* lies a large soft coral, *Sarcophyton glaucum*.

BOTTOM: 12 The cliff-like reef face may be only a couple of metres high or, as here, drop away out of sight. Corals cling to the reef; note the more rounded coral in the upper right, *Porites*, the most important contributor to the structure of the reef.

THE CORAL REEFS OF THE RED SEA

The description of coral reefs along the coast of Saudi Arabia and in the rest of the Red Sea is of course enormously complex and can only be seen by reference to detailed charts. Some indication of the occurrence of at least some of the well-developed reefs are given in the map (Figure 9), but a simplified account of the occurrence of reefs in the Red Sea area is as follows.

Essentially there is little coral growth either in the Gulf of Suez in the north-west of the Red Sea, or in its extreme south, say south of Massawa, the main port for Ethiopia, or of Hodeida, the main port of Yemen. In these two areas conditions are generally too shallow and sedimentary for luxuriant coral growth. In the coastal waters of most of the rest of the Red Sea, however, well-developed coral reefs are to be found. Off most stretches of shore there are well-established fringing reefs, and these extend into the Gulf of Aqaba past Haql, just about as far as Aqaba and Eilat at the head of the gulf. The fringing reef is broken by the series of creeks which occur on both sides of the Red Sea, (known in Saudi Arabia as a *sharm*, and in Egypt and Sudan as a *mersa*). The development of the fringing reefs is also limited or even suppressed within the small and large shallow bays which occur at various points along the coast, for example in Saudi Arabia in the bay in which Jeddah is situated and the various bays to the north of Yanbu, in Egypt within Foul Bay, or in Sudan within Dunganab Bay and the area of Aqiq.

Off many parts of the Red Sea coast, between a couple and ten or more kilometres from the shore, lies a further system of reefs. This may be typically considered to consist of interrupted sections of an outer barrier reef, behind which are distributed various numbers and patterns of patch reefs. Often there are islands on the line of these barrier reefs, or sometimes lying behind them. Such an arrangement appears to occur at numerous separated points along much of the Saudi Arabian coast, the northern part of the Egyptian coast to the Red Sea proper, and along most of the coast of Sudan. The actual form of these complexes is in fact enormously variable, but, for example, half a dozen or so of such sets of reefs occur off the Saudi Arabian coast between the entrance to the Gulf of Aqaba and Al-Wajh, and a further half a dozen or so such complexes between Al-Wajh and

Yanbu. North-west from Jeddah and opposite the coast to the north of Sharm Obhur, the reefs of Shi'b al Kabir, Abu Faramish and Eliza Shoals form such a complex, although here there is no development comparable to a barrier reef. In Sudan a fairly continuous series of barrier reefs, behind which occur sets of patch reefs, stretch from Muhammad Qol past Port Sudan to Suakin, including the reef areas of Wingate and Towartit to the north-east and south-east of Port Sudan.

These reef complexes basically occur on chains of underwater hills, extending parallel with the shore along much of the coast on a continental shelf type of area. Where these underwater hills are larger, their peaks may rise above sea-level, thus forming the occasional islands already referred to. These reef complexes have not depended for their presence on sea-level changes although their detailed form will obviously have been affected by them. Where an outer barrier reef is present, however, the extent of this may have depended on the upward growth of what were fringing reefs along the outer side of large but now covered islands. At the present time some of the best developed barrier-type reefs in the Red Sea are in part the fringing reefs of such offshore islands, for example that off the island of Mashabih, south west of Al-Wajh (Saudi Arabia) and that off the island of Mukuwah, just south of Dunganab Bay in Sudan.

At a few points in the Red Sea pre-existing shallow areas of sea bed extend much further out to sea, and in these cases extensive groups of shallow underwater hills have given rise to complex archipelagos of reefs and islands. The three most conspicuous of these groups are the Farasan bank and archipelago which stretches along the southernmost quarter of the Saudi Arabian coast, the Dahlak archipelago off Ethiopa, and the Suakin archipelago off the southern part of the Sudanese coast. As can be seen from the map, the Farasan and Dahlak archipelagos contain quite sizeable islands. In addition there are extensive islands and reef complexes where the Red Sea narrows, both at the southern end, and at the northern end at the entrances to the Gulfs of Suez and Aqaba. Thus off the coast of Yemen lie the islands of Jebel Zuqar and Hanish, although as mentioned above coral growth is not very luxuriant in this part of the Red Sea. At the entrance to the Gulf of Aqaba are the islands of Tiran and Sinafir; and at the entrance to the Gulf of Suez lie the group of islands including the island of

Shadwan: both these groups include well-developed coral reefs.

Finally, independently of these island groups occurring on seaward extensions of the continental shelf-like area, there are isolated reefs and islands arising from rather deeper water. The origin of these has not been investigated using modern techniques, but it seems quite likely that they have depended in part upon sea-level changes, and are reefs which have grown up with a rise in sea-level from somewhat lower pre-existing submarine peaks. Such isolated offshore reefs are El Akhawein or the Brothers, over halfway out into the centre of the Red Sea off the coast of Egypt, Abu el Kizan or Daedalus reef, almost exactly halfway between Egypt and Saudi Arabia, and Gezeirat Zabargad or St John's Island somewhat further to the south. Some of the deeper water reefs have developed the typical atoll-like formation, as has for example Sanganeb reef about twenty kilometres offshore to the north-east of Port Sudan. To what extent if any the development of this atoll-like reef has depended upon sea-level changes has not been established.

ZONES AND ANIMAL COMMUNITIES

So far we have considered the gross forms that coral reefs usually take, but the more detailed shape of the reef as one goes across it also tends to have characteristic features. The direct action of the environment and the development of animal and plant communites, as well as others of the factors considered above, often result in the appearance of a series of distinct zones at different depths and positions across the reef.

It is easiest perhaps to describe in detail the zonation on a well-developed Red Sea fringing reef. This is illustrated in Figure 10, from which it can be seen that there are a series of zones, from the shoreline out across the reef into deeper water, each zone running parallel to the shore. The shore itself may be sandy or rocky, and depending on its nature characteristic animals are to be found in the narrow intertidal zone.

Below the shoreline on the fringing reef commonly lies a sandy lagoon. On the shoreward side of the lagoon the water often becomes quite warm and here few if any corals are to be found; rather there is often growth of brown or green algae or of sea grasses in this zone, especially during the spring and early summer months.

BELOW TOP: 13 Brilliant sponges encrust the steep reef face where a pair of pennant fish *Heniochus intermedius* are also sheltering. Beyond, a sandy terrace scattered with coral clumps and mounds.

BELOW BOTTOM: 14 From the bottom of the drop-off the reef slope descends more gradually. Where they meet, caves and overhangs are often formed, bedecked with soft corals and sea fans.

FIGURE 10 Showing the zones and features characteristic of a typical fringing reef.

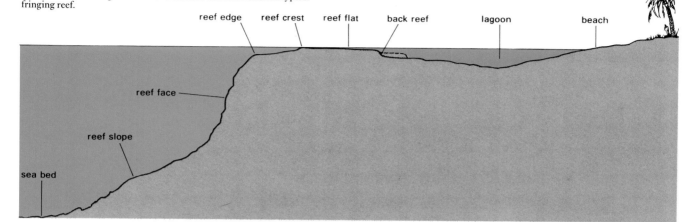

The deeper central part of the lagoon mostly appears to have a bare sandy bottom, and the majority of fish and animals found here are those characteristic of this type of habitat. However, occasional mounds of coral may be found in this zone and often small groups of some of the fish species characteristic of shallow coral areas may be found living here. In particular these coral mounds tend to be based on the growth of large isolated colonies of rounded massive corals, especially the brain coral, *Platygyra* (Plate 28), and the principal reef-building coral, *Porites*. On and around the base of these large massive colonies smaller colonies of branched and other coral may develop, especially where part of the massive coral has died off to expose a patch of coral rock suitable for settlement. The outer side of the lagoon slopes gently upwards again towards the reef proper. This part of the lagoon often has a partly hard bottom of areas of fairly smooth coral rock covered by a fine layer of sand. An increasing number of corals are to be found in this area, for example scattered colonies of two small bushy forms, *Stylophora* (Plate 9) and *Seriatopora*.

On the outer side of the lagoon there may be a distinct step up of perhaps half a metre or so on to the top of the reef. This step may be termed the *back-reef* and an increased variety of corals may be found growing in this area (see Plate 12). While the back-reef may run parallel with the shore in places, it is often highly broken up and dissected with numerous channels running further into the reef from the lagoon, branching and rejoining.

Above and stretching out from the back-reef is a

LEFT: 15 Sharm Obhor, north of Jeddah, a popular recreation area. Along the coast extends a well developed fringing reef, while corals are also scattered in the shallow water along the edge of the *sharm*, forming a coral fringe.

fairly level very shallow area known as the *reef flat*. Depending on the state of the tide this may be almost uncovered by the sea. Some parts of the reef flat may indeed be almost smooth and level, but in other areas there may be accumulations of pieces of rock or coral rubble, and some of the channels from the lagoon extend right into the reef flat while more or less enclosed deeper pools may also occur here. The reef flat is usually too shallow to swim across, but with care can normally be walked over, although this is more easily done wearing a pair of gym shoes or plimsolls rather than in a pair of flippers. Alternatively occasional channels from the lagoon may run right across the top of the reef to the outer side, and on getting to know a particular reef well it may be possible to find a route which can be swum, particularly in winter when the water level is slightly higher. These channels between the lagoon and the open sea are partly kept open as places through which on the falling tide heated and partly deoxygenated lagoon water is drained from the lagoon; this process keeps the channels open, by exposing corals on the sides of the channel to unfavourable conditions.

At some point, often towards the outer side, the reef flat may become particularly shallow, forming the highest point of the reef, known as the *reef crest*. This zone is often too shallow for fish to cross and is often well covered by colonies of the organ-pipe coral, *Tubipora musica*, and by incrustations and nodules of the pink calcareous algae *Porolithon*. Such calcareous algae appear as a thin smooth but almost rock-hard veneer, coloured a coralline or purplish pink, over the surface of rock and rubble. Towards the edge of a patch and when the algae die the skeleton turns white. Such coralline algae play a very important part in the formation of a reef in that by growing over adjacent pieces of substrate and rubble these are bonded together, even after the algae are no longer alive.

Beyond the reef crest lies the *reef edge*; this may be little lower than the crest, or the reef may drop down slightly as it extends outwards before the reef edge is reached. Between these two points (see Plate 13) a rich coral community develops within which are especially abundant the squat bushy coral *Pocillopora danae*, recognisable by its thick warty branches and characteristic pink or purple coloration (Plate 7) and the pale yellow plate-like Fire coral *Millepora platyphylla*. These are both corals which are comparatively well able to

withstand exposure to the wave action which is greatest on this outer edge of the reef, *Pocillopora* by virtue of its thick squat form, and the Fire coral as a result of the orientation of its plate-like fronds which lie parallel to the direction of the oncoming waves.

Dropping away from the reef edge is the *reef face*. Depending on the degree of development of the reef and on the pre-existing submarine topography, the reef face may either be comparatively small, perhaps dropping just a couple of metres onto a sandy sea bed, or alternatively it may drop in cliff-like fashion for up to twenty or more metres (see Plate 12). Such a reef face is often known among divers as a *drop-off*. Also the reef face may end in or be interrupted by a *terrace*, an almost level or sloping step interrupting the fall of the reef.

The upper part of the reef face is generally the zone of greatest coral growth; up to 90 per cent or more of the surface area of the reef may be covered by living coral. Depending on the conditions the coral zone may be dominated by massive banks of *Porites* (see Plate 12), or by a selection of the many species of *Acropora*, fine branching corals such as are shown in Plates 8 and 10; or perhaps under the most ideal circumstances there may be an immense variety of different forms and types of coral, with few species noticeably much more abundant than others. The upper fore-reef is also the zone where fish life is most abundant. In particular the newcomer to the reef is often startled by the swarms of small colourful fishes, each but a few centimetres long, which appear to dance in the sparkling water off the main points and outcrops along the reef edge (see Plate 11).

Where there is a terrace the extent of coral cover on this is much less than on the upper reef face; seventy or more percent of the area of the terrace may be bare rock, dusted in pockets with a thin layer of sand. The coral that does occur is to a large extent often organised into clumps and mounds (see Plate 13); often these groups centre around growths of massive rounded coral upon which further settlements of a few branching corals has taken place. Among the massive mound-building corals species of *Goniastrea* (family Faviidae) (see Plate 8) may be especially noticeable, and here too are most often found the more elegant forms of *Acropora*, open staghorn-like arrangements, umbrella-like structures, and large single-legged tables. Presumably from such coral mounds may grow up the larger knolls and pinnacles which may also be found on a reef terrace or towards the bottom of the fore-reef. These knolls may reach to the surface and develop their own reef-edge communities, and of course may be considered as constituting a stage in the development of a patch reef, some of which may be found where shallow water extends out from the fringing reef. Such large rounded knolls are increasingly becoming known among divers as 'bommies', a term first used in Australia and apparently derived from the Australian aborigine word *bombara*.

Beyond the reef terrace, or at the bottom of the reef face, the terrain often gives way to an area that is gently sloping, at perhaps 20° to 50°, and is known as the *reef slope* (see Plate 14). The terrain may be much more rugged than on the upper parts of the reef, with ridges and cuttings extending downwards and sometimes giving way to small cliffs and amphitheatre-like depressions. Corals of the reef slope tend to be encrusting or plate-like in form, such as *Montipora, Podobacia crustacea* or *Oxypora lacerta*. The fish in this region are generally fewer in number than in shallower waters, but include some species not so often seen there, such as the species of the wrasse *Bodianus* (see Plates 96 and 97). At the same time some of the species most conspicuous in deeper water are also in fact as common around the reef crest, for example the wrasse *Cheilinus fasciatus* (see Plate 98) and the parrotfish *Scarus ferrugineus*.

The zones which are characteristic of the other types of reef, patch reefs, barrier reefs and atolls, can to a large extent be compared with and derived from the zones just described for the fringing reef. Thus the simplest patch reefs can be derived by placing back to back, as it were, two sections of fringing reefs from the reef crest down to the bottom of the reef face. As the patch reef becomes larger, a reef flat and then a lagoon appears. By this stage the difference between windward and leeward sides of the reef may become apparent.

Drawing the above zonation on a much larger scale one can develop the zoning typical of atoll-like reefs. The lagoon area becomes much larger and deeper, with its own recognisable zones, and there may be separate knolls and patch reefs within the lagoon; and on both windward and leeward sides the reef face and reef slope may drop away to considerable depths. In addition, on atolls, especially on the windward sides, may be found a number of extra features or zones which are characteristic of reefs exposed to the swell and wave action of the open ocean. The upper parts of the reef face are characterised by the development of what is known as a *spur and groove system*; that is, along the reef edge and extending downwards for some way are a series of deep gullies, cut back into the reef between an alternating series of outgrowing points. The gullies are eroded and maintained by the wave action which is dissipated within them, while the outgrowing points, in the face of constant supplies of fresh seawater, develop a rich growth of coral. Often the tops of the gullies below the reef edge are extended backwards into caves, and even into blow-holes which emerge on the top of the reef some metres back behind the reef edge. On calm days when the more exposed areas are accessible to diving these caverns and blow-holes provide great fun for the snorkeller or diver. Their roofs are covered by a great variety of brilliantly covered encrusting sponges and other organisms, and within the caves themselves various fish are characteristically seen: groups of brilliantly coloured snappers (such as *Lutjanus kasmira*, Plate 115), and gaterins (*Gaterin gaterinus*, Plate 116) rest here by day; the entrance may often be guarded by a large red soldierfish, *Holocentrus spinifer* (Plate 129) and groups of the smaller red large-eyed squirrelfishes, *Myripristis murdjan* (Plate 128) or transparent cardinal-fishes may cluster in the deeper recesses.

Meanwhile on the most exposed reefs the reef edge itself may be cut back by wave action to form an erosion terrace a few metres below the sea's surface. Such a terrace may be five, ten or more metres across before the reef rises to a set back reef edge. This terrace may be comparatively bare of corals, save for scattered, mal-formed and small colonies of *Pocillopora, Stylophora* and *Millepora*, and the area is instead covered by fine algal lawn and dominated, like parts of the reef flat, by surgeonfishes.

Also, on the most exposed reefs, some way behind the reef crest, may be a distinct rubble or boulder zone. This is formed where wave action has broken off small pieces and even quite sizeable heads of coral from the reef edge area, and carried them back over the reef crest to a point where the wave action dies away. Another feature of the top of exposed oceanic reefs in other parts of the world, the so-called *algal ridge*, is not very apparent on Red Sea reefs. Where it does occur this feature takes the form of a ridge built up along the reef crest, largely by the activity of calcareous algae. The lack

BELOW: 16 A more distant aerial view of Sharm Obhor. Such creeks, thought to have been formed by rivers in a previous much wetter geological period, are common on both sides of the Red Sea. In Saudi Arabia such a creek is known as a *sharm*; in Egypt and Sudan as a *mersa*.

of algal ridge development in the Red Sea probably has to do with the calmer conditions that tend to prevail there, and with the lack of any significant tide. Thus there are always some periods when fishes and sea-urchins are able to graze the algae even on the reef crest, and there is little intertidal zone in which algae, able to tolerate periods of daily exposure to the air, can build up.

Finally, considering the zonation across barrier reefs, we may say that barrier-like reefs in the Red Sea generally resemble deep fringing or even exposed atoll-like reefs on their outside, whereas the landward side shows zonation more characteristic of a small patch reef. There may be an element of shallow lagoon formation, or else the reef flat may lead directly to a small leeward reef face, dropped on to a sea bed that slopes gradually away.

OTHER COASTAL HABITATS OF THE RED SEA

Although this book is primarily about coral reefs, some mention must be made of a few of the other habitats which occur in close association with reefs in the shallow waters and coastal area of the Red Sea. Often these other habitats interdigitate so closely with coral-dominated areas that they cannot fail to be seen by a visitor to the reef. They hardly compare in terms of immediate beauty or interest, but to the biologist or indeed to the interested amateur they are full of fascinating life-forms. In addition some at least have potential economic significance. The characteristic plants and animals to be found in these other areas will not be described separately, but occasional reference will be made in the following chapters on fishes and invertebrates to some such species.

BELOW: 17 Several kilometres offshore, barrier reefs are often found, formed
by coral growth on submarine hills. These may be dangerous to shipping
approaching the coast, as here where a freighter is stranded. The lower half in
the picture shows the top of the reef (the reef flat); this is covered by half a
metre or so of water despite the island-like appearance. White waves are
breaking on the outer edge of the reef which is dissected by gullies and surge
channels characteristic of such exposed situations.

Most closely associated with the reef are often areas
of sandy or soft-bottomed sea bed; indeed, as we have
seen, sandy areas actually develop naturally on many
reefs, and their fauna constitutes part of the fauna of the
coral reef in the broadest sense. To the diver the off-reef
sandy areas may appear to be comparatively bare of life,
but of course many of the animals typical of coastal and
on-reef lagoons are to be found there also, as well as a
great variety of additional species. Many shellfish and
worms occur in the sand, and many fish forage over the
sea bed, although they are often cryptic or do so only at
night. Of particular importance may be the sandy areas
occurring within the coastal bays and creeks. In many
parts of the world such enclosed soft-bottomed areas
have been shown to be important nursery grounds,
where spawning may occur and the young stages grow,
for a variety of fish of commercial importance and for
some of the commercial species of shrimp. The significance of these areas in Saudi Arabia and other parts of
the Red Sea has not been fully established, but it is

clearly important that such areas should be where
possible conserved, rather than invariably used for the
development of ports, commercial centres or residential
or recreational areas.

Another habitat, created by the growth of sea
grasses, may develop on shallow sandy areas. These sea
grasses resemble in general appearance terrestrial grasses
in that they produce sets of narrow upright standing
blades; they are not related to one another, but sea
grasses are nevertheless true flowering plants, and not
seaweeds or algae. A dozen or so species of sea grass
have been recorded from the Red Sea, three of which are
particularly abundant: *Halophila stipulacea*, *Halophila
ovalis* and *Halodule uninervis*. The sea grasses provide a
home for numerous invertebrates and many fish. Some
of these feed directly on the sea grass although most
depend directly or indirectly upon the food made
available when the old blades of sea grass decay. Again
the sea-grass beds provide feeding areas for commercial
shrimps and the young stages of various food fishes.

One rather remarkable animal of considerable interest is sometimes to be found feeding on the grass. This is the Sea-cow or dugong (*Dugon dugon*). The dugong is a mammal somewhat resembling a large seal. However, its flippers are small and it is unable to leave the water, so that as regards its degree of attachment to the sea it lies biologically somewhere between the seals and the dolphins. The dugong, known in Arabic as *arus-el-bahar* or the bride of the sea, are the animals which gave rise to the legend of mermaids. They suckle their young in somewhat human fashion from glands positioned below their flippers. However, they could only attract a sailor who had been at sea for a considerable time, for the face resembles that of an elephant, the eyes being small and the broad snout somewhat elongated. Indeed, elephants are the terrestrial group of animals to which the sea cows are most closely related. The snout is used in feeding to dig up from the sand the roots of sea grasses, which are consumed. The dugong feeds by night, spending the day in deep water, and only coming close to the shore as dusk is falling, generally the only time when these rare and elusive animals are ever seen. Save in a few parts of the world the dugong is very much a threatened animal and in the past it was almost certainly more numerous in the Red Sea than it is today. Nowadays just the odd individual or pair of dugong are very occasionally seen at particular bays or creeks where they may come to feed on the grass beds.

Apart from the grass beds, another habitat may develop in soft-bottomed areas along the shoreline. These are the mangrove areas. Mangrove areas are not well developed in the Red Sea and scarcely deserve the common name of swamps, but intermittently along its length, especially at the back of the bays and creeks, sizeable stands of mangrove trees may be found. The term 'mangrove' covers a variety of trees from a number of different families, all of which are able to grow in shallow or salty water, in some way overcoming the high salinity which to other plants would prove fatal. Two species of mangrove tree generally occur in the Red Sea. The commonest is *Avicennia marina*, easily recognisable by its numerous aerial roots which stick up through the mud around each tree like sets of sharp-tipped spears. Also common, more in the southern part of the Red Sea, is *Rhizophora mucronata*, sometimes referred to as a candelabra mangrove because its roots appear to branch out from its trunk well above the water-level to provide an intricate array of props apparently supporting the tree. The mangrove swamps contain a great variety of invertebrate life, much of it as in the sea-grass beds depending for food upon the old leaves which fall into the water and decay. In this way the mangrove may feed populations of commercial fishes at various stages. In addition the mangroves provide nesting sites for a variety of interesting maritime birds, such as various species of heron and egret.

Finally the islands should be mentioned, which, as described above, often occur on or within reef systems. These islands are interesting places in their own right, but they also provide breeding grounds for animals and birds which are very much part of the marine and even the coral-reef ecosystem. Turtles nest on some of the sandy shores, especially the hawksbill turtle (*Eretmochelys imbricata*) which is an invertebrate feeder, and also the green turtle (*Chelonia mydas*) which feeds on algae. These species are not infrequently to be seen under water, searching for food along the reef face or reef slope. Also nesting on the islands may be found colonies of half a dozen or so species of tern, which may feed on small surface-dwelling species of fish not only at sea but near or over the reef, and odd nests of the fish-eating eagle, the Osprey. This Osprey is the same species which is a rarity in Europe; in the Red Sea it feeds mostly over coral reefs, dropping down to snatch with its talons surgeonfishes and other shallow-water species.

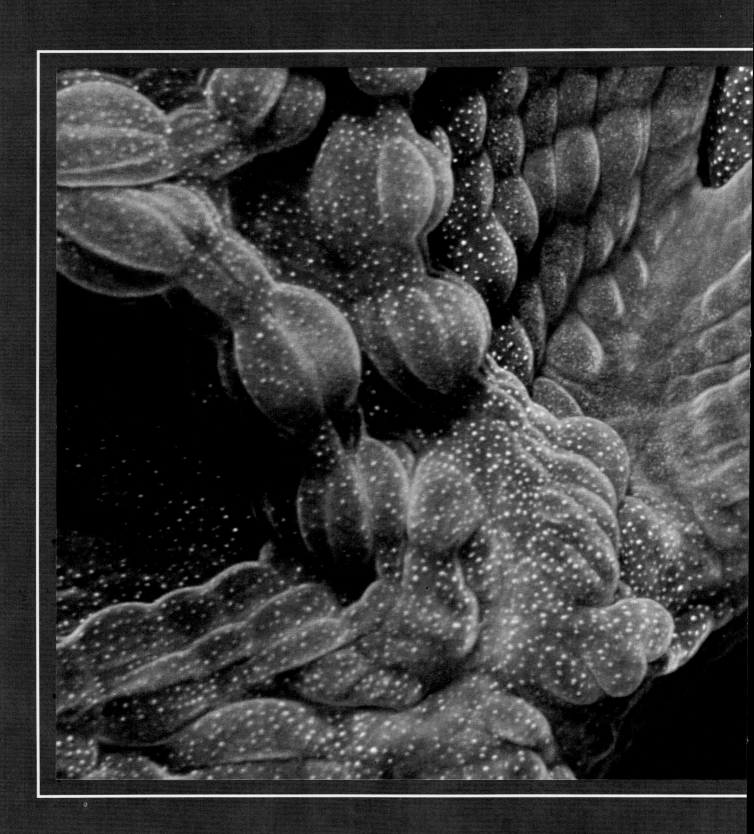

3 The Coral Animal

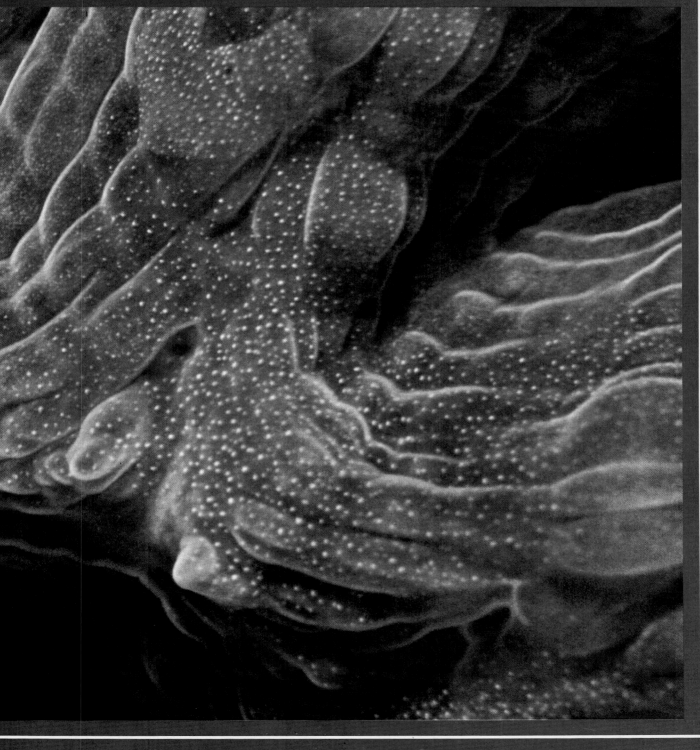

RIGHT: 19 Coral polyps, the anemone-like individual colonies which compose the living tissue of the coral. Each polyp has a cylindrical body surmounted by a ring of tentacles surrounding the mouth. In most hard corals these polyps are small and contracted by day, but they are easily seen in this coral, *Goniopora*.

Corals create coral reefs; but what sort of animals are corals? To the uninitiated this may not be at all clear. To those less familiar with living coral reefs the idea of coral brings to mind the bleached white coral skeletons of different shapes, sculptured branches and domes, to be obtained from tourists' souvenir or aquarium shops, not only in coral areas but throughout much of the world. Sometimes it is not even realised that these are the remains of a living animal; they are thought of as fossils or stones created by the sea as reefs accumulate. And even to the aquarist or the visitor to the reefs, familiar with living coral, the exact nature of the animal may not be really clear, since in most cases the living coral has much the same form as does the dead skeleton, but instead of being white it is coloured in shades of beige or pink, blue, green, mauve or brown. Of an animal there may be no sign.

The shrub-like form of many corals, their lack of movement, and the absence of any apparent animal life certainly confused many early biologists. Until a few hundred years ago writers about such things confidently believed that corals were plants. Even when the animal nature of corals was established, it was uncertain what sort of animals corals were. Sometimes they were referred to as coral insects; perhaps it was thought that corals were built like ant-hills or termite mounds. At other times they were classified with starfishes and the like. But in the last two hundred years or so the true nature of corals has been clearly established. They are in fact close relatives of the sea-anemones, and they fall in the biological group (or phylum) known as the coelenterates, a group within which are also placed, surprising though it may seem at first, the jellyfishes.

Within the coelenterates there are in fact several groups of animals which are called corals in the looser sense of the word, and which are also to be found on coral reefs; thus at an early stage we must distinguish between these. The corals about which we have been talking so far, that is those with sizeable white calcareous skeletons, may be more precisely defined as the hard corals or Scleractinia. There are many different forms and species of these, but all have the white limey skeleton. In addition there are to be found on coral reefs the soft corals, stinging corals, black corals, and sea-fans or gorgonians (sometimes called fan corals). These other types of coral, as well as a variety of other different organisms, form separate groups within the phylum Coelenterata. For the present we shall talk principally about the hard corals (Scleractinia) before coming later to discuss the nature of these other groups.

The hard corals are in fact very closely related to the sea-anemones and may be looked upon as being colonial sea-anemones which secrete a hard calcareous skeleton beneath them. The living part of the coral colony consists of a thin layer of animal tissue composed of numerous tiny anemone-like individuals joined together side to side and covering the surface of the coral skeleton which they have secreted. Each anemone-like member of the colony is known technically as a *polyp*. In many corals these polyps are only apparent on close inspection, but in some, such as *Goniopora* (see Plate 19), they are comparatively obvious.

The structure of such polyps can be seen most clearly by looking at a sea-anemone. The typical sea-anemone, as shown in Figure 11, basically resembles in form an inkwell with a series of tentacles arranged around the top. The sides of the sea-anemone (or inkwell) are known as the *column*, the base as the *foot* or *pedal disc*, and the top part with the mouth in the centre as the *oral disc*. The whole inside of the animal forms a single large stomach or gastric cavity which thus has but a single opening to the outside world, that through the mouth. The stomach is however divided by a series of vertical partitions, or septa, which radiate in from the sides but which do not meet in the middle. There may be a large number of such septa, but in sea-anemones

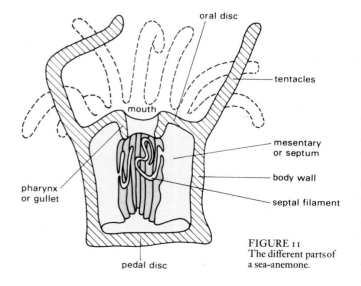

FIGURE 11
The different parts of a sea-anemone.

and hard corals they are commonly arranged to maintain a sixfold symmetry. From the mouth may hang down a short collar of tissue, which thus forms a throat or *pharynx* leading into the stomach. This completes the structure of the animal, which, as can be seen, is basically very simple, the coelenterates being amongst the simplest of multi-celled animals known.

The body wall of the polyp is composed of very few types of cells; there are gland and digestive cells on the inside, and on both sides there are primitive nerve cells and muscle cells. There is also one further important type of cell: the stinging cells or nematocysts. Nematocysts are characteristic of coelenterates and have played an important part in establishing the relationships of the different groups of coelenterates to each other. Each nematocyst consists of a small nematocyst capsule within a larger cell. The capsule is prolonged into a long hollow thread which turns back and is coiled up within the capsule. There may be a variety of barbs arranged along the thread, while the pointed tip may be open or closed. When the stinging cell is activated, either by a mechanical or a chemical stimulus to the outside of the cell, the nematocyst thread is suddenly whipped out through the side of the animal to lash at any predator or food which may be at hand. This shooting out action is achieved quite simply by turning the whole thread inside out in an explosive fashion, driven by hydrostatic pressure maintained in the nematocyst cell. It is the

activation of such nematocysts, filled with irritating poison, which is responsible for the stinging of the human visitor to the reef by fire corals and jellyfish.

Having described the form of the polyp we can now look more closely at the relationship between the coral animal and the skeleton which it secretes. We can do this by imagining first how an individual anemone might secrete such a skeleton. It must be emphasised that the skeleton produced by corals is strictly an external skeleton and not one which is produced within the body as is the case with man and the other advanced animals. Thus in the case of an anemone the cells on the outside of the column and base might secrete the calcium carbonate of which the skeleton is made. This would result, as shown in Figure 12, in a cup-shaped skeleton on and within which the anemone was sitting and into which the anemone could withdraw. To this simple picture we need to add two further features to approach the conditions found in some living corals. Firstly, the top of the outside of the coral grows down over the outside of the skeleton so that the wall of the skeletal cup is in fact secreted by an infolding passing up through the wall of the column. Secondly, much as the outside of the skeletal cup would now support the wall of the polyp, it might be valuable for the skeleton to help support the septa which project in from the wall partially subdividing the stomach. This is done by infoldings of the base which project up in the space between each adjacent pair

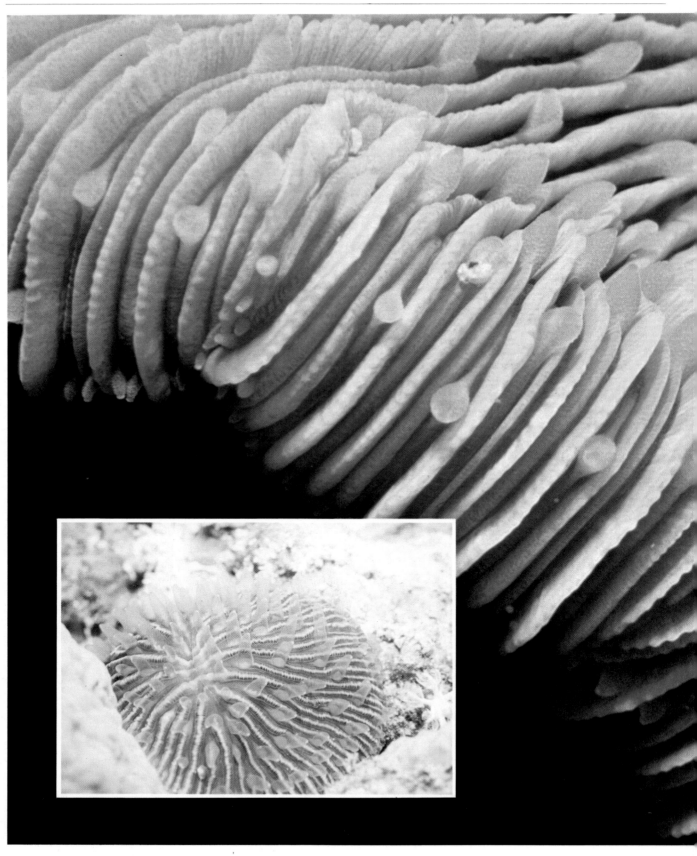

INSET LEFT: 20 The mushroom coral, *Fungia fungites*. This coral consists of a single large polyp with a single central mouth (closed in the picture) surrounded by several series of small tentacles.

LEFT: 21 A close-up of the side of a mushroom coral (*Fungia fungites*), showing the calcareous plates, or septa, which radiate from the mouth.

of septa, and which secrete skeletal partitions which thus keep the septa apart. The complete skeleton thus secreted by a coral polyp is known as a *corallite*, the wall of the skeleton is known as the *theca*, and the skeletal septa are known as *sclerosepta*.

There are in fact some corals which consist in this fashion just of a single anemone-like polyp which has secreted just such a corallite for itself. The main group are the cup corals, one of which, a species of *Balanophyllia*, is illustrated in Plates 22 and 23. Superficially the cup corals look just like anemones, but within foldings in their wall and base is secreted a simple thin skeleton, part of which may be visible, as in Plate 23, on the bottom of the outside of the coral. The cup corals are one form of what are known as ahermatypic corals; these are corals which are true hard corals or *Scleractinia*, but which unlike the better known so-called hermatypic forms, do not produce a sizeable skeleton. Instead the skeleton is only very poorly formed. The ahermatypic corals are found throughout the classification of hard corals, rather than being a separate sub-group, and correlated with their poor skeletal development are several other features. Among these we may mention at this stage that although some species are found on coral reefs, the ahermatypic corals, in contrast to the hermatypic corals, are found in all the world's oceans, and at great depths rather than being limited to shallow waters. The reason for these important differences will become clear later.

While the cup corals possess but a single corallite, there are other ahermatypic corals which are colonial forms and where a number of corallites, developed by branching of the original, together constitute the simple skeleton. On the other hand there are a few hermatypic corals which like the cup corals have a skeleton consisting of a single corallite. The most important of these are various species of *Fungia* or mushroom coral, one of which is shown in Plates 20 and 21. The basic form of such a *Fungia* is essentially similar to that of the cup corals. However, the *Fungia* are much broader and flatter, being typically fifteen or more centimetres across; instead of one circle of tentacles, rows of tentacles are arranged across the broad oral disc, while the mouth is restricted to the very centre, and in Plate 20, where the mouth is closed, it is discernible only as a small depression in the centre of the coral. Also the skeleton is much better developed, accounting for most

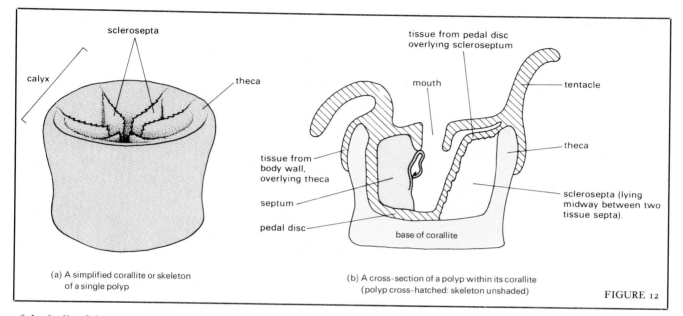

(a) A simplified corallite or skeleton of a single polyp

(b) A cross-section of a polyp within its corallite (polyp cross-hatched: skeleton unshaded)

FIGURE 12

of the bulk of the coral, and there is a very large number of septa, visible as plate-like structures radiating from the centre of the coral. The sclerosepta are shown especially clearly, together with the serrated edges of their tops, in Plate 21, which is a close-up of the rim of the *Fungia* colony. *Fungia* is also an interesting coral in that unlike most other corals, hermatypic or ahermatypic, it is not in the adult form attached to the substrate. Rather the separate corallites are found in suitable areas scattered over the surface of the reef and among the other corals, like a number of fancy biscuits which have been dropped there. The young *Fungias* begin life in an attached form, but only the initial point of attachment remains on the underside of the disc, developing into a thin stalk which is soon broken. The mature form may be moved about by wave action, and apparently has the power to turn itself over should it land upside down, and even to some extent to move short distances under its own steam.

While most typical *Fungias* consist of a single corallite formed by a single polyp, there are some species in which the polyp divides or partially divides to form two or more daughter polyps, and to give rise to a more complex skeleton. For example in *Fungia echinata* the original corallite becomes elongated and several mouths appear end to end within a groove-like depression in the centre of the top of the coral. The great

variety of more normal hermatypic corals are formed in an essentially similar way by the development of colonies of polyps which arranged side by side spread over the surface of the coral skeleton. Thus if one looks closely at the skeleton of a typical coral, such as may be bought from a souvenir shop, it is possible to see that scattered over the surface are numerous small cups or depressions. These may be closely adjacent to one another, giving a honeycomb-like effect, or may be separated widely. Usually each of these cups is slightly smaller than the typical anemone, measuring from perhaps a few millimetres to a centimetre or so across, although in some cases these cups are barely visible as tiny pores a millimetre or so across, while in others they may be several centimetres. In any case these cups are the visible portion of each of the corallites belonging to the polyps of the living colony, and closer examination of each cup will usually show that within it are a series of small radiating plates which are the sclerosepta. Each polyp lives within its own secreted corallite but is connected with its neighbouring polyp by the extension of the tissue which grows out from the top of the column over the top of the theca.

We may now imagine how a rounded coral colony might develop, a process illustrated in Figure 13. The colony would begin life as a single polyp sitting within a single though well developed corallite. The polyp con-

INSET BELOW: 24 Coral tentacles, expanded to feed, surrounded by plankton. In most hard corals there is no noticeable column to the polyp, just a dense set of short tentacles, which are apparent when the animal is feeding, but are otherwise contracted within the skeleton. Although most coral species feed only at night, quite a few do so by day.

BELOW: 25 Close-up of the live bushy coral *Acropora eurystoma*. On branching corals there are usually many polyps on each branch, each within its own small cup-like calyx.

tinues to secrete skeletal material, particularly beneath its pedal disc. However, as the skeleton grows up the polyp itself subdivides into two separate polyps, and the changing structure of the base of these polyps results in the branching of the original corallite so that near the surface of the expanding skeleton there are now two separate corallites. As the process of growth of the colony continues so the polyps further subdivide, and at the same time, as the secreted skeleton grows upwards and outwards, its surface becomes composed of more and more corallites (see Plates 26 and 27). Eventually a large rounded mass is formed over the surface of which are distributed the many corallites, each corresponding to a daughter polyp within the living surface layer of the coral.

Although it is easiest to envisage the formation of a rounded colony of this type, on reflection it can be realised that by modifying the pattern by which one polyp arises from another, and by varying the speed of skeletal disposition beneath the polyps on different parts of the colony, different distribution of polyps and different skeletal forms can be produced. The two most familiar forms are the solid rounded colony (generally termed *massive*) which we have just been considering, and the upright branching form which develops into a small bush-like shape (see Plate 25 and Figure 14).

Alternatively, production of new polyps and growth of the skeleton may occur mostly around the edges of a colony and this results in an expanding mass of coral with an encrusting growth form. If the edges of such an expanding skeleton rise away from the substrate or

FIGURE 13 Showing in a simplified way how a massive coral colony may develop from a single polyp.

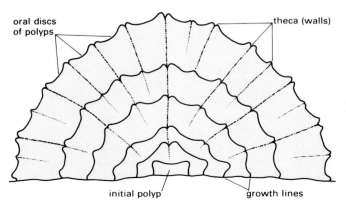

oral discs of polyps   theca (walls)

initial polyp   growth lines

INSET BELOW: 26 Close-up of the surface of a rounded faviid coral (*Favites species*) showing how the calices of the polyps cover the surface.

INSET CENTRE: 27 Close-up of two polyps of the massive coral, *Galaxea fascicularis*. The calices and polyps are moderately large; each calyx appears as a ring of teeth-like septa between which the swollen white-tipped tentacles project.

INSET BELOW: 28 A close-up of the brain coral (*Platygyra*). In the small 'brain' or meandrine corals the calices are elongated to form valleys, each of which houses a series of polyps. The surface of the coral thus resembles the fissured surface of the human brain.

INSET BOTTOM: 29 An encrusting coral, *Turbinaria mesenterina*; the small polyps are scattered over the surface of the coral and have attractive yellow tentacles.

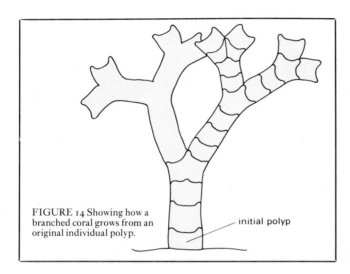

FIGURE 14 Showing how a branched coral grows from an original individual polyp.

initial polyp

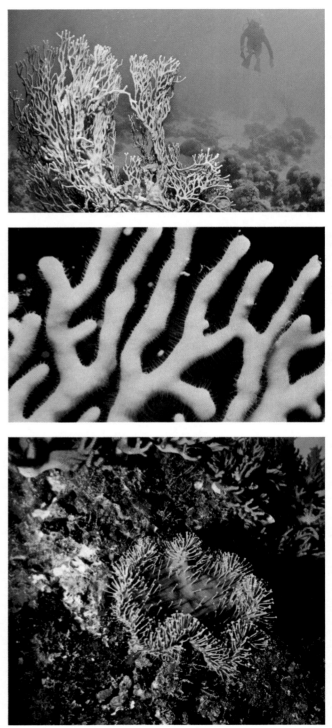

extend beyond it, then a plate-like or shield-like colony results; or encrusting or plate-like colonies may expand to give complex foliar forms, with undulating and interdigitating sheets.

More detailed variation in growth pattern can result in other fairly conspicuous differences in appearance. For example, we have already described the typical semi-massive coral with a honeycomb-like arrangement of small polyps over its surface; such corals include species of *Favia*, *Favites* and *Goniastrea*, all members of the family Faviidae. In some corals of this family, however, longitudinal groups of daughter polyps arise without walls or thecae separating off the adjacent mouths; instead rows of mouths become contained within very elongated calices. In this way are formed the principal group of corals known as brain corals. A coral of this type, *Platygyra*, is shown in Plate 28. Such corals have become known as brain corals because the long sinusoidal valleys thus formed cause the often head-size piece of coral to resemble the human brain with the numerous meandering fissures that wander over its surface. As with other growth forms, the form of such brain corals is not the result of a random process but is thought to be an adaption to dealing with sedimentary conditions. Sand and silt settling on to the coral can be removed by the action of small hair-like cilia, the beating of which carry the sediment along the length of each calyx until it drops away at the edge of the colony.

HOW CORALS FEED

More will be said about the variation in form of corals when we come to consider the difficult problem of coral identification, but first let us turn to consider the question of how corals feed. This is an important question in regard to any animal group. It becomes of particular interest in relation to corals in that their feeding activities are not obvious to the casual observer, and also in that the full details of how they obtain the energy they require for life are somewhat surprising. Basically corals, like sea-anemones, are carnivores in that they feed on small animals which are trapped, often with the aid of tentacles, and passed to the mouth for consumption (see Plate 24). Much of the animal food thus taken is in the form of very small organisms which constitute part of the plankton, but corals only feed on the animals of the plankton (the zooplankton), and they do not make use of the planktonic plants (phytoplankton). However, at the same time corals actually obtain much of their energy requirements through the process of photosynthesis, that is the process whereby energy in the sun's light is used to produce food substances, a process characteristic of all plants, but not achieved by any animal tissues. This they do by virtue of the presence and activity of very large numbers of small individual algal cells, known as *zooxanthellae*, which are present within the cells of the coral, and which live in harmony with them. Such an arrangement whereby two different types of organism live in an association from which both appear to benefit is known as a symbiosis (see chapter 7). In that corals are thus able to obtain part of their food requirements in a fashion characteristic of plants, they resemble plants in a way which would have gratified the ancient writers who believed that this is what corals were.

The symbiotic zooxanthellae benefit from being with the coral tissue in that they thus have direct access to the waste products of the coral. Animal waste pro-

35–42 A miniature fantasy world. Studies of the soft coral *Dendronephthya*, one of the most attractive of its kind, characteristic of steep faces and overhangs. There are eight tentacles on each polyp, and large spikey coloured calcareous spicules embedded in the polyps and body of the coral serve for defence as well as support.

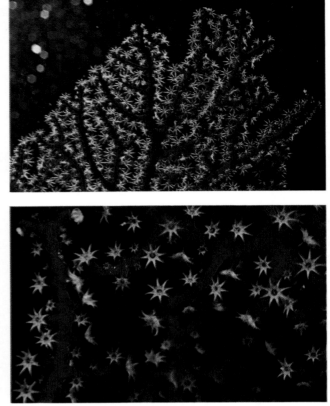

ducts contain elements, especially nitrogen and phosphorus, which of course act as fertilisers for plant growth. But such animal excretions will be widely diluted in the marine environment, whereas by living within the coral cell the zooxanthellae will have ready access to higher concentrations of these nutrients. At the same time the coral itself benefits not only by the energy-rich food it gains from the algae, but because these nutrients, in being re-utilised by the algae, are changed to a form where they may again be used by the coral itself. Thus, in effect, important nutrients like nitrogen and phosphorus are constantly recycled between the coral and the algae, only a very small proportion being lost to the outside environment.

This recycling of nutrients between the coral and their symbiotic algae is the most extreme example of the efficiency with which recycling of nutrients takes place on the coral reef. Coral reefs are in fact communities adapted to living in marine areas characterised by low levels of nutrients. In many if not most natural communities a large proportion of the nutrients excreted by animals is dispersed through the environment and may be lost, only a small proportion being immediately taken up by the community. But corals in particular, and the coral reef community more generally, appear to have developed certain mechanisms, the result of which is that as much as possible of the limited supply of

nutrients is actually retained within the system.

Apart from the supply of food and nutrients, there is yet one further benefit which the presence of zooxanthellae confers upon the corals. It is in fact as a result of the presence of these algae that the hermatypic corals are enabled to form such large skeletons in relation to the limited amount of their tissue. The way in which this works cannot properly be explained without going into details of chemical reactions, but in a more simple way it may be said that the effect probably depends to a large extent on the way in which the algae use up carbon dioxide during the process of photosynthesis. Calcium carbonate, the chemical of which the calcareous skeleton of the coral is made, is comparatively soluble in sea water, and is present in solution in the sea in large amounts. But a principal way in which it dissolves requires the presence of extra carbon dioxide, and thus by reducing the concentration of carbon dioxide within the cells of the coral the zooxanthellae make it much easier for the coral cells to precipitate solid crystallised calcium carbonate out of solution. It can be seen that this process requires both the presence of the zooxanthellae, and high light-levels to enable them to photosynthesise. It is this fact which explains the principal difference between the hermatypic and the ahermatypic corals, introduced in chapter 2.

FAR LEFT TOP/LEFT TOP/FAR LEFT BOTTOM/LEFT BOTTOM/BELOW:
43/44/45/46/47 Studies of sea fans (gorgonians, *Gorgonia* sp.). The sea-fans,
like the soft corals, are octocorals, with eight tentacles on each polyp. The fan
is supported by a central skeleton of a horny-like material, called gorgonin,
and by additional calcareous spicules.

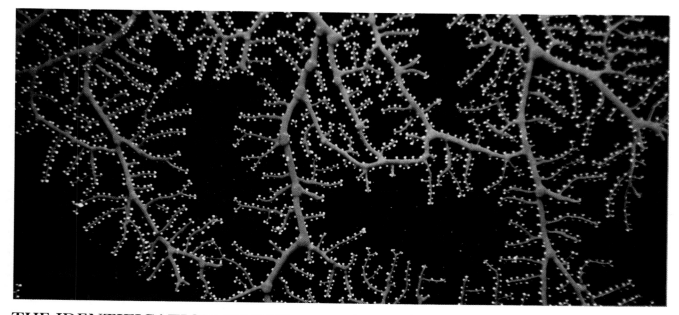

THE IDENTIFICATION OF RED SEA CORALS

Unfortunately, although corals are easy to find and take samples of, their identification is a very difficult subject. Many species of coral vary both in colour and, within limits, in their gross external form; thus a species of coral cannot be identified readily by its general appearance. Instead it is necessary to look at the structure and arrangement of the corallites. In some cases sufficiently detailed examination requires inspection of the skeleton under a low-powered microscope, so that exact identification cannot be achieved in the field. Nevertheless, it is possible to identify a proportion of the corals, at least to the extent of deciding to which genus they belong, especially when their abundance is itself taken into account as a characteristic. Clearly the precise identification of all the Red Sea corals is a subject far beyond the scope of this book, but it does seem worth-while to indicate how some of these commoner corals can be identified, and to enable the reader to do so with the aid of the photographs.

If one considers only the commonest corals, a small regularly branching shrub-like coral is likely to be one of only about four genera: *Acropora*, *Pocillopora*, *Stylophora* or *Seriatopora*. Of the last three genera, there is really only one species of each which is common, whereas there may be as many as a dozen species of *Acropora* that are fairly abundant (see Plates 10 and 189). The four genera can be characterised as follows. Both *Acropora* and *Pocillopora* have branches covered with small warts or knobs, but in the case of *Acropora* each of these knobs corresponds to the calyx of a single polyp (see Plate 25), whereas with *Pocillopora* there are numerous tiny pore-like calyxes scattered over the branches irrespective of the position of the knobs. The common species of *Pocillopora* is *Pocillopora danae*, which is usually pinkish or purplish and is highly characteristic of the reef edge area (see Plate 7). *Stylophora* and *Seriatopora* both have smooth branches; the common species of *Stylophora* is *Stylophora pistillata* (see Plate 19) which has finger-thick branches covered with small pore-like calices, while *Seriatopora histrix* is readily recognisable by its very thin delicate branches, a half centimetre or less across, which end in very fine spiky points.

The common massive corals include *Porites*, *Goniopora* and several genera of the family Faviidae. *Porites* (see Plate 12) grows in very large smooth banks, often metres across, but the calices are very small and pore-like, only a millimetre or two in diameter. There are several species of *Porites* which are very difficult to tell apart. They are characteristically blue-grey or beige in colour. *Goniopora* (Plate 19) is closely related to *Porites*, but has larger polyps, half a centimetre or a little more across, which are unusual in that they may extend a couple of centimetres above the surface of the coral. This gives the colony, which is often a metre or two across and growing as a large lump on a sandyish substrate, the appearance of a soft coral; however, if the polyps are touched they immediately withdraw revealing the hard skeleton beneath. There are several not uncommon species of *Goniopora*, which is sometimes called daisy coral because of the daisy-like appearance of the polyps, but the commonest is *Goniopora planulata*.

The Faviidae are mostly massive or semi-massive corals characterised by calices which typically are from three or four millimetres to a centimetre or more across. These calices may be ring-like in form with slight gaps between, or they may be closely adjacent to each other, perhaps giving a honeycomb-like effect. Of the important genera, *Favia* has largish ring-like calices distinctly separated from each other, *Favites* (see Plate 26) has largish calices closely adjacent to one another, *Goniastrea* (see Plate 8) has medium or small calices closely packed to form a honeycomb-like effect, *Cyphastrea* has small calices each slightly standing out like a pimple and fairly well separated from its neighbour, *Echinopora* has largish separated calices which, however, are very rough and spiky, and *Platygyra* has calices which are elongated to give the brain-like form described above. Other corals which might perhaps be described as being massive or semi-massive are *Galaxea fascicularis*, which has crown-like calices, and a few species of *Montipora*, which like *Porites* have very small pore-like calices, but the surface of the *Montipora* is very rough and covered with nodules or wart-like formations, in contrast to the smooth surface of *Porites*.

Common genera which may include encrusting-like forms include *Montipora, Turbinaria*, and *Hydnophora. Montipora* has very small calices and a rough surface; *Turbinaria*, represented by a single species *Turbinaria mesenterina*, has an undulating surface scattered with individual medium-sized polyps which always have a characteristic yellow-green coloration (see Plate 29); and *Hydnophora*, which falls within the family Faviidae, is characterised by an apparent breakdown of the walls of the calices so that the polyps are only separated by an irregular arrangement of small elongated hills or collines.

Among the common genera which show shield or plate-like forms the following may be mentioned: *Podobacia, Oxypora, Mycedium* and *Pachyseris*. There is one common species of each of these genera. *Podobacia crustacea* develops a circular plate-like form up to thirty centimetres or more across, and generally with a pronounced dip in the centre. The upper surface is covered by a pattern of semi-regularly arranged fine and toothed septa radiating from the centre of the plate, superimposed upon which is a pattern of scattered star-like corallites, at each of which the nearby radiating septa appear to converge and then diverge again before continuing to the margin of the shield; thus there are no walls to the calices. *Podobacia crustacea* usually is of a uniform pale brown colour. *Oxypora lacera* has a similar general form but among other differences is much more colourful; often the oral surfaces of the polyps are orange or red while the intervening background surface of the coral is a pale green.

Mycedium elephantotus is closely allied to *Oxypora* and may also be fairly colourful. It is however much more convoluted in general form with the general appearance of being covered by much coarser spines. The fourth of these shield-like forms, *Pachyseris speciosa*, is readily recognisable on account of the series of well developed parallel ridges which run circumferentially around the plate rather than radially across it. *Pachyseris speciosa* is normally a pale beige in colour, and sometimes develops a more complex form with a series of plate-like forms interlocking and interfolding.

Some corals have more complex irregular foliar forms that are more or less their own. Thus *Pavona decussata* might be described as partly encrusting, partly branching and partly foliar; it throws up small branches which diverge and spread out into complex foliar tips. This and other species of *Pavona* are characterised by numerous small corallites, about three millimetres across, closely adjacent to each other, which however lack walls so that the septa from one corallite are continuous with the septa of one or other of the surrounding corallites.

Finally may be mentioned a few species of coral, colonies of which are composed of very large polyps and corallites. *Lobophyllia costata* has very large calices, five or so centimetres across, which rise up as thick individual branches, occasionally forking and dividing. Another species with similarly large polyps is *Symphyllia nobilis*. This forms semi-massive colonies in which, in contrast to *Lobophyllia*, the adjacent corallites remain fused. Moreover each corallite becomes very lobed and sinuous,

BELOW: 48 A larger type of gorgonian, reaching 2 metres in height.
Characteristically, sea-fans grow on vertical faces at depths of over three
metres, and are orientated broadside across the current passing along the reef.

ISSAM SHARABATI

containing several sister polyps, as may also happen in *Lobophyllia*. Finally may be mentioned an interesting and comparatively unmistakable coral, *Plerogyra sinuosa*. *Plerogyra* forms semi-massive colonies in which single corallites are again often very elongated, meandering and occasionally branched. Between each corallite runs a deep depression, while the corallite wall consists only of thickenings between the bases of tall blade-like septa with rounded tops. The rows of upstanding septa thus arranged in two closely adjacent parallel rows on the opposing sides of each corallite seem to resemble a mouthful of teeth, while the whole colony, when its skeleton is clean, gives the impression of a small jumbled collection of curiously shaped dentures. In life however the coral has very large thick although short tentacles which surround the row of septa, and protrude slightly beyond them.

OTHER TYPES OF CORAL

SOFT CORALS It has already been mentioned that there occur on the reefs, as well as the true or hard corals with their well-developed white calcareous skeletons, several other groups of animals which are also generally known as corals of various sorts. These include the soft corals, stinging corals, the black corals and the sea-fans, each of which constitute a different sub-group of coelenterate.

Of these other types, the soft corals are probably the most conspicuous, and in some places they may even constitute a larger proportion of the organisms covering the substrate of the reef than do the hard corals themselves. The soft corals, constituting the biological group Alcyonacea, are, like the hard corals, colonial animals, each colony being made up of numerous

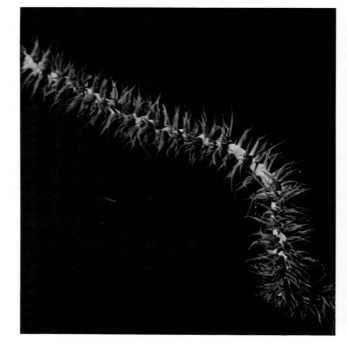

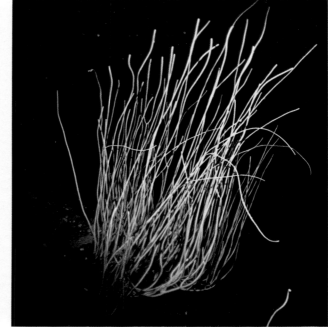

polyps. The soft corals vary in form and shape in some ways much as do the hard corals, forming colonies in some cases perhaps only ten or twenty centimetres across, or in others extending for five or even ten metres (see Plates 32, 33 and 34). The soft corals, however, as their name implies, differ from the hard corals in that the polyps cover the surface of a soft structure, which might be described as being basically fleshy, leathery or rubbery. In general form the colonies may appear thick and squat, almost semi-massive; an enlarged upper part may partly or wholly obscure a less thick stalk or base; or colonies may spread as thick sheets, lobed and ridged on their upper surface, over the substrate; or some species grow almost upright, with thick, tapering and occasionally dividing branches. Whatever its form, the main mass of the colony is made of a gelatinous material derived by enormous expansion of a gelatinous layer within the polyp wall. In the soft coral this gelatinous mass is further supported and strengthened by the presence of numerous small spindle- or rod-shaped spicules embedded there.

There is one other difference between soft corals and hard corals which deserves emphasis in that it is important in the classification and recognition of the different types of coral and anemone-like animals. This is that, as we have already mentioned, hard corals and anemones both generally show sixfold symmetry: their septa and tentacles number either six or a multiple of six. The soft corals and their allies normally show an eightfold symmetry, possessing eight septa and eight tentacles; moreover the tentacles of soft corals, in contrast to those of hard corals, are *pinnate*, possessing a

series of side branches so as to give a feather-like form. The arrangement of these eight pinnate tentacles is clearly shown in the pictures of the soft coral *Dendronephthya*, Plates 36 to 42.

There are about twenty species of soft coral which might be regarded as common on Red Sea coral reefs. The exact identification of some of these still depends on microscopic examination of detailed structure of the spicules, the feature on which their taxonomy was originally based. However it is possible to mention some of the points by which a few of the main genera may be recognised. Amongst the most noticeable soft corals are those of the family Xeniidae, genera *Xenia* (Plates 33 and 34) and *Heteroxenia*. These frequently draw attention because the eight long pinnate tentacles on each large polyp maintain in unison slow rhythmic opening and closing movements. Every couple of seconds or so the tentacles spread wide apart and are then drawn inward again so that their tips touch, the sustained movements almost giving the appearance of hands rhythmically opening and closing.

Another conspicuous group of soft corals is that of the family Nephthiidae, named *Nephthya* and *Dendronephthya*. These are typically upright, branching and plant-like in form with polyps carried scattered along the main stem and clustered towards the end of side branches. Whereas most soft corals are a very dull and drab yellow, brown or grey in colour, species of *Nephthya* and *Dendronephthya* are often semi-translucent and possess subtle shades of pink, purple, orange and red. They are thus often animals of considerable beauty, as is well illustrated in the series of photographs

shown on Plates 35 to 42. The Nephthiidae are also characterised by the presence of some comparatively large and spiny spicules, especially among those which are arranged around the sides of each polyp. These spicules develop a different, often deeper, shade of colour than the surrounding tissue, and they can clearly be seen in the photographs. They frequently project from the tissue, right through the epidermis to the outside of the animal, thus serving to protect as well as to support the animal. Because of their very fine shape, these spicules can become deeply embedded in the skin and cause unpleasant irritation if this type of soft coral is not handled carefully. Typically species of *Nephthya* and *Dendroephthya* are found growing on steep parts of the reef face, or on the sides and roofs of overhangs, caves or gullies, thus contributing to the beauty of these features on the reef. Other common genera of soft corals to be found on Red Sea reefs include *Sarcophyton* (Plate 32), *Lobophyton*, *Litophyton* and *Sinularia*.

SEA-FANS Comparatively closely related to the soft corals are the sea-fans, fan corals, or gorgonians which form the biological group known as Gorgonacea. Like the soft corals, the gorgonians have polyps possessing eight septa and eight feathered tentacles. The polyps of the gorgonians, however, are arranged on a thin, upright, plant-like colony which typically branches profusely, either in one plane to form a feather-like or lattice-like structure (the sea-fans) or in all directions to form a bush-like colony. These elegant structures are supported by virtue of a well developed skeleton which runs as a central axis along each branch of the colony, and is composed of a horn-like protein, known as gorgonin.

The most attractive gorgonians, with fine delicate branches forming large lace-like fans, are members of the family Gorgoniidae, such as the species *Gorgonia*. They are various shades of orange, yellow or red in colour, and especially in close-up form objects of considerable beauty, as shown in Plates 43 to 47. In these photographs the eight pinnate tentacles on each polyp can also be clearly seen. Such gorgonians are most typically found a little way down on steep cliff-like reef faces. They grow at a right angle to the direction of the current which passes along the reef at such sites, thus optimising their ability to trap food particles and absorb nutrients from the sea. In the Red Sea other larger shrub-like gorgonians are generally found at greater depth. It is worth mentioning here that the so-called precious coral, *Corallum rubrum*, which has a pink skeleton of which jewellery and prayer beads may be made, is in fact a gorgonian. However, atypically for a gorgonian, its axial skeleton is almost entirely composed of calcareous material. Precious coral is not found on coral reefs, but on rocky bottoms mainly in the Mediterranean and off Japan.

BLACK CORALS Of the other types of coral which we have previously mentioned, the black corals (forming the biological group Antipatharia) are more closely related to the hard corals, and typically they possess on each polyp six simple tentacles (see Plates 52 and 53). The black corals usually form large shrub-like colonies with very thin slender branches set well apart, as shown in Plate 51.

BELOW: 54 Close-up of the tentacles of a large sea-anemone. The tentacles are equipped with batteries of stinging cells or nematocysts of a variety of different types, some designed for grasping prey, others for injecting poison.

RIGHT: 55 The Berried anemone, *Alicia mirabilis*. The pink warts or berries contain batteries of stinging cells; the tentacles catch plankton at night.

INSET RIGHT: 56 Probably a species of *Cerianthus*. Distinct from true anemones, the cerianthids have two distinct types of tentacle, short ones close around the mouth and long ones outside.

In one group of black corals, however, the polyps are arranged along a single slender unbranched stem which may be a metre and a half long, and are characteristically found projecting out from steeper faces of the reef. The corals, such as *Cirrhipathes anguina* shown on Plates 49 and 50, are perhaps the animals most deserving of the name sea-whips.

Black corals are supported by a central axial skeleton made of a gorgonian-like protein, which however is brown or black in colour, giving rise to the group's name. Especially in Saudi Arabia, the thicker basal parts of the skeleton of the larger species have been used, like that of *Corallum rubrum*, for the manufacture of prayer beads and similar ornaments.

FIRE CORALS The final type of coral to be mentioned is the stinging or fire corals which comprise the biological group Milleporina and all belong to the single genus *Millepora*. As shown in Plates 8 and 30, the stinging corals all have large calcareous skeletons, which generally form upright plates, series of which are arranged parallel to the prevailing direction of surrounding water movement. The plates grow to a metre or more in height so that in general appearance the stinging corals very much resemble the true hard corals, along with which they are often considered. However the stinging corals are only distantly related to the other types of corals which we have so far described. They are most closely related to the small freshwater animals known as hydras and to the colonial forms of these, which are often known as sea-ferns.

In *Millepora* the skeleton actually surrounds the

LEFT: 57 A jellyfish (*Aurelia* sp.) drifting in the surface waters. Jellyfish are very closely related to corals, sea-anemones, and hydroids, some species having both polyp-like and jellyfish-like stages.

INSET LEFT: 58 Swarms of jellyfish concentrated by the current on the windward side of a Red Sea reef. Many of the elongated jellyfish are sea-gooseberries or Ctenophores. The reef crest is dominated by the yellow fire coral, *Millepora dichotoma*.

bulk of the animal, in contrast to the situation occurring in the hard corals where the tissue essentially rests on a large skeleton lying beneath it. To gain access to the surrounding water the polyps can project through individual pores in the surface of the skeleton, while within the skeleton the separate polyps are connected by a network of tissue tubes. The small pores through which the polyps project can be seen on close examination of a piece of fire coral: these pores are in fact different from the calices of hard corals, since they do not possess any sclerosepta and penetrate more deeply into the skeleton. It can also be seen that there are in fact two sizes of pore, and a pattern is apparent of larger pores, each surrounded by five or six smaller pores. Corresponding to this there are in *Millepora* two types of polyp. There are what might be thought of as comparatively normal polyps, which possess a mouth and stomach, but whose tentacles are reduced to a ring of knobs heavily laden with nematocyst batteries; these polyps are termed 'gastrozooids' or stomach animals. Also there are highly modified polyps, which are termed 'dactylozooids', or finger animals, and these are thin and highly elongated (see Plate 31), with no mouth, but with a series of tentacle-like branches each bearing at its end a knob equipped with numerous nematocysts. It is the potent nematocysts carried in the nematocyst batteries which are responsible for the powerful sting of the fire corals.

There are two common species of *Millepora* to be found on Red Sea reefs, *Millepora platyphylla* in which the upright plates are rounded if somewhat irregular in general outline, and *Millepora dichotoma* in which the plates, on becoming so wide, branch, maybe fuse again and branch again, to end in hand- and finger-like projections.

THE CLASSIFICATION OF COELENTERATES

We have mentioned that all the different types of coral are coelenterates, members of the large biological phylum Coelenterata. Having got so far, it may actually clarify the reader's understanding of the differences and similarities between these different groups to provide a simple classification of the coelenterates within which can also be placed some other animal forms to be seen on and around coral reefs.

The coelenterates divide into three main subgroups or classes. The first of these is the *Hydrozoa*, which contains those animals related to the freshwater hydra and the colonial hydroids and sea-ferns. This group includes the fire corals and contains about three thousand known species. The second class, the *Scyphozoa*, contains the large jellyfish, of which about two hundred species are known. Some of these are not uncommon near Red Sea reefs (see Plate 57). The third group, the *Anthozoa*, contains the sea-anemones, hard corals and soft corals and their allies, of which about six thousand species in all are known. The *Anthozoa* are however further subdivided into two important subgroups or subclasses, and it is the first of these, the *Alcyonaria* or *Octocorallia*, which contains all those forms such as the soft corals and gorgonians with an eightfold symmetry, while the second subclass, the *Zoantharia* or *Hexacorallia*, contains those forms with an essentially sixfold symmetry, including the hard corals and the black corals. The Zoantharia also include the sea-anemones, of which there are quite a variety to be found on Red Sea reefs (see Plates 54 to 56), although by far the most conspicuous is the giant anemone *Stoichactis gigas*. Finally may be mentioned the Ctenophores or sea-gooseberries (see Plate 58) which are not true coelenterates but are usually classified in close association with them.

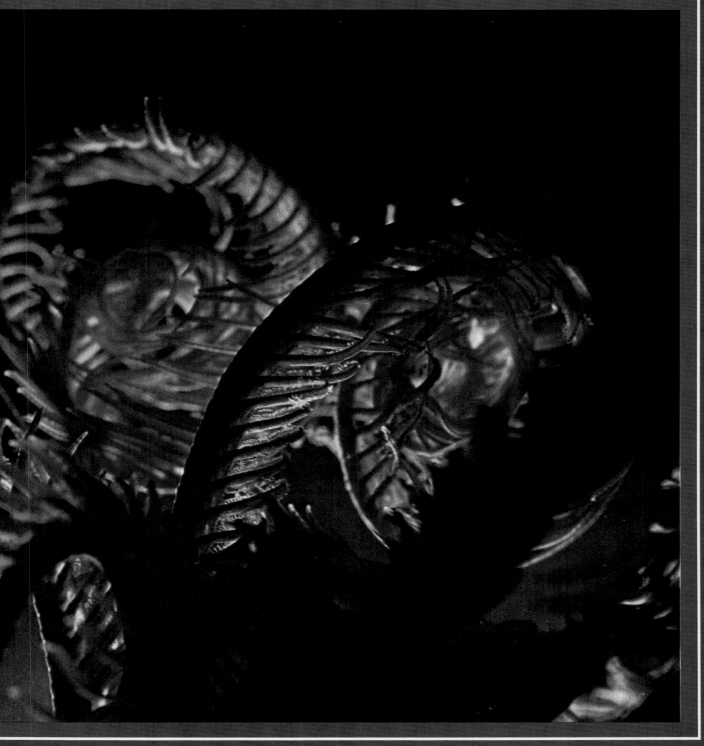

RIGHT: 60 The colourful starfish, *Gomophia aegyptica*; it feeds on sponges.

Having considered the corals and allied coelenterates at some length, in the next two chapters we turn to look at several groups of invertebrate animals (i.e. without backbones), which are conspicuous on Red Sea reefs. The aim is not to give a full list of all the animal types that may be found; still less to give an exhaustive account of the biology of coral reefs. Rather it is intended to discuss four or five of the most noticeable groups in such a way as to indicate how a variety of invertebrates of similar form are able to co-exist on the same reef by different adaptations of behaviour and form; and to point the way to the most likely identifications of many of the commoner Red Sea species. If the reader is able to appreciate how the study of almost any group of animals, ranged in their natural habitat, can with patience and thought become totally fascinating, our main hope will have been realised.

The animal groups that will be discussed in these chapters are the starfishes, sea-urchins and their allies (echinoderms), the crabs and shrimps (crustaceans), the sea-snails, sea-slugs and their allies (molluscs) and the variety of marine worms (especially the polychaetes). One really important group of coral-reef organisms will not however be discussed in detail, and these are the principal plants to be found on the reef, the marine algae. Sadly it must be admitted that however significant their presence on the reef, their lack of behaviour makes them distinctly less interesting to the average reader.

However, we cannot but emphasise the key role they play in the ecology of the reef. As plants, able to photosynthesise, the algae actually produce most of the food on which all the reef animals directly or indirectly feed. We have already mentioned the significant part that zooxanthellae, the symbiotic algae to be found within the corals, play in this respect. But algae occurring independently from the corals are equally productive.

It might seem at first sight that such algae are surprisingly scarce on the reef. This fact was even at one stage a slight puzzle to biologists since many of the commonest reef fishes, such as surgeonfishes and parrot-fishes, are algal grazers. But the most important group of algae on the reef are those which constitute the 'algal turf' or 'algal lawn', the brown-green fuzz that tends to develop on all the bare rocky surfaces of the reef. This is composed of many species of microscopic, blue-green and green filamentous algae. It is this turf on which the herbivorous fish mainly feed. Because they crop the turf as soon as it grows, it is scarcely apparent, but because it grows so fast, it is in fact the major food source for the reef.

In addition to the smaller species of the algal turf, a variety of larger algae also occur on the reef. These may be green, such as *Halimeda*, shown in Plate 7, or brown, such as the fairly well-known *Sargassum*, or the conspicuous *Turbinaria* which has fronds (or leaves) shaped like small inverted pyramids. These larger algae however tend to be common only in the early summer, and even then they are restricted to situations such as very shallow water, or crevices, where grazing fish are generally unable to get at them. These larger species are perhaps rather less important to the ecology of the reef.

Having thus briefly indicated the role of the algae, we begin by discussing that group which contains many of the largest invertebrates to be found on the reef; it is also the group which in fact contains the main invertebrates to graze on the algal turf.

STARFISHES, SEA-URCHINS AND THEIR ALLIES – ECHINODERMS

Starfishes and sea-urchins, together with related forms, constitute the scientific group known as the echinoderms. There are probably less than a hundred species of echinoderm to be found at all readily on Red Sea coral reefs, but because of their generally larger size the echinoderms are often amongst the most noticeable of the invertebrates.

That echinoderms are not more abundant on coral reefs may well have to do with the problems they face in avoiding predation by the large number of fish which also live there. The echinoderms are not capable of great speed of movement or complex behaviour, and thus have used to the full other means of combating this threat. Thus their main feature is their covering of spicules or spines, which gives rise to their scientific name, echinoderm, meaning spiny skin. Often these spines are equipped with poison, or the animal itself is toxic if consumed. The echinoderms are also protected by a skeleton lying beneath the skin and composed of calcareous plates or spicules. In the starfishes these skeletal plates are linked together in a flexible fashion, while in the sea-urchins the plates are actually fused to form a complete shell, known as the *test*. In addition almost all coral-reef echinoderms are nocturnal, hiding

as far as possible by day from the greater numbers of fish which are then active.

Also typical of most echinoderms are the tube feet, and the water vascular system to which they are linked. The tube feet are tentacle-like projections lying in rows along the underside of each arm. In the starfish they have little suction pads at the end and are used for walking. Among the echinoderms the tube feet may however also be concerned with respiration, with feeding, and they may also be modified as sense organs. The water vascular system is a set of water-filled tubes running through the body which in effect works like a small hydraulic system; they connect with the tube feet and by local changes in pressure serve to extend them.

There are five major groups of echinoderms, all of which are evident on Red Sea coral reefs. Starfishes (Asteroidea) and sea-urchins (Echinoidea) are well known. The brittle-stars (Ophiuroidea) are like small starfish except that the arms are of a uniform diameter and project from a clearly defined central disc. The sea-cucumbers (Holothuroidea) are largish sausage-shaped animals. And the feather-stars (Crinoidea) again have a similarity to starfishes except that the many arms are branched, giving the appearance of feathers, and the central disc is very small. Despite this variation these different forms can, as basic biology teaches us, be derived with a little juggling one from another, much as the polyp and jellyfish forms of coelenterates can be related to each other. Thus sea-urchins can be derived from starfish by bending up the five arms to meet each other at the top and fusing the resulting shell; and sea-cucumbers can in turn be derived from sea-urchins by elongating the sea-urchin from top to bottom and then lying the resultant animal down on one side. The mouth of both starfishes and sea-urchins is situated on the underside, and the anus, through which the digested

remains are voided, is on top; while the sea-cucumber has a mouth one end and an anus the other. Brittle-stars and feather-stars are more clearly related to starfishes, save that the feather-stars are normally active in the inverted position with their mouth uppermost.

STARFISHES – ASTEROIDS

There are about half a dozen fairly common starfishes to be found on Red Sea coral reefs. Like most starfishes they are basically predators, and they are able to feed by pushing the stomach out through the mouth, turning it as it were inside out to do so, and spreading it over some suitable food. Digestive enzymes are released and the products of digestion absorbed in situ before the stomach is retracted back in through the mouth and the starfish moves off. Probably the commonest of the Red Sea starfishes is the small *Fromia ghardaqana* which is a classic biscuit-like starfish shape, about five centimetres across and red with a network of small white patches. *Fromia* feeds on small encrusting sponges as probably does another common species *Gomophia aegyptica*, and both are often to be found in this situation, sitting on semi-vertical sponge-encrusted rock faces. *Gomophia* is shown in Plate 60 and it too is patterned red and white, although it is somewhat larger, about twelve centimetres across. It is possible that both these starfish are able to absorb toxic material from the sponges which they eat, and that this red and white coloration is a warning pattern advising potential predators of the danger.

Another abundant species of starfish, although one which is much less conspicuous because of its cryptic coloration and its general occurrence while hidden among coral rubble is *Linkia multiflora*. This starfish is about five centimetres in diameter and has hardly any central disc but five or so tube-like arms which are greyish-green in colour with a camouflaging mottled pattern of dark brown or sometimes fawn. The arms of this species are often of very unequal length, a fact which reflects the ease with which parts may be broken off. However, this species also has considerable powers of regeneration so that not only can the main part of the starfish regenerate a lost arm, as happens with many species, but also broken off arms can regrow the parts of the body which they miss. When this happens the new individual passes through a stage where one large arm has four or so tiny arms growing from its basal end, thus giving a so-called comet form.

THE CROWN-OF-THORNS STARFISH

The best known coral-reef starfish must be the now notorious Crown-of-thorns, *Acanthaster planci*, plagues of which during the late 1960s and early 1970s destroyed many coral areas on the Great Barrier Reef of Australia. The starfish itself, which is shown in Plates 61 and 62, grows up to thirty centimetres or more in diameter and has typically between twelve and twenty arms. It is covered in shortish stout spines which are surprisingly sharp at the tip. From any distance the body usually appears to be a shade of brown although this colour is in fact that of numerous small hair-like extensions projecting from the skin, the *papullae*, which are organs of respiration and are withdrawn if the animal is touched or disturbed. The underlying colour of the body and of the arms varies between a light grey-green to a dark grey-blue.

The Crown-of-thorns actually feeds on coral by climbing on to a suitable colony and inverting its stomach beneath its body over the surface of the coral. Digestive juices are secreted and digested coral material then absorbed before the stomach is retracted and the starfish moves away. The starfish is thus in fact able to circumvent the protective skeleton of the coral in a way which has been achieved by no other animal, for fish must either be prepared to take in a great deal of calcareous skeleton along with any material of nutritional value, as do some parrotfishes and triggerfishes for example, or must try to catch and pick at individual polyps when they are expanded, as do many butterfly fishes. The result of the starfishes' feeding is to leave a large white patch of skeleton conspicuous against the normal fawn, grey or blue coloration of the living coral. *Acanthaster* can in fact be more readily tracked down by watching for groups of these white patches, where an individual animal has been feeding, than by looking for the starfish itself, since the animal is active principally by night, while by day it generally hides in crevices within the reef.

The destruction of Australian reefs was due to the activity of hundreds of thousands of these starfish gathered together in immense concentrations which worked their way across many of the individual reefs of which the Great Barrier Reef is composed. By 1972 or 1973 considerable damage had been done to many of the reefs over a central section between Cairns and Towns-ville; some surviving herds of subsequent generations of the starfish worked their way much further south, but in

BELOW: 63 The needle-spined sea-urchin *Diadema setosum*; after sheltering by day it emerges at night to scrape algal strands off the coral rock. The conspicuous pink structure on top is not an eye, but the back end of the digestive system.

fact in the last few years only the occasional dense population has been reported, and the population explosion of this animal in that area appears largely to have died out.

Shortly after the Australian plagues had become well known, other plagues of *Acanthaster* were reported from reefs scattered widely across the Pacific and into the Indian Ocean. A few areas, such as the island of Guam, were indeed seriously damaged, but on the whole it is now clear that most of these reports were of much smaller aggregations of a few hundred or a couple of thousand starfishes. It now seems certain that such small aggregations occur fairly normally from time to time, and such groups have been found and studied in the Red Sea. However, on most reefs in the Red Sea as well as in the Indian and Pacific Oceans only occasional individual starfish are to be found and here they are likely to be playing a positive rather than a destructive role in the life of the reef.

Why such huge plagues should have occurred in Australia and parts of the Pacific is still not fully understood. Because of the many millions of eggs produced by each adult animal and the chances of larval existence, drifting in the plankton, the population levels of many marine invertebrates do in fact fluctuate wildly, sometimes in an almost cyclic fashion. The population of the Crown-of-thorns may be among those which behave in this way. At the same time man's activities through pollution, damage to the reef, or the taking of predators, may have greatly exacerbated this tendency. One suggestion is that in Australia the collection of the beautiful Triton shellfish, an established predator of the Crown-of-thorns, may have contributed to the increase in numbers of the starfish. In the Red Sea it has been shown that large triggerfishes and pufferfishes are important predators of *Acanthaster* and that small aggregations of the starfish may be controlled by them; thus it is clearly important that these fish species should not be taken from the reef, as they sometimes have been in significant numbers by spearfishermen to be made into lampshades and souvenirs.

SEA-URCHINS – ECHINOIDS Sea-urchins differ from starfishes not only in their body form but in their basic mode of feeding. On looking at the underside of a sea-urchin it can be seen that the mouth is surrounded by five large calcareous teeth; these are used to scrape

BELOW TOP: 64 The sea-urchin *Tripneustes gratilla*; this species is more characteristic of lagoon areas and often partly covers itself in disguise with pieces of sea-grass and algae.

BELOW BOTTOM: 65 The sea-urchin *Phylocanthus imperialis*. This is a primitive species with only one type of spine. Most other urchins, including the slate-pencil urchin, *Heterocentrotus mamillatus*, have small secondary spines as well as the main primary spines.

algal material from rocky surfaces. The sea-urchins are thus herbivores feeding in a somewhat similar way to the parrotfishes which, as described in another chapter, scrape at such algae with hard calcareous beaks. The sea-urchin's five teeth are suspended from an interesting small almost spherical structure lying within the base of the shell and known as Aristotle's lantern, after its discoverer. Also in contrast to starfishes, sea-urchins tend to use their spines for locomotion, stilt-walking as it were around on the stubby basal spines, while the tube feet play only a secondary role in this respect.

There are half a dozen or so species of sea-urchin which are common on Red Sea reefs. The most conspicuous of these must be the black needle-spined urchin, *Diadema setosum*, illustrated in Plate 63, the spines of which may be twenty-five centimetres or so long. This species is especially abundant in coastal lagoon areas where groups of them may be found by day sheltering under the sides of coral heads; by night they disperse to feed on the surrounding sand and rock.

The most abundant sea-urchin in the Red Sea, however, is probably the rather smaller *Echinometra mathei*, which indeed is probably the commonest urchin on most Indo-Pacific reefs. This species is about five centimetres across, is reddish-brown in colour, with fairly short but stout spines, and is easily recognised by the small white ring around the base of each spine. *Echinometra* is found all over the shallower parts of the reef among corals, rocks and rubble, where it tends to scrape out a small hollow to hide by day.

This tendency has been taken even further by the burrowing sea-urchin, *Echinostrephus molaris*. This is a slightly smaller sea-urchin, black in colour and looking superficially rather like a small *Diadema*. However, it is to be found on the more exposed and flat areas of the reef top within burrows through which only the upper parts of the dorsal spines project. Thus located these animals look rather like shaving-brushes sticking out of the reef. These urchins do not leave their burrows, and usually cannot do so because the body has grown within the burrow which they dig out by the action of their spines, while the mouth of the burrow remains fairly small. How the *Echinostrephus* could possibly manage to feed was for a long time a mystery but it is now known that it does so by catching with its elongated dorsal tube feet and spines small pieces of algae which have been broken off the reef by the wave action in the exposed areas in which they live. By living in their burrows these urchins are thus able to cope both with the rough water in such locations and to protect themselves from predators.

Another species of urchin is also found on the exposed part of the reef, and this has coped with problems of turbulent water and predation in a different way. This is the slate-pencil urchin, *Heterocentrotus mamillatus*. This species is brick red in colour and easily recognisable by its large chunky pencil-thick blunt-ended primary spines. When the animal is active these spines are rotated, giving the urchin the appearance of a miniaturised tank with so many long-barrelled guns. By day, however, or when disturbed, the spines are used to wedge the animal into crevices between corals and boulders, securing it as far as possible against wave action and attacks of predators.

Two other sea-urchins are likely to be seen by the snorkeller or diver on Red Sea reefs. The multi-coloured *Tripneustes gratilla* (shown in Plate 64) and the dark red *Echinothrix diadema*. *Tripneustes* occurs largely in coastal lagoon areas, where it is able to disguise itself fairly effectively by picking up with its tube feet and holding over its body numerous pieces of the algae and sea grasses on which they feed. *Echinothrix* is roughly similar to the needle-spined *Diadema* in general shape, but the spines are shorter and the overall coloration is a dark iridescent red, so that by the light of a torch they almost appear to be powered by small glowing fires within, or to be boiling over with anger!

SEA-CUCUMBERS – HOLOTHUROIDS As apparent on the reef as starfishes and sea-urchins, although generally evoking much less interest, presumably because they seem to be so inactive, are the sea-cucumbers (Holothuroidea), also known as *bêche-de-mer* or *trepang*. Nevertheless this group have been of rather greater commercial value in that some species are considered a gastronomic speciality in parts of the Far East and sea-cucumbers from the Red Sea have at times past been regularly exported to Japan and China.

Most of the noticeable sea-cucumbers are sausage-shaped, about thirty centimetres long and five to ten centimetres wide, and they are to be found lying about generally on rocky and sandy surfaces. Some species just lie on any side, whereas others have one side developed as a sole on which they move. There are no spines, but

spicules are embedded in the skin giving it a rough texture. The mouth at one end is surrounded by tentacles which in some species trap suspended food items; but in most common species the tentacles are used to shovel sand into the mouth and the animal obtains nourishment by digesting the various organic matter on and between the particles.

The commonest type of sea-cucumber in the Red Sea is all black and is found, often in large numbers, lying on the sand in shallow water. In fact there are several species which fit this description, all of which may vary somewhat in shade and may or may not cover themselves to some extent with sand. These species cannot be told apart in the field and can only be distinguished on microscopic examination of the spicules in the body walls; but much the commonest species involved is *Holothuria atra*, and for most purposes this one name is probably sufficient.

Some species of sea-cucumber can however be very readily identified, and three such species will be mentioned here. Not infrequently found moving over coral as much as across the sea bed is one animal which is rather more attractive than *Holothuria atra*. It is cream-coloured with many large chocolate-brown spots, each of which has a black centre and is also edged in black; there is an orange-brown area around the mouth and the tentacles are large and velvety black. This is *Bohadschia argus*, which appears to feed by picking mucus and food items off the surface of coral areas. The most visually striking of the sea-cucumbers generally found lying on the sea bed is perhaps *Thelenota ananas*; this is known in the *bêche-de-mer* industry as the prickly red fish and is the most highly valued, in part because the spicules of the body wall are very small, making the species that much more edible. The prickly red fish is orange-brown in colour, but is mostly covered by numerous wart or teat-like appendages each a centimetre or two long. These often grow in groups of two or three and perhaps give the animal the appearance of a shaggy red dog rather than a prickly red fish.

Striking in a rather different respect is another type found lying around on sandy bottoms in shallow water. Species of *Synapta* are longer and thinner than the average sea-cucumber with a more flexible body which may lie in twists and coils in a somewhat snake-like fashion. The body seems peculiarly sticky to the touch, because of the anchor-like shape of the spicules embedded in the skin, and the body is also capable of considerable elongation from the normal forty or fifty centimetres to over a metre or more. Thus the curious swimmer picking up this species may be taken aback to find the animal sticking determinedly to his body and becoming terribly entangled around his arms and legs.

BRITTLE-STARS – OPHIUROIDS The remaining two groups of echinoderms are much less conspicuous on the coral reef than the other three which we have so far considered. The brittle-stars (Ophiuroidea) are generally smaller in size than the others, up to ten centimetres or so across and with their fine filament-like arms are easily able to hide in small crevices among coral and stones. In some parts of the world brittle-stars are the commonest type of animal on parts of the sea bed, and may in fact cover it in a seething carpet up to five animals deep. Brittle-stars are nowhere so abundant on the coral reef, but they are nevertheless very numerous and to be found in almost every possible hiding-place. They can be very difficult to extract from such hiding-places, being very prepared to drop part of an arm so that they can make off, and when they are exposed in the open they can move with surprising speed. Two or three of the five arms propel the animal with rowing or snake-like movements, and the numerous club-spines which project from the arms, giving them a woolly bottlebrush-like appearance, give grip to the arms as they move over the surface.

On Red Sea coral reefs there are ten or twenty common species of brittle-star, most of which however are difficult to tell apart except on detailed examination. Some of them may be fairly well characterised by the situation in which they are found. Thus *Ophiocoma pica* and *Ophiocoma erinaceus* are found in some numbers living among the branches of almost every head of some of the bushy corals such as *Pocillopora* and *Stylophora*. *Ophiocoma erinaceus* is jet black all over, while *Ophiocoma pica* has a pattern of radiating gold lines on the disc.

A few species can be fairly readily recognised. *Ophiolepis superba* has no spines and is conspicuously patterned, a pale sandy grey with two or three dark bands on each arm and a dark star shape on the disc; it is found in sandy areas, often just buried under the surface. *Macrophiothrix demessa* is noticeable from its particularly long sinusoidal arms, which very easily fragment; it has a light and dark mottled pattern with five thick

dark lines radiating on the top of the disc. In particular, however, there can be no mistaking the so-called basket-star *Astroba nuda*. These magnificent animals reach as much as a metre in diameter with a scarcely apparent disc but many finely branched arms. They look more like, and in fact behave like, giant feather-stars for they hide themselves deep in coral crevices by day, emerging at dusk to cling to the reef edge with arms extended and catch small planktonic particles and organisms.

FEATHER-STARS – CRINOIDS The fifth and last group of the echinoderms to be considered here, the feather-stars (Crinoidea), are even less apparent to the average snorkeller than are the other groups. The feather-stars (see Plates 66 to 68) are only active by night whereas by day they are extraordinarily well able to secrete themselves deep within small holes and crevices. Shortly before dusk they emerge on to knolls and coral heads along the sides of the reef where there is a good current. They cling on by means of a ring of hook-like appendages called *cirri*, situated on the side of the body away from the mouth. The mouth is uppermost and surrounded by numerous feather-like arms, which in feeding are spread out as an array across the current, with the mouth and the tops of the arms facing downstream. The arms catch small planktonic plants and animals which are wrapped in mucus and transported to the mouth along grooves in the upperside of the arms by the action of small beating cilia. In fact this method of food collection is so efficient that there are some small polychaete worms and even a brittle-star which live largely by syphoning off this flow of food. The feather-stars can move around rather clumsily by walking-like movements of their cirri, or can swim in a rather spectacular fashion, each of the arms independently beating up and down with undulations.

By far the commonest of the feather-stars on Red Sea coral reefs is *Lamprometra klunzingeri* which occurs in densities of ten or more per square metre in some areas. It is fifteen to thirty centimetres across, has twenty-five to thirty arms, and may be dark red or black, sometimes with white banding across the arms.

CRABS, SHRIMPS AND WATERFLEAS – CRUSTACEANS

The biological class Crustacea, containing crabs, shrimps and their allies, is a subdivision of the larger group the

Arthropoda, which also includes such animals as insects and spiders. With very few exceptions, however, these other groups are not to be found on the reef, and thus we will limit our discussion here to the crustaceans. The shrimp is in many ways typical of the crustaceans, which are characterised by a segmented body, on each segment a pair of leg-like appendages which may be modified as walking legs, as mouth parts or as swimmerets, and a horny external skeleton, the front part of which is fused to form over the head and the front part of the body (the *thorax*) a large shield called the *carapace*.

Crustaceans are subdivided in turn into several groups, the most conspicuous of which is that containing the crabs, shrimps and lobsters and known as the Decapoda, meaning ten legs. The name refers to the five pairs of walking legs on the thorax, the front pair of which are often equipped with large claws. On the head the appendages are modified as mouth parts while on the posterior part of the body, the *abdomen*, these appendages are modified as swimmerets, save that in the crabs the whole abdomen is greatly reduced and curled up underneath the carapace.

CRABS On all coral reefs the family of crabs which is most characteristic and most conspicuous in the coral-rich zones is the Xanthiidae, a family which appears to lack any common name but which might well for our purpose be termed the coral crabs. The xanthiids are medium- to small-sized crabs, a few centimetres across, characterised by a flat, fan-shaped carapace. The most noticeable of these on Red Sea coral reefs are smallish crabs with a smooth, shiny, often brightly coloured carapace, to be seen lurking within the branches of

various corals. Of these, species of *Trapezia*, which may be pink or have a spotted pattern with a darker red, are to be found in *Pocillopora* coral; species of *Tetralia* occur in corals of the genus *Acropora*; and species of *Quadrella* are found on soft corals and gorgonians. In fact it may seem that almost every colony of the thick-branched purple or pink *Pocillopora danae* so abundant along the reef crest is inhabited by one or more species of *Trapezia* crabs, nearly always present in pairs; they shiftily inspect the diver as he looks down at them, or scuttle across the colony to nip the diver's hand should he be resting there. The legs of these crabs are modified so that they can move around their coral with surprising speed while still holding on, and so that they can grip on to a coral branch sufficiently tightly so that they cannot be removed without tearing the body away from the legs. These crabs feed both on the organic material that may settle on the coral, and also on the mucus which the coral itself produces to try and rid itself of this and other sediment.

A variety of other xanthiid crabs are to be found on Red Sea reefs but of these perhaps two deserve particular mention. *Pilumnus incanus* is readily recognisable as a species of hairy crab in which the carapace is covered with hair-like growths giving the appearance of a wooly coat; and *Lybia leptocheilus*, which again tends to be associated with living corals, is a species of boxer crab, holding with each pincer a small anemone of the species *Triactis producta*. With its claws thus gloved, the boxer crab waves its arms at any would-be intruder, threatening to sting them by virtue of the stinging cells on the anemone.

Showing an even closer relationship with living

BELOW: 69 The ghost crab *Ocypode saratan* among the burrows which it excavates on the shore, building up conical sand castles which also advertise its presence.

RIGHT: 70 A coral crab, a species of *Trapezia*, living among the branches of a coral *Stylophora*.

corals than do crabs like *Trapezia* are the rather remarkable gall-crabs of the family Hapalocarcinidae. These may be typified by the gall-crab *Hapalocarcinus marsupialis* which may be found in the Red Sea on the corals *Seriatopora*, *Stylophora* and *Pocillopora*. The young crab settles on a suitable coral and provokes the coral to modify its skeleton at this point so as to form a gall completely enclosing the crab, save for a few small apertures through which water may pass. The crab probably feeds on small plankton that it separates from the water with the aid of hairs along the edge of the mouth parts.

Other crabs characteristic of coral zones on Red Sea reefs include one or two species of porcelain crabs, *Petrolisthes*, and several species of hermit crab. The *Petrolisthes* are small crabs, one to two centimetres across, generally found under coral rocks and rubble where they feed on suspended matter. They have a generally porcine or pig-like shape which is thought to be the most likely derivation of the common name porcelain crab. The hermit crabs of course protect themselves by curling their abdomen into an empty gastropod shell and carrying this shell around on their back. They include several species of *Dardanus* which are usually a reddish colour and, together with the shell, may reach quite a moderate size. Most interesting of the hermit crabs however is perhaps *Pagurus asper* which occupies a shell five centimetres in length and covers this with ten or more anemones of the species *Calliactis polypus*, so that the shell itself is hardly visible. This remarkable combination of crustacean hermit crab, gastropod shell and coelenterate sea-anemones is not infrequently met with on night dives as the creature

trundles across a sandy patch on the reef. The crab benefits from this association or symbiosis through the added protection that the stinging cells of the anemone give it, in particular it is thought against such predators as octopuses; the anemones benefit in obtaining substrate on which to live and in being placed in all sorts of situations where they may be able to capture food with their tentacles – in particular when the scavenging crab is breaking up food with its pincers and smaller bits float about and are captured by the anemones. The *Pagurus-Calliactis* partnership is an excellent thing to have in a large general marine aquarium; not only is the hermit crab like all crabs of its type excellent fun to watch as it scans the scene with its beady stalked eyes, but the two species together provide an excellent cleaning service, the crab scavenging the bottom while the anemones filter the water.

More typical of lagoon areas are a number of swimming crabs (family Portunidae) which have the last two joints of the fifth pair of legs flattened and fringed with hairs so as to assist with swimming. These inlude several species of *Thalamita* and also *Lupa pelagica*. *Lupa* has a very broad almost diamond-shaped carapace seven or more centimetres across, and is almost invariably seen by anyone walking across shallower, muddy areas as it scuttles away with large conspicuously blue claws held wide apart in an aggressive threatening posture.

However, the crabs most likely to draw the attention of the snorkeller or diver in the Red Sea are those to be seen as he is entering the water from the shore. Where rocks predominate crabs of the family Grapsidae are to be found: in particular *Geograpsus crinipes* can hardly be ignored. Groups of these orange crabs scuttle like

LEFT: 71 A tiny spider crab living on a gorgonian. Many coral reef crabs and shrimps live in this way as commensals on other animals.

spiders around small cliffs on the shore and in particular on the concrete bases of jetties and light-beacons.

On sandy shores crabs of the family Ocypodidae are common. Largest of these are the ghost crabs (see Plate 69), pale, almost transparent, sandy or very light yellow or orange crabs with squarish carapaces about four centimetres across which run high on long legs along the shore. They have particularly tall eye-stalks with the eye positioned halfway up the stalk, and as with all crabs of this family, the stalks can be lowered to rest neatly sitting against either side of the front edge of the carapace. Ghost crabs dig large burrows in the sand, the males in particular piling the excavated sand near the entrance in conical-shaped towers which are probably important as beacons indicating the presence of a male's territory.

Finally in this section on crabs must be mentioned one crab which often occurs alongside the ghost crab, and which is not only most noticeable, but may even be most irritating in drawing attention to itself. This is the tiny land hermit crab *Coenobita scavola*, armies of which scurry along the tide line on many sandy shores, each individual protected in a small gastropod shell a centimetre or two long. Shells of *Nerita*, *Cerithium* and the small species of *Strombus* seem especially to be favoured. These crabs scavenge along the tideline and readily clear up scraps left by picnickers or are even tempted to nibble at their toes. Worse, if when camping out empty food tins are left lying on the beach, these are happily invaded by the little hermit crabs intent on scavenging out the last traces of food, but they rattle their acquired shells so noisily against the tin that they make a decent night's sleep impossible until the tins are placed out of reach.

SHRIMPS Shrimps are rather less apparent in coral-reef areas than are crabs. However, a large number of species are usually present, but doubtless because of the large number of fish and other predators around they are mostly small and well hidden. In fact, of the species of shrimp to be found on the reef, only a small minority are free-living, wandering around as best they can, the majority being associated to a lesser or greater extent with a very wide range of other animals from which they are able to gain food and protection.

The two shrimp families most typical of coral reefs are the Alpheidae and the Palaemonidae. The alpheid

shrimps are characterised by very large pincers, one larger than the other, sometimes as much as half the length of the body. The alpheids are known as pistol shrimps because with the aid of these pincers they can produce a snapping sound not unlike the crack of a small pistol. These frequent snappings are in fact one of the major sounds to be heard by the snorkeller in shallow coral areas. The sound is actually produced by a peg-like process protruding from the finger of the pincer and which is snapped into place in a matching hole on the thumb. This snapping action sets up a rush of water and it has been thought the shrimp uses this to stun small prey. There are ten or more species of pistol shrimp which are fairly common on Red Sea reefs. Perhaps the most conspicuous of these is *Alpheus sublucanus* which is a large generally orange species found inhabiting branched coral along with the variety of xanthiid crabs. The majority of *Alpheus* species, however, are free-living as is for example *Alpheus edwardsii* which gains protection by retreating to crevices on the reef. Amongst the most interesting of the associations shown by species of *alpheid* shrimp on Red Sea reefs is that of *Aretopsis aegyptica* which associates with hermit crabs of the genus *Dardanus* using for shelter the same gastropod shell as does the crab.

There is a great variety of shrimps of the family Palaemonidae to be found on the reef, almost all of which are commensals living in association with other larger animals on the reef. Each species of shrimp is specifically adapted to a particular host species or group of host species which include sponges, sea-anemones, corals and soft corals, bivalves and echinoderms. Large sponges on the reef are often found to provide a home for whole colonies; many of the different species of coral have particular tiny species of shrimps which may be found associated with them; and on careful inspection a majority of individual medium- or large-sized echinoderms are found to have one or more shrimps living on them. Often these shrimps may be completely transparent, save for the pigment of the eye, so as to be almost invisible against their host, or they may be remarkably well camouflaged against the background of their host. An example of the latter readily to be found in the Red Sea is provided by the little shrimp *Periclimenes soror*, which is found among the spines of the Crown-of-thorns starfish, *Acanthaster planci*; the shrimp is reddish brown in colour with a paler spine-shaped longitudinal stripe along its back which precisely imitates the appearance of the starfish's spines against its dorsal surface. By contrast shrimps which are species of *Stegopontonia* and *Tuleariocaris* are to be found living on the spines of the sea-urchin *Diadema setosum* which has long black spines; the shrimps are dark blue in colour, almost black, with a narrow white line along the side.

A few shrimps from other families are also comparatively noticeable on Red Sea reefs. *Stenopus hispidus*, with conspicuous red and white banding (see Plate 154), is probably the species most frequently noticed by divers, and is one of the so-called spiny prawns (Stenopodidae) where the third pair of spiny legs is much longer than the others. The banded shrimp is found usually in pairs living in shelves and crevices among the coral; it is also, as described in chapter 7, a species which gains part of its living by cleaning fish of ectoparasites and dead tissue.

SPINY LOBSTERS AND MANTIS SHRIMPS A group of decapods which are of culinary interest and are to be found on Red Sea reefs are the spiny or rock lobsters of the family Palinuridae. Spiny lobsters differ from true lobsters in that they lack the large pair of pincers which the latter have on the front pair of legs. The common Red Sea species of spiny lobster is *Palinurus penicillatus* which grows to fifty centimetres or so in length and is reddish brown with a series of pale transverse bands and numerous very fine dots on the dorsal side of the abdomen. This species is relatively frequent on many Red Sea reefs, especially those which are more exposed and are growing directly on volcanic rock as opposed to rock of coral origin; however, they are rarely present in commercial quantities. Much less common are *Palinurus versicolor* and *Palinurus ornatus*. The former species is readily indentifiable by its brilliant white antennae, striped legs and overall dark green coloration. *Palinurus ornatus* has a more or less uniformly coloured abdomen and transverse coloured rings around the legs. The spiny lobsters have generally been regarded as scavengers feeding on worms, shellfish and echinoderms, but there is evidence that they may also feed on algae to a significant extent. While by day it is unusual to see more than their long antennae flickering briefly from underneath a coral boulder, during the night they may be found in the open, and

particularly in the area behind the reef crest.

Another group of moderately large crustaceans are the stomatopods or Mantis shrimps which bear a clear resemblance to praying mantis insects in that they have a reduced carapace with an elongated abdomen, and the first pair of legs are very long and flex in clasp-knife fashion like the jaws of the praying mantis. In contrast to the insect, the abdomen is very broad and flat and ends in a well developed tail fan. As one might well imagine from a glance at the aggressive-looking jaws, mantis shrimps are carnivorous. They are found in areas of sand into which they can readily dig and often make permanent sloping burrows. Quite a number of species are to be found in Red Sea reef areas, some not infrequently in the lagoon areas behind the fringing reef. They vary in colour from sandy grey to light green to nearly black and are mostly species of *Gonodactylus* and of *Squilla* and related genera.

BARNACLES AND OTHER CRUSTACEANS Of the remaining crustacean groups, two (the copepods and the ostracods) are planktonic, while two more (the mysid and cumacean shrimps) are essentially semi-planktonic. The first two groups are really microscopic and not likely to be seen by the snorkeller or diver unless he stares very carefully at the water just in front of his face mask. These groups also contain the water fleas to be found in freshwater ponds and lakes. In the sea the copepods are very much the more important group, species of *Calanus* and *Pseudocalanus* being a major source of food for many fishes. The cumacean and mysid shrimps, the latter known as opossum shrimps, are small semi-transparent animals up to a centimetre or so in length, which look superficially like shrimps, but have eight or so pairs of apparent legs. They are usually seen swimming freely in mid-water, normally in small groups close by a coral head or other partial shelter.

The final group of crustaceans which cannot escape mention is the Cirripedia or barnacles. To the uninitiated it may seem very strange that barnacles, fixed in one place with their limpet-like form of shell, should be included among the crustaceans. But as those with any background in biology will know the barnacle form can be derived from that of the more typical crustaceans by cementing the crustacean down to the substrate on its back and allowing the animal's external skeleton to grow up around it in a conical form. To feed, the barnacle extends its feathered legs through the aperture at the top of the cone and with sweeping movements filters tiny animal items from the plankton. The most noticeable of the barnacles to be found in Red Sea reef areas are those occurring on hard surfaces along or just below the tideline. The largest of these, dominating the tideline in some areas, is the giant barnacle *Tetraclita squamosa rufotincta*. This is about three centimetres across and coralline pink in colour.

However, the barnacles most particularly associated with coral reefs are those which grow embedded in the surface of live corals. Barnacles of this type are very common on Red Sea corals. They are not so apparent on the living coral, but a good proportion of the coral skeletons taken from the Red Sea are found on subsequent examination to have one or more barnacles on them. These barnacles settle on the living coral tissue and, as the barnacle grows, coral skeleton grows up around the sides, bonding with the side plates, and leaving only a small aperture at the top through which the barnacle feeds. Further growth of the barnacle takes place in conjunction with the growth of the coral skeleton, the barnacle shell growing principally by expansion of the cup-shaped basal plate. In general, in encrusting and plate-like corals are found smaller barnacles which have a shallow base and a conical shell extending well above the surface of the coral. In more massive rounded corals are found larger barnacles with thicker shells that grow outwards to maintain their aperture at the level of the coral surface. The different species of coral-living barnacles show varying degrees of adaptation to this habit, for example in the degree of fusion of the plate forming the conical shell. The most modified of all is the parasitic *Hoekia monticulariae* which has been studied in the Indian Ocean. This species has a very small aperture, generally covered by the coral tissue, and only a single pair of ineffective feeding legs. It seems that the barnacle feeds on the coral tissue which grows over and down in through the aperture.

SEASHELLS, SEA-SLUGS AND OCTOPUSES – MOLLUSCS

To many people the variety of shells to be found on coral reefs are the greatest interest these reefs have to offer. The shells come in enormous variety, often most attractively coloured and beautifully patterned, and of course they are extremely collectable. But as the hobby of shell collecting becomes more and more popular, once-common shells are becoming scarce. Shells often have a patchy distribution and when their numbers reach a critical level below which reproduction may be difficult, whole populations may quickly become extinct. However, increasingly those interested in shells are taking time to study the live animals rather than the dead ones, and are becoming curious about how it is that such animals do in fact live. The challenge of building up a collection of photographs of the active animal is one to which it must be hoped more enthusiasts will turn.

The great variety of shells, and also the colourful sea-slugs, as well as the octopuses and their relatives all fall within the biological group known as the molluscs. In this section we will not only indicate the major different types of mollusc, but also point out some of the more interesting features of their biology. For so many different species of mollusc to occur together on the reef, they must have many different ways of feeding and of coping with the problems of the environment in which they live. It is not intended to list or describe all the many species of shell that may be found; there are a number of specialist shell books that tackle that problem, but many of the commonest shells to be found on Red Sea reefs will be mentioned, so as to enable the more generally interested snorkeller or diver to guess what at least some of his finds may be.

The molluscs to be found on Red Sea reefs almost all fall within four major subdivisions. These are the chitons (Amphineura), the snails and slugs (Gastropoda), the bivalve shells (Lamellibranchia), and the octopuses and their allies (Cephalopoda). Despite their great variety of form these groups have, as might be expected, a number of features in common, and these need to be briefly mentioned before we can discuss the different types in more detail. All may be considered as consisting of three parts, the head, the foot, and the main part of the body. All these parts are soft and are not supported by an internal skeleton. Surprisingly and ironically the name Mollusca means 'soft-bodied', despite the common image of the mollusc as a hard shell. The main body has around it a skirt of tissue, known as the mantle, and between the body and the mantle is situated the mantle cavity which contains the gills (which in terrestrial forms has developed as a lung). It is the mantle which on its outside secretes the familiar shell.

CHITONS The chitons are a rather curious group of somewhat primitive shellfish. At first they may be easily overlooked since they live clinging, almost moulded, on to rocks around the water's edge. However, once seen, they are easily recognisable in that while having a superficially limpet-like form, the shell is in fact composed of eight parallel transverse plates, giving the animal something of the appearance of a woodlouse. These plates do not extend the whole way across the animal, the mantle projecting beyond the bottom of the plates to form a tough skirt-like girdle which is strengthened near the edges by numbers of calcareous scales or spicules. It is because the transverse plates articulate with each other so well that the animal can bend its body to cling close to an uneven rock surface while still gaining a measure of protection from a solid shell. Also the animal can, if dislodged, curl up, again like a woodlouse, to help protect itself from a predator. As well as suiting the chiton to life on the roughly cut rocks around the tideline, the transverse plates are of interest to the biologist as being an indication of the evolutionary origin of the molluscs as a whole, from more primitive animals that were transversely segmented in the manner of the segmented worms.

With few exceptions the chitons are herbiverous and feed by means of a long narrow chitinous tongue or *radula* which is covered by numerous rows of many teeth. The teeth, containing significant amounts of iron, are very hard, and are used to scrape the thin algal film of the rock. As the animal feeds, the rock itself is also partially ground away. The radula is also the principal feeding organ of the gastropods and in some groups, as we shall see, has become highly specialised. There are ten or so kinds of chiton which might be found in Red Sea coral-reef areas, but much the largest and most conspicuous, and perhaps the commonest, is *Acanthopleura haddoni*, which is about five centimetres long.

SEA-SNAILS AND SEA-SLUGS – GASTROPODS

The shellfish with snail-like shells (in fact both aquatic

BELOW: 73 *Cypraea exusta*, one of the attractive species of cowrie to be found in the Red Sea.

forms and those which occur on land) are placed together in the same biological group as the sea-slugs. Members of the group are known as gastropods. We will discuss the shellfish first.

The commonest sea-snails in Red Sea areas contain representatives of almost every major family of shells, and it is probably best to consider these in the order of their biological classification, since this order also reflects major differences both in feeding behaviour and in the type of habitat preferred.

TOP SHELLS AND TURBAN SHELLS The most primitive sea-snails are classified as Archaeogastropoda (meaning quite simply the old gastropods). These include the top shells (Trochidae), common Red Sea species of which are *Trochus* (or *Tectus*) *dentatus*, *Gena varia*, and *Clanculus pharaonis*; the turban shells (Turbinidae) among which *Turbo petholatus* is common on Red Sea reefs; and the nerites or slipper-winkles (Neritidae) of

which a number of species such as *Nerita polita* and *Nerita undata* are common in the Red Sea, especially around the tideline on rocky shores, which they may completely dominate. These families are all algal feeders. They have a rather primitive organisation of their mantle cavity and also feathery gills, as a result of which the cavity and gills are particularly prone to clogging by silt and sediment. Because of this the species generally avoid sandy areas and are either to be found on rocky shores, or else, as with the *Turbo* and *Trochus* species, mainly on the fore-reef, including the reef face. This distribution contrasts with that of most other shellfish groups; they are more often characteristic of reef flat and lagoon areas where they may be better able to hide, and where perhaps the threat of predation by fish may be less.

The *Trochus* species are of particular interest in that they have been of considerable commercial value because of the mother-of-pearl in the shell. Mother-of-pearl is

is carried out in totally traditional manner from large dhows (*sambuk*) which are based at a number of Red Sea ports, especially Massawa and Suakin. The sambuks sail the length of the Red Sea on expeditions lasting many months. Each sambuk carries half a dozen or so dug-out canoes (*huri*). At each new reef area the sambuk finds an anchorage, and, from dawn to dusk, one or two men or boys in each huri paddle from reef to reef searching for *Trochus* through a glass-bottomed tin. In the hot salty conditions the life is an exceptionally arduous one, and these days the financial returns are very poor. Almost worse than anything else, if the fishermen are at all successful, they must tolerate on board the unbearable stench from the increasing piles of *Trochus* shells, within which the animals slowly decay month after month until the ship can return to her home port.

While the *Trochus* shells themselves are not particularly attractive, one smaller member of this family to be found on Red Sea reefs is rather beautiful. This is the aptly named Strawberry top (*Clanculus pharaonis*), which grows to two or so centimetres across, and is strawberry red in colour with two or three rows of black dashes running along each whorl. Some of the Turban shells are also fairly attractive; *Turbo petholatus*, known in arabic as *abu imma* (father of the turban), is reddish brown, with further light and dark markings. Snorkellers, however, are perhaps more likely to be aware of its presence because of its highly polished *operculum*, the disc on the foot which blocks the aperture of the shell when the animal withdraws inside. In most shells which have an operculum this is of a horny slightly flexible nature; in *Turbo*, however, the operculum has become calcareous, and is coloured to give the effect of a catseye with a dark centre and paler surround. No doubt in life the sudden appearance of such an eye as the animal withdraws may sometimes serve to frighten off a predator. However, loose catseyes of this sort lying on the sand quite often attract the attention of the snorkeller long after the animal itself may have passed away.

HORN SHELLS AND SPIDER CONCHS The next group of shells are also herbivorous, mostly feeding on algae, and are classified within the Mesogastropoda (or middle gastropods). This group includes worm shells (Vermitidae), horn shells (Cerithidae), strombs (Strombidae) and cowries (Cypraeidae). These animals all have a more advanced arrangement of the mantle cavity, a

the inner shiny white layer of the shell which in these species is particularly thick, and can therefore be cut out for the manufacture of mother-of-pearl shirt buttons and other ornaments. This inner or *nacrous* layer owes its lustre and shiny appearance to the optical properties of the numerous fine horizontal calcareous plates from which it is formed. In the late nineteenth and early twentieth centuries, when mother-of-pearl was particularly in fashion, large fortunes were won (and lost) in extensive fisheries for these shells in different parts of the Indo-Pacific. Nowadays however plastics have largely replaced the need for mother-of-pearl, although a moderate amount is still taken.

In the Red Sea *Trochus* shells are fished for commercially over quite an extensive area. The main commercial species is *Trochus dentatus*, which grows up to eight centimetres high, rather than the larger and inappropriately named *Trochus niloticus*, which is much commoner in the Indian and Pacific oceans. The fishing

BELOW TOP: 78 Beauty in detail: the small patterns on the mantle of a sea-slug, illuminated by a strobe light from behind.

BELOW BOTTOM: 79 The coiled ribbon-like egg masses of a sea-slug: a fascinating problem in identification for non-biologist and biologist alike.

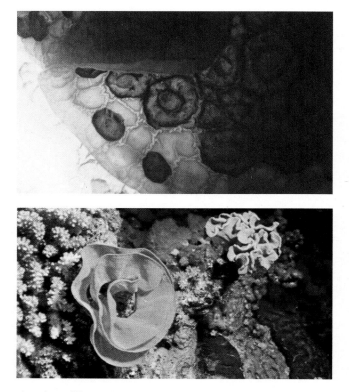

simpler gill, and other features which enable them to cope with sediment more effectively. This has equipped them for the possibility of moving into sandy and lagoon-like environments, a step which has already been taken by the horn shells and the strombs.

The horn shells actually creep and burrow within the surface layer of the sand and often feed by filtering suspended material out of the water. Among the common Red Sea species *Cerithium caeruleum*, grey with rows of dark blue knobs, is perhaps the most conspicuous.

Among the strombs, particularly noticeable Red Sea species include several smaller ones (up to three or four centimetres long) such as the white, Purple-lipped stromb *Strombus gibberulus albus*, the striped *Strombus fasciatus* (an endemic Red Sea species), and the more irregularly banded *Strombus mutabilus*. Somewhat larger, growing to ten or more centimetres with the main whorl elongated into a single flair, is *Strombus tricornis*; and even larger of course are the well-known spider conchs, *Lambis lambis* and *Lambis truncata*. In the latter the main whorl is not swollen in bulb-like fashion, as in

Lambis lambis, and the spines are nowhere near as long. *Lambis truncata* seems to be more characteristic of very shallow water near the shore, while *Lambis lambis* is found in greater numbers on the reef flat of outer reefs. The spines presumably are defensive in nature, but, despite this, these large shells are sometimes found broken open, apparently by fish, probably by the larger triggerfish such as *Balastoides viridescens* or by the huge Hump-headed wrasse *Cheilinus undulatus*. Apparent in all strombs is the highly characteristic notch on the edge of the flange of the shell; this notch is known as the stromboid notch. Also characteristic of strombs is the horny claw on the foot. This claw is developed in fact from the operculum, and, by extending the foot, digging in the claw, and then contracting the foot, the animal can move itself along. In this way also the spider conchs can, surprisingly, right themselves, should they be overturned. The claw is so shaped that it may still when necessary act as an operculum in blocking the slit-like entrance to the shell.

WORM SHELLS Worm shells, in complete contrast to the spider conch, rarely attract the attentions of the collector since the shells look much more like the casts of worms, and moreover they are typically found embedded within the coral. Nevertheless they are an extremely interesting group, and one species, *Dendropoma maximum*, is extremely abundant and conspicuous to snorkellers and divers on Red Sea reefs. They characteristically occur in areas where the reef crest is flat and rocky and extends back for some way a metre or so below the surface and where there is a moderate amount of current or wave action. In such areas the coral rock or the large massive heads of *Porites* coral often appear to be pock-marked with small regularly shaped tubes, about two centimetres across, and often blocked by a horny disc at the entrance. The horny disc is in fact the foot of the elongated shellfish which lives within, while the shell-lined tubes left by deceased *Dendropoma* are often inhabited by small fish such as blennies.

On closer inspection it is possible to see how the living *Dendropoma*, thus entombed within the rock, nevertheless manages to gain a living. Spreading out from around the entrance to the tube may normally be seen a sheet of mucousy material; this mucus is produced by the shellfish and with the help of wave action is spread out over the surrounding rock to a distance of

about eight centimetres. The mucus net thus formed traps floating plankton and other material, and this is consumed by the shellfish when every ten to fifteen minutes or so it hauls in and swallows both the contents of the net and the net itself. A new net is then secreted. In this cunning way *Dendropoma* is able to live on a part of the reef which is hazardous to most animals, whilst protecting itself both from the force of the waves and from potential predators. It is fascinating that this solution is fairly similar to that arrived at by the small sea-urchin *Echinostrephus molaris*, described in the last chapter, which is also abundant on the same part of the reef.

COWRIES In contrast to worm shells, cowries need little introduction, being amongst the most popular souvenirs of a visit to the sea. Despite the familiarity of their shape, however, few people stop to give thought to the problem of how such a different form might be developed from the more usual spiralled coil of other shells. In fact the shape is obtained by enclosing the earlier smaller parts of the spiral within the final large body whorl, as can readily be seen by cutting open an old shell. When they are active the mantle of cowries is generally extended up over the outside of the shell, and it is for this reason that the shells of cowries tend to remain, to the great convenience of souvenir collectors and shops, shiny and lustrous, rather than becoming encrusted with algal growth and small organisms. The egg-like shape of the shell gives great mechanical resistance to predators attempting to crush it; nevertheless the Hump-headed wrasse is able to deal with cowries, either by crushing them with the aid of calcareous plates in the throat, or by swallowing them whole. The elongated shape of the aperture of the shell makes it more difficult for predators to enter or insert a claw. But it may also make it difficult to fit an operculum, which is absent in the cowries. Further defence is however obtained by the extended mantle, which, in some species at least, is able to secrete sulphuric acid, and this presumably makes the cowries a bit too hot for some predators to handle.

Among the common Red Sea cowries are *Cypraea pantherina* (the Red Sea form of the very familiar

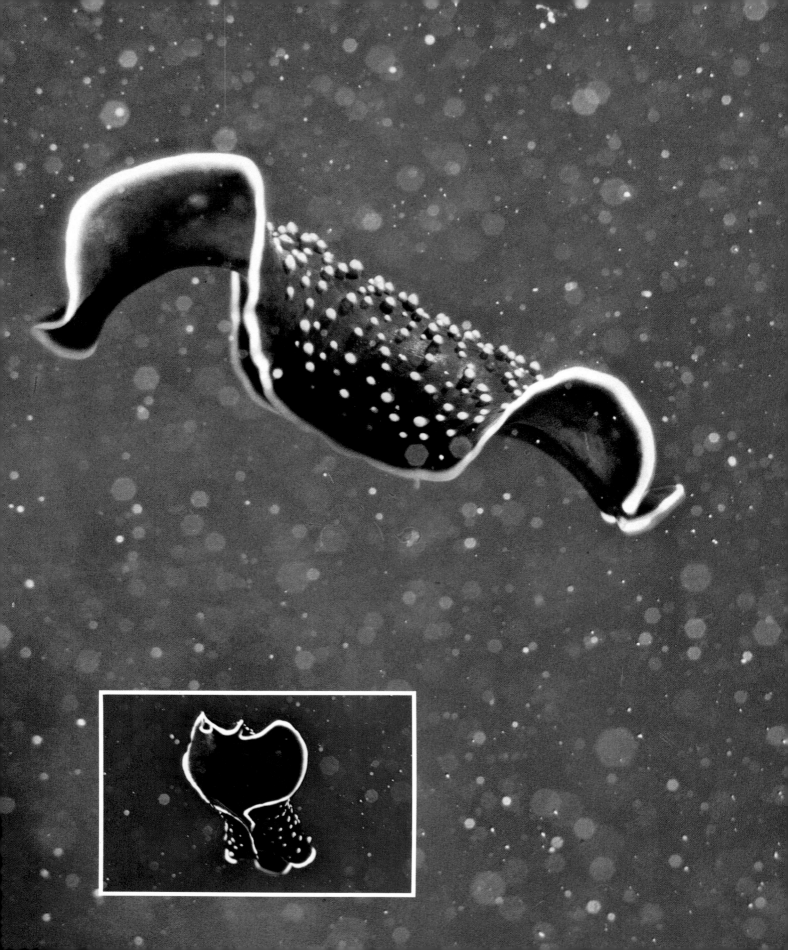

LEFT/INSET LEFT: 81/82 A brilliantly colourful flatworm, *Thysanozoon flavomaculatum*. Some of the larger species swim well with undulations of the body and may be mistaken for swimming sea-slugs such as the Spanish dancer.

BELOW LEFT/BELOW: 83/84 Close-up of the spiral feeding gills of the coral fanworm *Spirobranchus giganteus*, the variously coloured twin spires of which are commonly scattered over large mounds of coral, such as *Porites*.

Cypraea tigris), *arabica grayana, caurica, turdus, carneola, nebrites, isabella, lynx, gracilis* and *annulus*. Among the more subtly attractive of these are *Cypraea carneola* and *Cypraea isabella*. Two rather less common cowries of interest, which are both beautiful and unique to the Red Sea area, are *Cypraea camelopardalis* and *Cypraea pulchra*. *Cypraea camelopardalis* is pale brown with a regular array of pale blue spots, while *Cypraea pulchra* is a dark fawn colour with a pair of black blotches on the top of the lip at either end of the shell – these latter, looking like a pair of eyes, giving the shell when viewed from some angles the appearance of a comical little baby pig.

TUNS AND TRITONS A second group of mesogastropods are predatory. These include the tuns (Tonnidae) among which the grinning tun *Malea pomum* is quite common in the Red Sea, and the tritons (Cymatidae) which include in the Red Sea, as well as the large and famous giant triton *Charonia tritonis*, a few small species such as *Cymatium pileare*. The giant triton is not abundant in the Red Sea, but it is not uncommon; its beautiful shell is justly prized, but in the light of the information that this shellfish is a significant predator of the coral-eating Crown-of-thorns starfish (see chapter 4), collection of this species in particular must be frowned upon. *Charonia* is able, in rather dramatic fashion, to hold down the starfish with its foot while penetrating the spiny skin with its radula. The innards of the starfish are often scraped out through a single wound leaving the body like an empty sack with its fate readily apparent.

ADVANCED PREDATORS The third of the three subdivisions of the marine snails is the Neogastropoda

(or new gastropods). This group contains a variety of families, all of which are predatory. The main families with some of their common Red Sea representatives are as follows:

> The dye shells (Muricidae), e.g. *Murex tribulus* and *Chicoreus ramosus*;
> The dog whelks (Thaiidae), e.g. *Morula granulata* and three or four species of *Drupa*, such as *Drupa morum*;
> The whelks (Buccinidae), e.g. *Engina mendicaria*;
> The tulip and spindle shells (Fasciolaridae), e.g. *Fasciolaria trapezium, Latirulus turritus* and *Fusus polygonoides*;
> The olives (Olividae), e.g. *Oliva bulbosa*;
> The harps (Harpidae), e.g. *Harpa armouretta*;
> The mitres (Mitridae), e.g. *Pusia* spp.;
> The cones (Conidae), species of which will be listed below; and
> The augers (Terebridae) among which *Terebra maculata* is especially abundant in the Red Sea.

Many of these families, for example the tulips, the olives, the harps and the mitres, are principally characteristic of sandy areas. It is interesting to realise that this has provided the initial impetus for the development of a very important new feature, the syphon. The syphon is a small tube extending from the opening of the mantle cavity and reaching up above the head of the shellfish. In this way water can be drawn into the gills from above the level of the sand and sediment. But secondarily this syphon has become an essential chemosensory apparatus, for smelling the presence of prey at a distance. The opening of the syphon is waved about in different directions and the water drawn in is tested as it enters the mantle cavity. The testing is performed by a sense organ which initially was merely concerned to detect the presence of sand or sediment in the inflow. As well as detecting the presence of prey, the syphon may be used to detect the approach of a predator, such as a starfish. After ascertaining the direction of approach of the threat, the syphon swings through 180° to be followed at full speed by the rest of the animal, as it beats a hasty retreat.

While the syphon was developed initially to cope with conditions prevalent in sandy areas, various species and families have become more adapted to other reef zones. Thus *Murex tribulus*, *Chicoreus ramosus*, and *Fusus polygonoides* are found among rocks and corals on the reef, while the dog whelks are more characteristic of the rocks and boulders near the tide-level, and the cones have diversified to occupy a variety of situations.

The neogastropods have other features equipping them for a predatory life. The Muricidae are sometimes known as dye shells because they, and to an extent the whelks, possess a poisonous excretion which they may inject into their prey to subdue them. This poison, which is bright purple in colour, is known as *purpurin*, and became famous as the dye used to colour the imperial cloaks of the Roman Emperors. Also the radulas of these families have become adapted for drilling holes through the shells of other molluscs and similarly protected animals. In this task the radula is helped by a secretion of acid, now used in offence rather than defence as in the cowries. Thus many of the shallow water whelks feed on mussels, limpets and barnacles; they may drill a hole through the shell of the mussel or limpet, or may inject purpurin between the valves of the mussel or between the plates of the barnacle, forcing the muscles to relax and the shell to open.

CONES Probably the most specialised of these predators are the cones. In this family the radula has become greatly reduced to form a series of separate elongated darts which are held one at a time in a proboscis. Associated with radula is a large salivary gland modified to produce poison with which each of the darts is charged. The proboscis is capable of sudden extension for almost as far ahead of the animal as its own length, and in this way the dart is shot into a prey item. Many of the cones are extremely poisonous and it is for this

reason that they should be handled with considerable care, and never, for example, popped into one's bathing trunks until one reaches the shore. The cones fall into three groups with regard to appropriate prey, some preferring worms, some feeding on other molluscs, and some preying on small fishes. It is the cones in this latter group, particularly *Conus textile* and *Conus geographus*, which are especially dangerous to man, since their poison is adapted to stun their vertebrate prey, and a number of human fatalities have been recorded as a result of the stings of these two species of cone.

The cones which may be considered as being common in the Red Sea include the following: *Conus textile*, *sumatrensis* (the regional form of the better known *vexillum*), *virgo*, *striatus*, *terebra*, *arenatus*, *flavidus*, *lividus*, *tesselatus*, *achinatus*, *frigidus* and *quercinus*.

SEA-SLUGS We now come to the sea-slugs, which are the major component of the second of the two divisions into which the gastropods are divided. The name sea-slug suggests a rather unattractive animal; but however attractive and colourful may be some of the shells familiar to the shell collector, they are surpassed in intensity and variety of coloration by many of the sea-slugs. Despite this, presumably because they cannot readily be preserved, they are very much less known to the non-specialist. However, they would make an excellent subject of study for the snorkeller or diver equipped with a camera (even a land camera) and a close-up lens; they can easily be photographed in a dish of water before being returned to the sea. There is not such a great variety of sea-slugs as of shells, but nevertheless there are probably several dozen species which may be found not too infrequently in the Red Sea. There is, of course, not room to deal with many of these here, but some of the commonest and most colourful examples will be described, and mention made of several rather interesting aspects of their behaviour and physiology.

In some ways it is surprising that while the shell has been the hallmark of success for such a great variety of gastropods, there should be others which have actually abandoned it. However in the right situation there may be distinct advantages in doing so. On the one hand a shell is heavy, and may become a bit of a burden when the animal is trying to climb up and feed on slender or flexible sea-anemones, hydroids or sponges, as do many of the sea-slugs. Also, freed from the weight of its shell,

BELOW: 85 The largest of the fanworms to be regularly found on Red Sea reefs, *Sabellastarte indica*.

many sea-slugs have developed the art of swimming. A shell may not be an effective defence against a predator: many fish, especially wrasses, are able to crush shells, and carrying a shell makes it more difficult to enter and hide in a suitable protecting crevice. If the crevice is too small, the shell will not fit, while if the crevice is big enough or too big, a predator can often get inside as well. In a similar way, loss of the shell enables some sea-slugs to squeeze into cracks and crannies in search of such prey as small sea-squirts and encrusting sponges.

To make up for the loss of one means of protection, the shell, the sea-slugs have developed a range of other defensive features. The bright and even gaudy coloration of many, such as *Chromodoris quadricolor* (see Plate 76), is certainly a warning indicating at the least a very unpleasant taste and possibly the presence of very effective poisons. Particular patternings may also serve to influence any potential predator to first attack various comparatively dispensable appendages in which the poisons or defences may in fact be sited, while ignoring the much more vulnerable head and body. Other sea-slugs are attractively coloured as a means of camouflage against their preferred backgrounds, even mimicking the presence of encrusting organisms on their backs. At the same time swimming may be an especially effective means of escape, not so much from fish as from persistent predators of molluscs such as the starfishes,

which would be unable to see warning coloration and perhaps be less affected by particular poisons.

TECTIBRANCHS The slug-like form has in fact evolved several times quite independently within the gastropods. This is true even within the main group of sea-slugs, as indicated by the fact that within a number of different families some species of intermediate form are found in which some sort of shell is in fact retained. These shells are usually rather smaller, and, in life, are partially or completely covered by the edge of the mantle. Such shells are present especially within the first of the three groups of these sea-slugs, the tectibranchs (meaning covered gills). The shells of some of these may even be present in the collections of shell hobbyists. An example of these are the so-called bubble shells, one of which, *Bulla ampulla*, is not uncommon in the Red Sea. This shell is thin and light and very rounded, appearing from the top almost like an egg; in colour it is mottled and striated with different shades of tan. The shell is about four centimetres long, while the whole animal, which is greyish flesh-coloured, is about twice this length and unable to withdraw completely into the shell. *Bulla* is usually found on fine sand, ploughing along through the surface layer.

Much more reduced are the shells of two other common Red Sea tectibranchs. *Aplysia oculifera* is a species of sea-hare which is large and olive-green to olive-brown in colour. It is related to the European and Atlantic sea-hares which get their name from the long upright pair of tentacles on the head which look like the ears of a hare. Sea-hares feed on algae, and are able to produce a variety of very unpleasant secretions, a whitish slime or a purplish liquid, in self-defence. *Berthilina citrina* is a smaller smooth yellow species with a dome-like mantle usually found under stones in shallow water. It feeds on sea-squirts and secretes sulphuric acid if disturbed.

SACOGLOSSANS The second group of sea-slugs are the sacoglossans (meaning sharp-tongued), of which the most apparent Red Sea species is probably *Elysia grandiflora*. This is a small slug-like animal up to three centimetres long, smooth, with in-rolled edges of the mantle, and coloured dull green mottled with darker spots. It is found under stones and on algae along the reef edge. In the sacoglossans the radula has become modified for incision, there being but a single line of scalpel-like teeth with which *Elysia* can slit open single algal cells prior to sucking out the contents. *Elysia* is also able to supplement its rations in a rather remarkable way. The chloroplasts, that is the light-fixing photosynthesising components of the algal cell, are digested intact and are passed to lobes of the liver closely beneath the dorsal surface of the sea-slug. Here they are able to function, at least for a time, producing carbohydrates just as they did within the algae, but to be used by the sea-slug. *Elysia* has thus become a photosynthesising green animal by a different route and perhaps in a truer sense than are the corals and another group of molluscs to which we shall presently come.

NUDIBRANCHS The third, largest, and most attractive group of sea-slugs are the nudibranchs (meaning naked gills). These are characterised by various feathery or filamentous appendages to their mantle. In particular one group, the dorids, carry a tight group of tufted secondary gills near the rear end of the middle of the mantle, while another group, the aeolids, carry rows of pointed filaments along either side of the mantle. These pointed outgrowths are known as *cerata*, and in the aeolids have become adapted to add to the defences of these sea-slugs. This group feeds typically on anemones and hydroids, and is apparently, in some cunning way, able to ingest the nematocysts or stinging cells from their prey without discharging them. They are digested whole and passed to outgrowths of the liver which reach the cerata. Here the nematocysts are stored until, if the slug is attacked, they are ejected through a pore in the end of the outgrowth so that, on coming into contact with the seawater, the actual stinging threads are discharged in the face of the predator.

There is only room to mention a few species of nudibranchs. There are five or six fairly common species of *Chromodoris*, all of which are brightly coloured (see Plates 75 and 76) and feed on sponges. Some of these are only a centimetre or two long, but the species illustrated reach five to seven centimetres in length. Somewhat different in shape, being broader, thicker and flatter, with reduced appendages, are several species of *Discodoris* and *Platydoris*, which are usually found on the underside of large stones on the reef. Also found under and around rocks where they feed on sponges are similar species of *Kentrodoris*, one of which is illustrated in Plate 77.

The most spectacular of the Red Sea nudibranchs must be the giant scarlet sea-slug *Hexabranchus sanguineus*. This grows up to twenty centimetres in length and is a dark red save for a white edge to the mantle. A very similar form occurs in the Indian and Pacific oceans and is widely known as the Spanish dancer; this has a second white ring around the mantle and within this again a pattern of white lobulation, so that when the animal swims, which it does with a series of well-organised undulations of the mantle passing backwards along the body, the waving red and white rim looks the swirling skirts of a Spanish dancer. The two forms are probably of the same species, although this has not been clearly established. Certainly the Red Sea dancer swims as well. *Hexabranchus* feeds on the soft coral *Sarcophyton*.

A final interesting point on the sea-slugs generally concerns their method of reproduction. Nearly all of the sea-slugs are simultaneous hermaphrodites, that is, they possess functional male and female reproduction organs at the same time. Cross-fertilisation is however normal and in some species, notably *Aplysia*, this may lead to the formation of chains of spawning individuals, each member of the chain acting as the male for the individual in front of it and the female for the individual behind it. Subsequently the eggs are laid contained in a gelatinous mass which is often coiled in an attractive pattern characteristic of a particular family or species (see Plate 79). Indeed for some species these conspicuous egg masses attract more attention from visitors to the reef than do the sea-slugs themselves.

CLAMS, OYSTERS AND MUSSELS – LAMELLIBRANCHS We now come to the third major group of shelled molluscs which are called the lamellibranchs or bivalves. These species, such as oysters or clams, have a shell consisting of two saucer-shaped plates or valves which are hinged to each other at one side, and are able to shut together so as to completely enclose the animal. With few exceptions, such as the giant clams, the bivalves are not so apparent on the reef as are the gastropods, but they are usually present there and in the surrounding areas in at least as great a number. Although many shell collectors, for example, tend to ignore the bivalves, they are most interesting animals which, by means of their different body form, are able to develop different solutions to the problem facing mollusc-like animals, or to take advantage of different opportunities and move into new habitats.

The shell of lamellibranchs is still lined by and secreted by a mantle, and between this and the body still lies the mantle cavity. Within the much broader mantle cavity, however, the gills have been able to become greatly enlarged. Thus they can now function not only for respiration, but also for feeding, by filtering out food particles carried with the current of water into the mantle. This change of body shape has however generally resulted in the animal being much less able to move itself about than is the case with the gastropods. Accordingly the foot itself has typically been reduced in size to a columnar organ, normally held within the shell, although in most species the foot can still be extended outside to push or pull the animal along, albeit in a somewhat clumsy fashion.

As they are less able to move away from potential predators, bivalves generally occur partly or completely protected within the substrate, in mud or sand or among coral. It is for this reason that they are so much less conspicuous to the non-biologist than are the gastropods. Bearing in mind this typically close association of bivalves with the substrate it is perhaps easiest to consider in turn the different situations in which different species may occur.

The largest number of bivalves around the Red Sea reefs are undoubtedly to be found living buried within the areas of sand or mud that may occur on or adjacent to the reef. These bivalves belong to those same families which dominate soft-bottomed areas throughout the world. These include the carpet or venus shells (Veneraceaa), such as species of *Dosinia*; the wedge shells or tellins (Tellinaceaa), such as species of *Tellinella* and *Macoma*; and the trough shells (Mactraceaa), such as species of *Gari*, *Donax* and especially the very abundant *Mactra olorina*. Venus shells are mobile animals which occur just beneath the surface and have thick rounded shells. Tellins have slightly elongated rather flat thin and polished shells and they burrow deeply and are notable for the length of their syphons. Trough shells also burrow fairly deeply, have smooth thin shells that may be slightly elongated and are commonly tinted in delicate shades of pink or orange. Most of these sand-dwelling bivalves are suspension feeders; through a syphon projecting above the surface of the sand they draw water into their mantle cavity where suspended food material is extracted by the gills. However, the tellins are deposit feeders and with their long syphons

they explore the surface of the surrounding sand and draw in organic matter that has settled there. In addition to this difference in feeding technique, other interesting variations in strategy are apparent between the different families. Deep burrowing makes the shell safer from predators, but this may require more energy and specialised adaptations and makes it less easy to move from place to place. Equally, laying down a thin shell makes it possible to grow faster, but at the same time renders the animal more susceptible to predation by certain types of animal.

In more muddy areas, such as may occur adjacent to fringing reefs, similar though different species of bivalve are common, and in particular *Gafrarium pectinatum* is often superabundant. Also in such areas may be found a shell which often attracts the attention of visitors, the fan shell *Pinna muricata*. These shells are a little like giant mussels, being up to thirty centimetres long and about half that width, with the shape of a partially opened fan. They lie upright, buried in the mud, with the top quarter or so of the rounded end showing at the top, and the bottom pointed end attached by horny thread-like secretions, the *byssus*, to some stone or piece of hard substrate. It seems that the projecting blade of the fan is regularly broken, but the animal can readily withdraw into the remaining portion and is able to quickly repair the damage.

In coral areas themselves a surprising range of bivalves is to be found on careful search. Many of these are attached to the dead lower parts of branches of large bushy corals or to the underside of massive corals by means of byssal threads. There are comparatively primitive arc shells (Arcidae) such as *Barbatia ovata* and *Arca avellana*, thick rough elongated shells with a boat-shaped depression surrounding the hinge. There are scallops (Pectinidae) of the genus *Chlamys*. There is the tree oyster *Isognomon acutirostris* with characteristic vertical parallel grooves on the hinge, and a greatly compressed and tapering shell. And there are the pearl oysters *Pteria aegyptica* and *Pinctada margaritifera*. *Pteria* is smaller, about five or so centimetres across, with a greatly elongated or winged hinge. *Pinctada margaritifera*, the black-lip oyster, can reach twenty centimetres in diameter. The mother-of-pearl oysters, like the *Trochus* shells, have a particularly thick inner nacreous layer to their shell, and they also may be collected for the mother-of-pearl trade. More impor-

RIGHT/INSET BOTTOM/INSET TOP: 86/87/88 The fine structure and variety of colour of sponges. Water is drawn in through many tiny pores (ostia), filtered for food particles, and pumped out through a smaller number of larger pores (opercula). A small cryptically coloured juvenile fish rests on the yellow sponge.

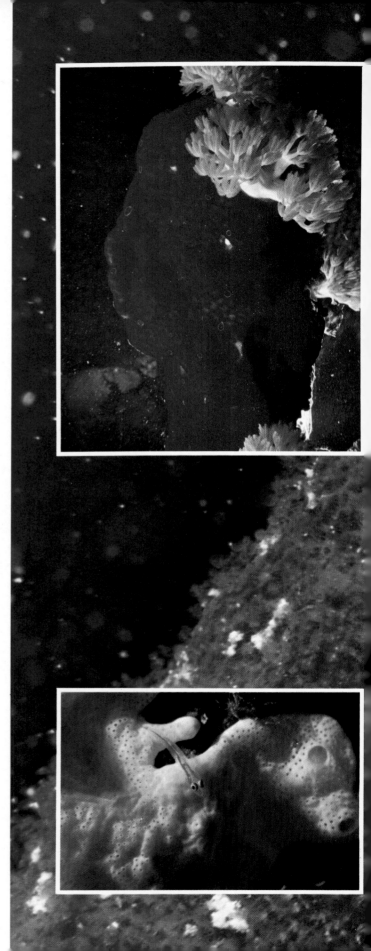

tantly, however, a particle of grit lodged against the mantle may be surrounded by separate layers of nacreous shell to form an infinitely more collectable item, a pearl, and for centuries until the development of artificial pearl culture in Japan the Red Sea was one of the areas famous for its pearls. *Pinctada margaritifera* has been cultured successfully in the Red Sea, notably at Dunganab Bay in Sudan, principally for the mother-of-pearl alone, but trials with pearl culture have also been initiated.

While all the above species attach themselves by means of byssus threads, some other species actually cement one of their valves to the coral branch or head. Particularly conspicuous is the thorn oyster *Spondylus gaederopus* (see Plate 74), deep red with rows of elongated barbs projecting from both valves; it is most characteristically seen below ten metres on a steep reef slope cemented onto the lower lobe of a head of *Porites*. Often found in similar situations and nearly as conspicuous is the coxcomb oyster *Lopha cristagalli*; this has a flattened shell, a dull purple in colour, but usually overgrown by encrusting sponges. The feature which most generally draws attention is the deeply zigzagging edge of the two valves where they meet, giving the impression of a wickedly grinning, viciously toothed mouth. Also cemented by its shell on Red Sea reefs is a true oyster, *Ostrea cucullata*, as is *Charma limbula*, one of the so-called jewel boxes which are characterised by thick rough shells, one valve of which is markedly smaller than the other and almost appears to fit within the top of it like a lid.

For living securely positioned among coral there are, however, alternatives to becoming tied or glued to coral branches and heads. One such alternative, that of actually boring into the coral rock, has been followed by species belonging to two different families of lamellibranchs, the mussels (Mytilidae) and the flask shells or gaping clams (Gastrochaenidae). The latter are represented in the Red Sea by *Rocellaria* (=*Gastrochaena*) *ruppelli*. *Rocellaria* borings are readily recognisable by the fact that the entrance is extended upwards by calcareous secretion into two flask-shaped tubes for the inhalant and exhalant syphons. The most important of the boring mussels are the date-mussels, *Lithophaga*, so called because both in colour, having a dark brown thick outer layer to the shell (the *periostracum*), and in form they bear an extraordinary resemblance to dates. Several species occur on coral reefs in the Red Sea and they live

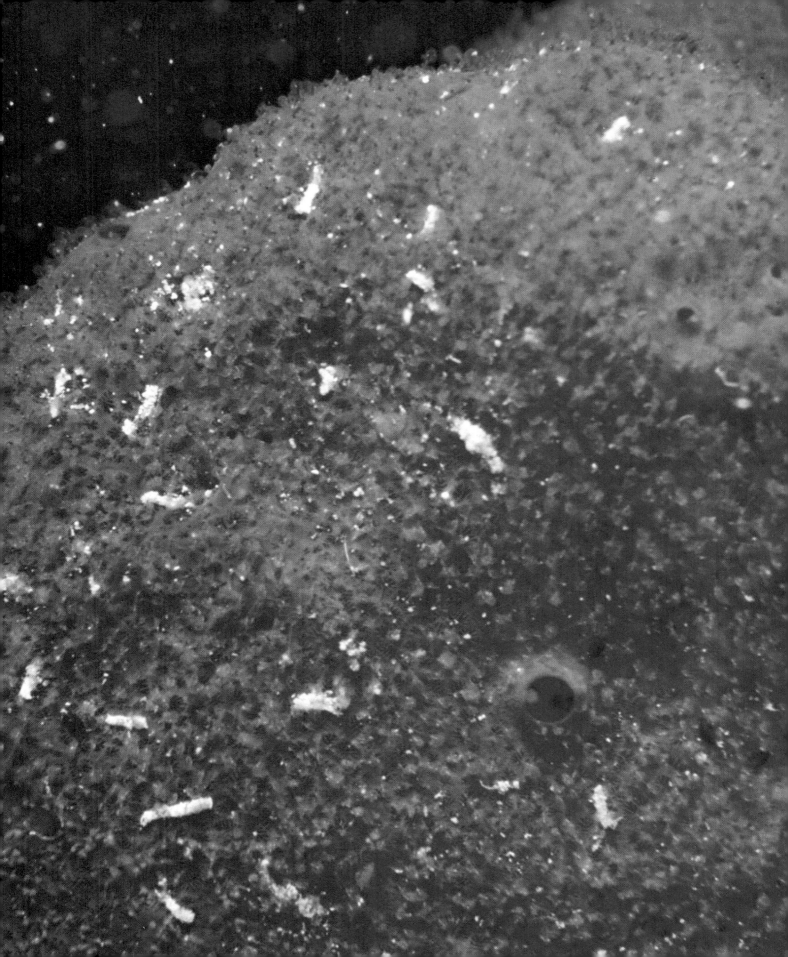

in rounded tube-like borings up to twice the length of the shell which itself may reach three centimetres.

A number of other species of mussels have become adapted to boring into coral rock in a very similar way, including in the Red Sea *Modiolus cinnamomeus* and species of *Botula*. But the most extraordinary boring mussel to be found in the Red Sea is the tiny *Fungiacava eilatensis*, not long ago discovered and investigated by the eminent coral biologist Tom Goreau. *Fungiacava* lives buried within the base of various species of mushroom (*Fungia*) corals with its syphon opening directly into the stomach of the host coral. The thin shell of the bivalve is completely covered by the mantle which secretes and absorbs calcium carbonate as necessary to provide a snug fit for the growing shell within the skeleton of the coral. *Fungiacava* feeds by taking in the planktonic plants brought into the gut of the coral by the latter's feeding activity.

The final solution to the problem of securing a firm attachment among coral is to settle between closely opposed heads or branches and allow the coral to grow up around one. This procedure is followed most completely by the scallop *Pedum spondyloideum*. This bivalve, with a big chunky torpedo-like shell, attaches itself to the bottom of crevices between lobes of the massive coral *Porites*, and as the shell grows it comes to be completely surrounded by the expanding coral. The animal is well camouflaged and most likely to be noticed by the snorkeller or diver when, on placing his hand on what appears to be the lobe of *Porites*, this suddenly snaps shut against the next lobe with a distinct 'chunk'. For a moment this can be a slightly alarming experience, as if the gape of the scallop was the mouth of a quite sizeable coral-like animal which is about to attack one.

Also secured among the lobes and heads of coral are, by contrast, almost certainly the most conspicuous of coral-reef lamellibranchs, the giant clams (Tridacnidea). Two species are common in the Red Sea, *Tridacna squamosa* and *Tridacna maximum*; the latter reaches thirty or more centimetres across, but the largest of the giant clams, *Tridacna gigas*, which in Australia reaches sizes of over a metre, has not been recorded from the area. These clams are, of course, conspicuous for the brightly coloured tissue which gapes through the rim of the open shell; this is a specialised area of the mantle which in different individuals varies

in colour from various shades of fawn to ultramarine and turquoise. The large size which these animals are able to reach is almost certainly due to one unusual and fascinating aspect of their biology. Their mantle tissues are packed with millions of tiny single-celled algae, zooxanthellae, closely resembling the symbiotic algae found in corals. Moreover, scattered over the exposed surface of the mantle are large numbers of small lens-like structures which allow light to penetrate to deeper tissues in which zooxanthellae are also contained. By contrast the colourful pigments protect the superficial tissues from damage by the intense tropical sunlight. As with corals, the zooxanthellae gain nutrients from the waste products of the clam; the clam however probably actively digests surplus zooxanthellae so that these algae are, in effect, truly farmed by the bivalves. The energy supply thus gained, along with the manner in which the zooxanthellae are able to facilitate calcification of the shell, accounts for the huge size which these animals are able to reach, probably exceeding the combined biomass of all the other gastropods occurring in the coral zone.

WORMS
FLATWORMS, RIBBON WORMS, BRISTLE WORMS AND FANWORMS

FLATWORMS The word 'worms' in popular use is in fact applied to quite a few different major animal divisions or phyla. Of these, three are of importance on the reef. The most primitive of these groups are the flatworms or Platyhelminthes. They are leaf-shaped animals, varying in size from a few millimetres to a few centimetres in length, which normally glide over the substrate with the aid of a ciliated underside. To the biologist they are in fact not so far removed anatomically from the coelenterates, the corals and their allies, which we discussed in chapter 3, in that the body wall merges with the gut without an intervening cavity as in higher animals, and there is only one entrance to the digestive system, the mouth being used to void digested material as well as to take in food.

Only a limited number of species of flatworm are to be found on coral reefs, most commonly under boulders on the reef flat. Many of them, however, are brightly coloured in mosaic-like patterns or with stripes of black, white and orange. As well as crawling some of them, as shown in Plates 81 and 82, are able to swim, working the sides of their bodies in graceful undulations. In fact, with their bright colours and manner of swimming, they are often mistaken for small swimming sea-slugs, such as the 'Spanish dancer' described above.

Flatworms are carnivorous, capturing prey even larger than themselves by entangling them with mucus; the mouth is then expanded to secrete digestive enzymes onto the prey so that it can be consumed. The colour of brownish or greenish flatworms is however often due to the presence of symbiotic algae, a phenomenon that we have now met with in several different invertebrate groups, and additional nutrition is obtained from these plant cells.

RIBBON WORMS The second phylum of marine worms to be met with on the reef are the Nemertina or ribbon worms. These worms are thin but may be very long, reaching up to ten or twenty centimetres or more; they may be flattened like a narrow ribbon or be round in cross-section like a bootlace. They are not uncommon on the reef but burrow into sand and mud and under rocks and rubble, and also they are extremely fragile,

OCTOPUS AND CUTTLEFISH – CEPHALO-PODS We now come to the fourth subdivision of the molluscs which deserve some mention here. This is the Cephalopoda, the group containing the octopuses, cuttlefish and squid. One or two species of each of these forms are not uncommonly to be met with on Red Sea reefs. Small octopuses may sometimes be seen on the flat reef or reef face, usually as they rush for cover, when one is snorkelling or diving; but as they are somewhat nervous animals the best chance to watch them often arises accidentally when one appears underneath a boat or a jetty and can be viewed through the surface of the water. The commonest species are *Octopus macropus* and *Octopus aegina*. The cuttlefish *Sepia pharaonis* is not uncommon in lagoon and sandy areas, swimming away with undulating movements of the mantle around the edge of the body, and squid (see Plate 80) such as *Sepioteuthis lessoniana* are sometimes seen, often in groups, swimming in midwater above or near the fringing reef. The cephalopods are a fascinating group; they have a well-developed brain, and an eye bearing a remarkable resemblance to the eye of vertebrates. They have an extraordinary ability to change colour to match almost any background, and this is used to the full during the surprising and attractive courtship behaviour of the octopuses. Unfortunately the minor importance of cephalopods in coral-reef communities does not allow us enough space to give a more detailed description of these features here.

commonly breaking when one attempts to pick them up for closer examination. In fact, by this means ribbon worms are able to reproduce asexually, broken pieces regenerating into a complete worm.

The different species may be dull sandy or brown in colour, or some are more red or orange; but exact identification often requires detailed examination of the shape of the head and the arrangement of the eyes. One species, however, which may be readily recognised on Indo-Pacific coral reefs is *Euborlasia quinquestriata* which is white with several black lines running the whole length of the body, and is to be found among coral rubble. Like the flatworms the ribbon worms are carnivorous.

BRISTLE WORMS – POLYCHAETES Much the most significant group of worms on the coral reef, however, are the polychaetes, a group which is closely related to earthworms and leeches. Polychaete worms, like earthworms, are segmented from head to tail, a feature which distinguishes them from ribbon worms, and they take their name from the numerous *chaetae* or bristles which project from parts of the body surface. Up to a hundred or more different species of polychaete, belonging to twenty or so different families, may be found on a typical Red Sea coral reef. For the average reader of this book, however, it is probably appropriate just to describe some of the more important families and mention a few of the very commonest or most conspicuous species. Among these families some may generally be distinguished which include highly active free-living worms, which are generally predators. By contrast other families contain sedentary species which live in permanent or semi-permanent tubes or burrows, and which feed on food particles suspended in the water or deposited nearby on the surface of the substrate.

Among the carnivorous families two may be mentioned in which the side of the segment extends into a paddle-like structure known as a *parapodium*. These two families are the Nereidae and Amphinomidae. The Nereidae are often known as rag-worms and are large and active predators up to twenty centimetres or more in length, and often green or greenish-brown in colour. When disturbed they can swim rapidly with graceful movements of the body, aided by the effect of the paddle-like parapodia. They have a distinct head with tentacles and jaws carried on a mouth which can be

further protruded to grab at prey. One of the commonest Red Sea species is *Perinereis nuntia* which is found near the tide-level on sandy shores. The fairly similar Amphinomidae have especially dense sets of bristles which are crystalline and brittle, so that it is best to avoid handling them since the bristles easily break off in one's skin and can cause unpleasant irritation. Two species of this family, *Eurythoe complanata* and *Hermodice carunculata*, are especially common on Red Sea reefs and are to be found beneath many boulders and coral heads. *Hermodice carunculata* is of special interest since it is known to feed on corals, especially *Porites*. It emerges at night and when feeding extends its mouth area over a small patch of coral for several minutes and appears to suck out the living coral tissue beneath.

FANWORMS Turning to the sedentary tube-dwelling worms we come across a species which can hardly be missed by any visitor to the reef; this is the small brightly coloured fanworm *Spirobranchus giganteus*, individuals of which are scattered like flowers over many

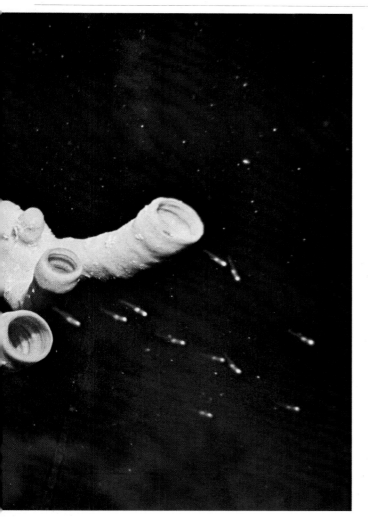

corals along the crest of Red Sea reefs (see Plates 83 and 84). The visible part of each worm consists of two small spiral fans, each about a centimetre across, forming a cone-shaped structure a centimetre or so high; these fans are, in fact, the gills which are used for filter feeding as well as for respiration. There is great variety in the colour of these gills between different individuals which range from red and orange to blue and grey. Should a shadow, possibly indicative of a predator, fall across the array of gills they are instantaneously withdrawn into the small calcareous tube in which the worm lives, and the entrance to the tube is blocked by a door or operculum which is in fact the end of a small trumpet-like structure carried on the head of the worm. The upper side of the entrance to the tube bears a small projecting spur on which, no doubt, fish attempting to snap at the tentacles may very easily injure themselves; certainly a snorkeller leaning on a head of *Porites* may easily jab himself on an unnoticed *Spirobranchus* tube. The bright colours displayed on the gills may well be a warning of this mean device, and should a fish succeed

in snatching off some of the gills they may probably soon regrow, the worm itself not being easily injured. The actual body of the worm is relatively plain, with reduced bristles, save that the front portion is surrounded by a conspicuous membranous collar. This is characteristic of the family Serpulidae, all of which have calcareous tubes, although in most cases these, rather than being embedded, are cemented to the outside of rocks and other surfaces. One such familiar group of worms are the species of *Spirorbis*, which although not so readily seen on the reef, are almost certain to be found on the bottom of the diver's boat. These are the small worms which have little calcareous tubes arranged in a small flat spiral a third of a centimetre or so across.

The fanworms of the family Sabellidae possess tubes of mucus embedded in the sand or mud instead of calcareous tubes. These are rather larger than the Serpulidae, the worm growing to twenty or more centimetres in length, and the fan of gills being several centimetres across. In some of these worms, such as *Sabellastarte indica* (see Plate 85), which is fairly common on Red Sea reefs, there appears to be just a single circle of gills, although this is in fact composed of two semicircular clusters, one attached to either side of the head. In others such as species of *Bispira* each cluster forms its own circular array. Again the body itself is relatively plain, each segment bearing small bundles of chaetae. In some species there are actually two or more eyes on each gill filament, and these no doubt assist in triggering the withdrawal response to the arrival of a possible predator.

A final group of tube-dwelling polychaetes which deserve mention are the Terebellidae. These lack the colourful fans of the other two groups but can be the cause of considerable fascination. The typical terebellids are very plain and plumpish flesh-coloured worms ten or twenty or more centimetres long, living in membraneous tubes in the sand or beneath stones or coral rubble. The head, however, bears two types of filamentous appendages; there are shorter branching red-coloured gills, and in addition there are many longer fine white tentacles which the animal uses to search the surrounding sand for organic matter on which to feed. In most species, such as *Polycirrhus plumosus* which is fairly common in shallow sandy areas in the Red Sea, these tentacles do not reach much more than five or so centimetres in length. However, in one remarkable

RIGHT: 92 A diver inspects a coralline sponge, a layer of sponge tissues lying over a coral-like calcareous pillar. The opercula are visible as pores on the outside.

species, *Reteterebella queenslandia*, there are tentacles reaching for a metre or more. These tentacles are not infrequently noticed by snorkellers swimming along in the shallow water behind the reef crest. At first only a single tentacle is noticed, a very fine white thread stretching across the sand between corals; it might be taken for an old piece of fishing line, or, when it is seen to move slightly, for an entire worm in itself. But when the thread is followed to see how long it is, it is found that at one end half-a-dozen or more such tentacles converge to a single point, and enter and vanish into a crevice in the rocks or under a coral. Despite their length, these tentacles convey particles of food back to the worm which lies hidden in the crevice to which the tentacles converge, the food being moved by ciliary action along a groove-like infolding in the tentacles. By peering through one's face mask close enough to the tentacle, such particles can in fact often be seen trundling slowly along this miniaturised conveyor-belt system.

THE SPONGES – PORIFERA

The sponges are a group about which one would like to be able to write in as much detail as we have treated the molluscs or the echinoderms, for they are among the most conspicuous and vividly coloured animals on the reef. Many are brilliant shades of red or orange, purple or yellow. But although some species tend to develop particular forms, cups or funnels, spheres or branching tubes, many grow as irregular masses, coating the substrate, or pendulous from coral cliffs or overhangs. Thus the identification of sponges is a most difficult and complex topic, depending on microscopic examination, and only now is the classification of the common Red Sea sponges being really sorted out, by the dedicated work of one or two scientists. And since recognition is an essential first step to further investigation, little is known about the ecology of even the most conspicuous species. Nevertheless a few points may be made of potential interest to the general reader.

Sponges are of course very simple animals, of an even more primitive type than the coelenterates. In some ways they may be seen as a blind alley in the evolution of multicelled animals from single-celled organisms. The structure of the typical sponge may be briefly described. Throughout its form there is little variation in the composition of the main tissue of the sponge – the *mesenchyme*. This consists of a gelatinous mass through which are able to move various wandering or amoeboid cells, some of which are packed with granules of the pigments which give the sponges their colour. Also embedded in the matrix are numerous spicules or fibres which constitute the skeleton of the animal and serve to support it. The spicules are composed of calcium carbonate or of silica, and typically consist of a single long spine, or of several such spines, often four, radiating from a point. The fibres are made of a protein known, predictably, as *spongin*.

The sponges feed by filtering plankton from the water. The water is drawn into the tissue of the sponge through numerous small pores or ostia which cover its surface (see Plates 86 to 88), and from a subdermal space the water is then drawn through a series of *incurrent canals* into numerous small *flagellated chambers*, within which the food particles are trapped. This is done by some very distinctive cells, the *collar cells*, which line the chambers. Each collar cell has a whip-like flagellum projecting into the chamber, while around the base of the flagellum is a collar-like structure within which food particles are absorbed. From the flagellated chambers the water is carried through *excurrent canals*, branching into larger canals, which open onto the outside of the sponge through another pore or *osculum*. The oscula are generally much larger than the ostia, but fewer in number. It is the movement of the flagella which maintain the flow of water through the sponge, although the exact mechanics of this is not fully understood, since the flagella do not all beat in unison. Possibly each may beat in spiral fashion so that they operate independently, like numerous tiny outboard propellers. In any case, a considerable volume of water passes through a sponge, even the smallest often filtering twenty litres or more a day.

Because of their hollow form and porous nature, through which is maintained a constant supply of fresh seawater, sponges make ideal homes for many small animals. A large number of species, especially shrimps and worms, may be found living as commensals within them, including a variety of small fish, such as blennies, which are often of identical colour to the sponge, so as to be camouflaged against this background. Sometimes very large numbers, as many as 10,000, of a particular species of shrimp or worm may be found within a single sponge. On the other hand comparatively few animals eat sponges, perhaps because the sponges contain sub-

stances which are toxic or unpleasant to them. Some sea-slugs browse on sponges, some crustaceans may nibble at their tissues, and just a few fishes also feed on them; and it often seems probable that these predators may be able to absorb whatever noxious compound may be present in the sponge, and use it in their own defence.

Three groups of sponges perhaps deserve special mention. The horny sponges (subclass Keratosa) some-times puzzle people because they seem unlike the typical sponge, their surface being covered with a rough leathery membrane. They lack the silicious spicules characteristic of most coral-reef sponges, and the small ostia are hidden among numerous tiny conical mounds which give the sponge its surface texture. Equally puzzling can be the coralline sponges, which at first sight appear to be fairly normal, brightly coloured, brick-sized sponges, but which are solid to the touch and heavy to hold. It often seems as though the sponge has completely overgrown a head of some sort of coral, and yet completely moulded itself to the coral's form. In fact the coralline head is a calcium carbonate skeleton built by the sponge itself, and such sponges can thus make a contribution to the growth of a reef.

By contrast one other group of sponges are important among those processes which erode the structure of the reef. These are the boring sponges of the family Clionidae. The tissue of these sponges bores and occu-pies channels within coral heads and coralline rock, and even within mollusc shells. Usually the sponge is not apparent from the outside, but, on splitting a coral head, fine channels occupied by strands of species of *Cliona*, which are often bright green or suphur yellow, may be found. Mounds of massive coral may become so riddled with the borings of these sponges, as well as those of boring molluscs and worms, that they may readily crack and split as their upper parts become overgrown, or under the pressures of wave action.

Here we must draw to an end our discussion of the most important groups of invertebrates to be found on the reef. It goes almost without saying that there are many other invertebrate groups represented on Red Sea reefs. With most of these groups however only occasional examples of relatively few species are found. Or, with a few groups, a variety of species are in fact extremely abundant, but these animals are either very small or otherwise inconspicuous and unlikely to be noticed by the ordinary visitor to the reef. Nevertheless all these groups may repay study. They can stimulate much interest and fascination. Always the same theme is apparent – the variety of ways in which the different species within a group have made use of the basic equipment of the group to solve problems and adapt to new styles of living in the 'struggle for survival' on the reef. And often the animals on their part, when one takes a close look, provide cunning examples of mecha-

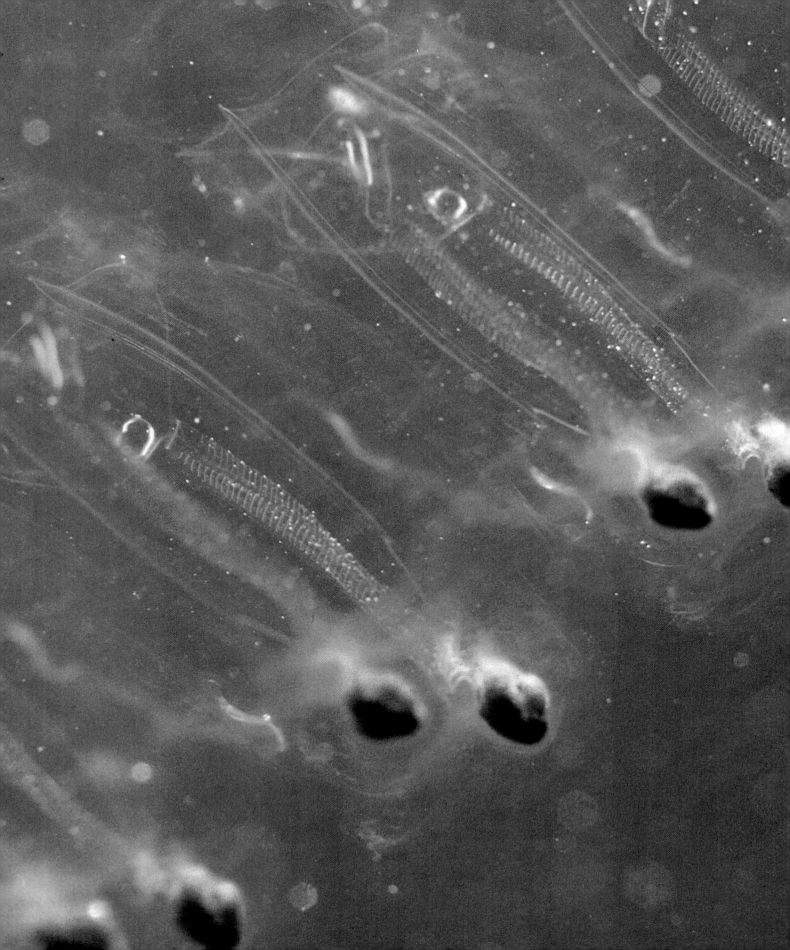

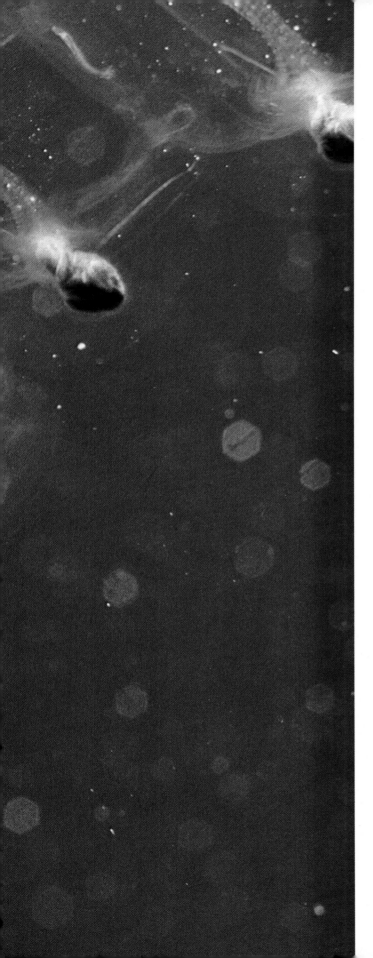

LEFT: 93 A chain of the colonial planktonic sea-squirt, *Salpa maxima*. New individuals form by budding from older individuals, and often remain attached.

nical and biological engineering, or turn out to be objects of considerable beauty.

Perhaps to illustrate all these points two examples may briefly be mentioned, one taken from each end of the great spectrum of invertebrates. On most surfaces of the reef, on the rock and on the sand, are to be found very large numbers of one of the very simplest types of animal. These are the Foraminifera, tiny single-celled organisms related to the Amoeba. Although a few Foraminifera may be a millimetre or more in size, most are much smaller. Yet although each foraminiferan consists of but a single cell, a single 'blob' as it were of protoplasmic jelly, when looked at beneath a microscope it is at once clear that they are objects of great interest and beauty. For each is surrounded by a delicate calcium carbonate shell, sculptured with numerous spires and windows, by which protrude strands of protoplasm from the core of the cell. With the aid of these strands the animals capture the tiny single-celled plants on which they feed, while the Foraminifera themselves are a major source of food for slightly larger invertebrates, and their dead shells are a major component of the calcareous sand around the reef. Yet most non-biologists, and even many biologists, visiting the reef are unaware of their presence.

At the other end of the range of invertebrates, there are sometimes to be found around the reef animals which, while lacking backbones, nevertheless give some indication of the origin of the vertebrates, and of animals more closely related to man. For example, at certain times of year and with particular currents and winds, strings of large jelly-like organisms, as shown in Plate 93, are to be found drifting in open water along the windward side of the reef. These are salps, which are in fact a type of sea-squirt. The body of each salp has the form of a gelatinous capsule on which are apparent an inhalant tube or syphon, through which seawater is drawn in, and an exhalant syphon, through which the water is expelled. The plankton filtered from the water is processed by a muscular gut. Salps can reproduce by budding, and the new individuals often remain attached to the older ones so that a string of salps is formed. On the other hand, sexual reproduction may occur, and in some sea-squirts this gives rise to a tiny tadpole-like larva; in the tail of the larva is present a flexible rod-like structure, the forerunner of the backbone, the diagnostic feature of the vertebrates to which we now turn.

Few things are more dazzling or bewildering to the snorkeller or diver on his first visit to a coral reef than the overwhelming variety of fishes which drift and dash in seemingly countless numbers all about him. They seem to come in every shape and form and in every pattern and coloration. In fact on a typical Red Sea coral reef there are likely to be several hundred different species or types of fish, perhaps three quarters of which are obviously visible swimming around, while the remainder are small and cryptic species which live within the branches and crevices among corals and boulders.

Exactly why a habit like a coral reef should be able to support so many different types of fish is at the moment the subject of a great deal of interest among biologists working in the field. The question is one not only of great theoretical interest, but is also a practical one, since if we want to try to conserve coral reefs together with the many different types of fish and other animals present on them, it obviously helps if we know what factors have enabled all these creatures to co-exist together in the first place. This great variety of fishes on a coral reef is somewhat similar to the great variety of birds which can be found in tropical rain forests, but in none of the other habits of the world can so many different species of backboned animals be found living together.

To the snorkeller and diver on the reef this great variety of fishes is of course the main source of interest and is also something that provides a great deal of aesthetic pleasure; while trying to identify these different fish, which naturally is what the human visitor to the reef sooner or later wants to do, can be a very baffling and frustrating matter, simply because there are so many different types to be considered. At the same time most people have not had a great deal of experience in comparing differences in shape as between one fish and another, so that differences which seem fairly obvious under water often prove to be very difficult to pin down when one is back on dry land again. The best approach for the beginner is to start by trying to recognise whether a particular fish is a member of fifteen or so different families, for in fact the great majority of the reef fish do belong to one of quite a small number of families, such as the butterflyfishes or wrasses, or groupers, or surgeonfishes. The fish of each family tend to have their own highly characteristic shape, and once

this is recognised, the different members can be told apart by differences in their coloration. In this chapter we intend to introduce the reader to at least some of these families. Some of the prominent or more interesting species within the families can be mentioned or illustrated, but it will also be worth mentioning some of the ways in which these fish obtain a living, how they find their food and how they protect themselves. As we have suggested, each type of fish tends to develop its own specialised way of doing things, for it is only thus that it is able to survive in the competitive world of the coral reef. Discovering exactly how each species is adapted in its form and behaviour to the situation in which it finds itself often provides the greatest fascination to those who become deeply involved in the life of the reef.

WRASSES – LABRIDAE It is hard to say whether the honour of being the family most characteristic of coral reefs would fall to the wrasses, the butterflyfishes, the parrotfishes or the damselfishes, but certainly there are more different types of wrasse to be seen on the reef than there are fish in any other family. They range from the huge Hump-headed wrasse (*Cheilinus undulatus*), which grows up to two metres in length and can weigh up to 90 kilogrammes, to tiny fish living among the branches of corals such as the little red and green striped *Pseudocheilinus hexataenia* which is only four or five centimetres in size. Nevertheless, despite such enormous differences, the wrasse can usually be recognised by their general shape, vivid but gaudy coloration, slightly elongated head often with thickish lips and slightly protruding teeth, and in particular by their characteristic mode of swimming which relies especially on a regular and often rapid up and down beating of the pectoral fins (e.g. those just behind the head). Three fairly characteristic species of wrasse are illustrated in this chapter, the Checkerboard wrasse, *Halichoeres centriquadrus* (Plate 95), the elegant brown and white *Bodianus anthiodes* (Plates 96 and 97), and the larger banded wrasse *Cheilinus fasciatus* (Plate 98). The most abundant wrasse on Red Sea coral reefs is almost certainly the Common green wrasse, *Thalassoma rupfelli*, which is about fifteen to twenty centimetres long and pale green with a pattern of longitudinal and vertical thin pink bars.

Most wrasse feed on a variety of hard-shelled invertebrates such as small shrimps, crabs, and shellfish.

BELOW: 95 The checkerboard wrasse, *Halichoeres centriquadrus*, a typical medium-small wrasse feeding on small crabs, shrimps and worms.

RIGHT/BOTTOM: 96/97 The wrasse *Bodianus anthiodes*, adult and juvenile; this species is commoner on the deeper reef face and reef slope than in shallower water. Note a fan-like hydroid behind the juvenile fish.

BOTTOM RIGHT: 98 The wrasse *Cheilinus fasciatus*, one of the most approachable fish on the reef, common in shallow water and at depth. It spends its time searching for shellfish in sand and rubble.

TOP RIGHT: 99 The large parrot-like beak of the parrotfish, in this case a female *Scarus gibbus*, is formed by the fusion of two teeth in each jaw, and used principally for scraping microscopic algae off the coral rock.

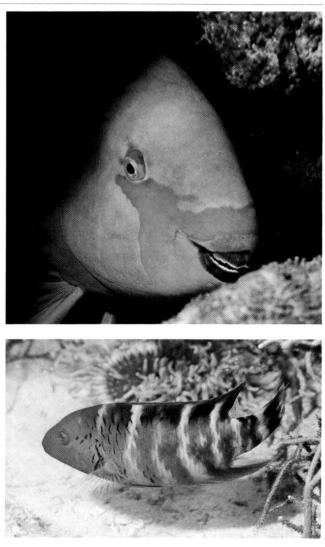

This they are able to do by using their well-developed teeth, and also the pair of hard bony plates in their throat which can be used to further grind up the food. The exact size of the prey obviously varies a great deal with the size of the wrasse – the Hump-headed wrasse can feed on large shellfish such as cowries and even on spiny sea-urchins, whereas the medium-to-small-sized wrasse such as the Common green wrasse and Checkerboard wrasse feed a great deal on the small crabs and shrimps which live among corals.

Wrasse are well known for being highly opportunistic and very able to exploit any chance of obtaining food that may come to hand. For example, some of the coral-reef wrasses spend a great deal of time following other larger fishes which may be overturning coral or rubble, or digging in the sand on the reef. Thus the Lagoon ray (*Taeniura lymma*) feeds in the lagoon by digging in the sand with its snout and wing-like fins, and near by are often one or two Checkerboard wrasse which wait to grab any invertebrates which may be unearthed by the digging of the ray.

At the same time many of the wrasses have developed specialisation of form or behaviour to enable them to capture food. One of the most conspicuous of these is the Elephant wrasse or Bird wrasse (*Gomphosus caeruleus*), a smallish wrasse about twenty centimetres long with a very elongated snout: the males are dark blue all over, while the females are pale green above and a yellowish white below. The elephant-like snout is used for probing into coral heads and small crevices to detect and winkle out the shrimps and other small animals on which this wrasse feeds. A more elaborate device of this type is shown by the Sling-jaw wrasse (*Epibulus insidiator*), a medium-sized wrasse with a grey head, a red central band, and a conspicuously elongated dark blue tail. The Sling-jaw wrasse gets its name from the fact that it is able to apparently 'unhinge' its jaw and extend its mouth into a long tube, almost as long again as its head. This it does to suck up small shrimps and tiny fish from coral interstices and crevices on the reef, rather in the fashion of an animated slurp-gun or suction-gun used by some divers to collect small aquarium fish.

Another specialisation of behaviour can be seen in some species of *Cheilinus* who are known to tackle large spiny sea-urchins by carrying them to a suitable rock against which they can bang the urchins until their spines and shells are broken. Perhaps the most cunning ploy, used by several species of wrasse, including the Sling-jaw wrasse, is to mimic in colour and behaviour other non-predatory species which may be present on the reef. In this way they can approach food items such as shrimps or small fish, which mistaking the predatory wrasse for a harmless species may fail to take evasive action necessary to ensure survival.

PARROTFISHES – SCARIDAE Parrotfishes are perhaps the most easily recognisable family of fish of the Red Sea reef. They are all of a fairly standard torpedo-like shape, but as shown in Plate 99 they have clearly discernible beaks formed from the development and fusion of their teeth; it is the resemblance of these beaks to the beaks of parrots which give these fishes their name. Many of the parrotfishes are brightly and gaudily coloured and they swim, like the wrasses to which they are in fact closely related, by up-and-down movements of their pectoral fins. In fact their gaudy

BELOW: 100 Thoughtful eye? Parrotfish sleep at night resting securely among coral branches, when they can easily be approached and photographed. This is the head of the pink-chinned male *Cetoscarus bicolor*, a species which takes small amounts of coral as well as algae.

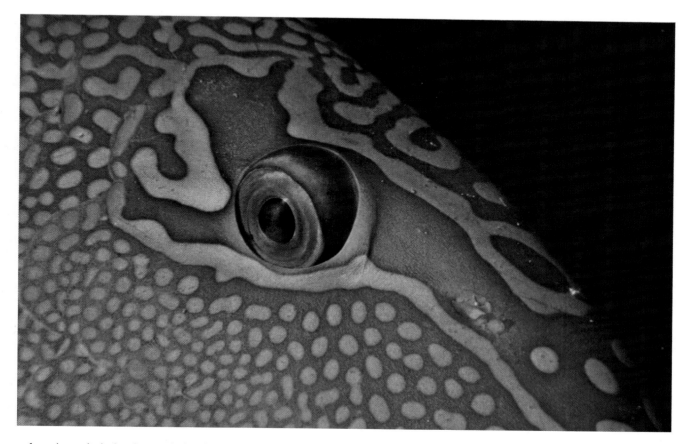

coloration, their beaks, and the flapping movements of their pectoral fins as they swim along the reefs can make them seem extraordinarily like a flock of parrots flying through a forest clearing.

The identification of the species of parrotfish is rather difficult and complicated by the fact that often male and female have a completely different coloration. Frequently the different sexes of a species were in the past given quite different scientific names and only recently has it been possible to work out which female belonged to which male. Perhaps the two commonest species of parrotfish of Red Sea reefs are the orange-cheeked *Scarus sordidus* and the green-saddled *Scarus ferrugineus*. The male of *Scarus sordidus* is mainly a brownish green, but there is a very conspicuous orange cheek and a violet or pale blue forehead; the female of the species is almost a dull black although sometimes there are a number of white spots on the flanks, or a white patch at the base of the tail. The male of *Scarus*

ferrugineus is basically a dark browny green but there is a pale green/blue saddle over the middle of the body and the top of the head is a brownish orange while the cheeks are a paler orange; while the female of the species is a rusty pink colour with bright yellow fins and tail.

There has in the past been some confusion over the exact feeding habits of parrotfishes, in that it has been thought that parrotfish used their heavy beaks to feed entirely by scraping and breaking off pieces of live coral. In fact most parrotfish feed on the layer of fine algae that grows on most of the partly bare rock surfaces of the reef. They use their beaks to scrape at the rock, getting off the thin film of algae which other fish, which can only pluck at algal strands, are unable to remove. In scraping at the rock they also take in a great deal of the rock itself, and this is ground up into fine particles by the bony plates in their throat which, in common with wrasses, they possess. These fine calcareous particles are voided from the body in large amounts, and in this way

parrotfishes are in fact one of the major agencies responsible for the formation of sand on the reef. At the same time some of the larger parrotfishes, especially in some areas including the Red Sea, take significant amounts of coral. They may leave characteristic scrape marks on the surface of the larger rounded corals, especially the mounded banks of *Porites*. The largest parrotfish of all, called the Donkeyfish (*Bolbometopon muricatus*) feeds entirely on coral and does so by breaking off chunks of massive and branched corals with its huge beak. In the Red Sea schools of thirty to sixty of these large fish (they grow one and a half metres or so) are not uncommon on most reefs. However, they are fairly nervous animals, and not infrequently the most apparent sign of their presence is the large 'smoke screen' of sand which they excrete as they swim off.

Both parrotfishes and wrasses hide themselves on the reef at night to sleep, and with the aid of a torch they may be found resting among the dead lower branches of a mass of bushy coral (see Plate 100). Parrotfishes often secrete a mucus envelope around themselves as an added protection, it is thought, perhaps against nocturnal predators which hunt by smell, such as moray eels, or perhaps against some of the poisonous cone shells which feed on fishes by night.

BUTTERFLYFISHES AND ANGELFISHES
CHAETODONTIDAE Butterflyfishes and angelfishes are amongst the best known of coral-reef fishes because of their attractive shape and coloration, and in particular because they are highly prized as specimens for marine aquaria. As can be seen (Plates 101 to 111), all these fish are very flattened from side to side and have a basic disc-like shape. They have a small snout projecting out of the front, and enlarged dorsal and ventral fins and tail projecting from the back. Angelfishes are slightly more rectangular in outline than butterflyfishes, and their mouths project from lower down on the front part of the fish. The flattened shape of these fishes enables them to wind their way amongst the corals; it also enables them to retain their stability when manoeuvring at low speed to pick up items of food, in much the same way as the keel of a sailing boat helps with its steering, and prevents it from turning over.

Most butterflyfishes and angelfishes, in the Red Sea at least, are conspicuously territorial, and the former are usually seen in pairs wandering around their territory

FAR LEFT TOP/LEFT TOP: 104/105 The blue-cheeked butterflyfish, *Chaetodon semilarvatus*, one of the largest of the butterfly fishes and another species unique to the Red Sea area. It mostly feeds at night.

BELOW LEFT/BELOW: 106/107 The pennantfish or bannerfish, *Heniochus intermedius*, is closely related to the butterflyfishes, but not to the very similar Moorish Idol to be seen in the Indian Ocean.

BELOW: 108 The angelfish, *Pomacanthus maculosus*, light blue with a yellow crescent on its flank. Species of *Pomacanthus* feed mostly on sponges.

feeding and patrolling the border. The broad sides of the fishes are also of value in this respect in that they are used to display the bright and attractive coloration which is so typical of this group. Each species has its own characteristic colour pattern, which enables members of the same species to recognise each other for purposes of social behaviour, pair formation, and in particular so that a pair can recognise others of the same species who intrude into their territory.

Despite the general similarity in shape and form within this family, the different species of butterflyfish and angelfish show a range of feeding behaviour. Some of the butterflyfishes, including the brown-faced *Chaetodon larvatus* (see Plates 102 and 103) and the white-backed *Chaetodon austriacus* feed mostly on coral; however, unlike some parrotfishes, which scrape up the coral with their beaks, these butterflyfishes pick at the individual polyps of the coral with their small elongated mouths. Since, when a part of a coral is attacked in this way, the surrounding polyps tend to withdraw as far as they can into their protective skeletons, after picking at a few polyps the butterflyfish has to move on to the next coral; thus the pairs of butterflyfish keep on the move, working their way from coral head to coral head across

their territory. These butterflyfishes may also gain a significant portion of their food requirements by taking in the mucus which is secreted by the coral, especially when it is irritated.

Other butterflyfishes, such as the white-browed *Chaetodon fasciatus* (see Plate 101) feed on a variety of small soft-bodied invertebrates such as hydroids and polychaete worms. Also while most of the butterflyfishes feed by day, some are nocturnally active: the blue-cheeked *Chaetodon semilarvatus* (see Plates 104 and 105) appears to feed entirely at night, and *Chaetodon fasciatus* probably does so to some extent, as does the conspicuously shaped and coloured Pennantfish or Bannerfish *Heniochus intermedius* (see Plates 106 and 107). For this reason these last three species are often seen by day resting fairly motionless in mid-water in the shelter of small coral faces and overhangs.

Of the angelfishes, the larger species, including the light blue *Pomacanthus maculosus* (see Plate 108) and the very similar dark blue *Pomacanthus asfur*, feed almost exclusively on sponges, whereas the small species of angelfish feed much more on algae. By far the most dramatically coloured of the small angelfishes must be the Royal Angelfish (*Pygoplytes diacanthus*) (see Plates

LEFT/BELOW/RIGHT: 109/110/111 The Royal Angelfish, *Pygoplytes diacanthus*, one of the most strikingly coloured fish on the reef.

109 to 111). However, the commonest angelfish in the Red Sea is a small brown species, *Centropyge multispinis*, which is scarcely fifteen centimetres long, but which being dull in coloration and secretive in habits is often completely overlooked.

A number of the species of butterflyfishes and angelfishes are of interest in that they are endemic or unique to the Red Sea area, in some cases including the north-west Indian Ocean. These endemic species include *Chaetodon austriacus*, *Chaetodon larvatus*, *Chaetodon semilarvatus*, *Chaetodon fasciatus*, *Chaetodon mesoleucus* and *Pomacanthus asfur*. This may reflect the particularly close association of these fishes to coral reefs, but also the particular attention paid to this group by aquarists, which has led to the recording of small differences between closely related forms.

DAMSELFISHES – POMACENTRIDAE Coral-reef fishes can scarcely be described without mention of the damselfishes which, on Red Sea reefs at least, must constitute the most numerous family in terms of numbers of individuals. The swarms of small fishes which hover above the reef crest, along the reef face, and over every coral knoll are, with one exception, damselfishes. Particularly abundant are the two small species of *Chromis*, the pale green *Chromis caeruleus* and the grey-green *Chromis ternatensis* (see Plate 11). Another species of *Chromis* is *Chromis dimidiatus* which is especially noticeable because its front half is black and its back half white. Also often present in smaller numbers on the outskirts of these groups are the larger (about twelve centimetres) so-called Sergeant-majors, conspicuous because of their black and

white vertical banding. But there are ten or fifteen other species of damselfish which are common on Red Sea reefs and occur scattered as individuals or small groups in or around the corals. All of these are of very similar shape and size, between about five and fifteen centimetres in length, but perhaps the best known is the clownfish (*Amphiprion bicinctus*) (see Plates 154 to 157) whose close association with the giant sea-anemones will be described in the next chapter.

Most of the damselfishes feed on the minute drifting animals which form a major part of the plankton; thus the *Chromis* shoals are largest and thickest where good currents bring plenty of such food to the reef. Some of the damsels are however more generalist feeders and some specialise in feeding on algae. One such of these specialist algal feeders is the small common black damselfish *Stegastes nigricans* which has earned itself a reputation as the most aggressive fish on the reef because of its habit of fearlessly, if harmlessly, attacking the hands or feet of snorkellers and divers who come too close to its home. This aggressive behaviour is part of its mode of living. Colonies of these fish are found especially on the reef top in areas of rubble which are overgrown with long filamentous algae, each individual damselfish defending a small area of its own, less than half a metre across. In fact this algal cover is present as a direct result of the aggressive behaviour of the damselfish, for they try to drive away any other fish, including many much larger, that might try to feed on this algae; hence the aggressive behaviour of the damselfish towards human intruders. In fact these damselfish may be considered as farming their small fields of algae

BELOW: 112 The silver-grey damselfish, *Amblyglyphidodon leucogaster*, a species which feeds in the water column a metre or so above the corals.

RIGHT: 113 The yellow-edged unicornfish, *Callicanthus* or *Naso litturatus*, a relative of the surgeonfishes.

BOTTOM: 114 A rabbitfish, *Siganus stellatus*, an algal browser. As with many Red Sea fish, the scientific latin name originates partly from the local arabic name for this type of fish, *sigan*.

FAR RIGHT: 115 The blue-lined snapper, *Lutjanus kasmira*. Like many snappers, this species feeds at night; by day groups are found sheltering near gullies on exposed reef faces, but by night they disperse to feed.

to the extent that they have been observed throwing out species of algae which are probably less suitable as food, thus as it were weeding their little cultivated plot.

Because of their small size and interesting behaviour the damselfishes, like the butterflyfishes, are popular aquarium subjects. Amongst the most frequently kept must be the little Banded pullers or Humbugs (*Dascyllus aruanus*) which are conspicuous with broad black and white vertical banding, and live in small groups among the branches of several species of bushy coral in shallow water (see Plate 9).

SURGEONFISHES – ACANTHURIDAE – AND RABBITFISHES – SIGANIDAE The surgeonfishes and rabbitfishes are fairly similar families which mainly feed by browsing on the algae growing on the reef. The surgeonfishes get their name from a pair of knifeblade-like structures which project from both sides of the stem of the tail and which are sharp enough to cut deeply into the fingers of fishermen who are not careful when trying to disentangle such fish from a net. There are several common species of surgeonfish, the most conspicuous of which is the white-cheeked *Acanthurus sohal*, a fish about twenty-five centimetres long that is basically pale blue with fine grey horizontal lines along the body and pale grey sides to the face; this species is endemic to the Red Sea. The rabbitfishes interestingly get their scientific name, Siganidae, from the arabic word for this type of fish, *sigan*; at certain times local fishermen may fish specially for *sigan* using large woven traps which look like lobster pots or baskets, and are commonly baited with stale bread. Such traps have found a more recent function as rather attractive lamp shades. The one

species of rabbitfish which is really common on Red Sea coral reefs is *Siganus stellatus*, which is illustrated in Plate 114.

There are two notable side branches of the surgeon-fish family. There is the genus *Zebrasoma*, sometimes called the tangs, of which there are two common Red Sea species, the black Sailfin tang (*Zebrasoma veliferum*) which sometimes has pale vertical banding on its side, and the Yellow-tailed tang (*Zebrasoma xanthurus*) which is a uniform pale blue with a bright yellow tail. The other sub-group, the unicornfishes (species of *Naso*), are easily recognisable in that most of them carry a unicorn-like horn projecting from their forehead. They are generally a greenish-grey in colour, although one, *Naso litturatus* (see Plate 113) has an attractive yellow fringe. Whereas most of the surgeonfishes are algal browsers, the unicornfishes feed to a significant extent on the plankton, and are often seen in groups in open water off the reef.

The White-cheeked surgeonfish (*Acanthurus sohal*) is notable in that it shows behaviour similar to that of some of the damselfishes, excluding other algal grazing fishes from its territory within which the algae may thus grow. Consequently *Acanthurus sohal* may also be some-what aggressive towards the diver, nipping at his flippers or making pushing movements with the tail with scalpel blades extended; however there is no record of any diver ever having been properly hurt by them. By contrast some surgeonfishes, including in particular in the Red Sea the Sailfin tang (*Zebrasoma veliferum*), at times gather together in schools, and this enables them to invade by sheer weight of numbers the territories defended individually by *Acanthurus sohal* or by damsel-

LEFT: 116 The colourful 'leopard rubberlips', *Gaterin gaterinus*, allied to the snappers.
BELOW: 117 One of the common coral trout or small reef groupers, the attractive *Cephalopholis miniatus*.
BOTTOM: 118 A typical grouper, *Epinephelus areolatus*; the mouth and throat can be greatly expanded and the resulting inrush of water helps to suck in prey whole.
RIGHT: 119/120 The dazzling, almost fluorescent, *Pseudochromis fridmani* is only a few centimetres long, but is allied to the groupers. It is one of the most conspicuous fish close to coral cliffs and overhangs. It is unique to the Red Sea.

BELOW: 121 The white-spotted longfin, *Calloplesiops altivelis*, another small grouper-related species. This species does not appear to have been previously recorded from the Red Sea.

fishes. The development of the farming behaviour by the one group of species, of the invading behaviour by others, and also of the hard scraping beaks of the parrotfishes, can all be seen as the result of the considerable competition that exists among the herbivorous reef fish for the algae growing on the rocky surfaces. It is also as a result of this competition that the algae is cropped so heavily and grazed down in most areas until it is barely visible, except on close examination of the rock surface.

SNAPPERS AND EMPEROR-BREAMS – LUT-JANIDAE, LETHRINIDAE, ETC.

The snappers and emperor-breams are two closely-related groups of fishes, some of which are conspicuous on the reef, and which unlike the families already discussed make a significant contribution to the catch of local fishermen using hand lines. The most frequently caught snapper is the grey *Lutjanus bohar*, so called after the Arabic name for this fish, *bohar*. One or two of the snappers are particularly prized for the taste of their flesh, for example, the red snappers (species of *Aprion*, *Etelis* and *Pristipomoides*) and the mangrove jack (*Lutjanus argentimaculatus*); but these are more frequently found in deep water or creek areas. More conspicuous on coral reefs are one or two colourful species of snapper which are not generally caught and eaten; these include *Lutjanus kasmira*, illustrated in Plate 115, and the very similar *Lutjanus fulviflamma*, in which the horizontal lines are yellow instead of blue.

The emperor-breams, members of the genus *Lethrinus*, are very similar in shape and size to the snappers, but have a more elongated horse-like face. There are five or six species which are quite common on the Red Sea reefs and are important as a major component of the catches of local fishermen. However they are all rather drabbly coloured in buff and grey, and are quite difficult for the non-specialist to tell apart. The snappers and breams are all predators of medium-sized invertebrates such as shrimps and small crabs and large worms, and a few occasionally take small fish. They normally catch their food by waiting motionless in mid-water or resting close to the sand until an incautious movement gives their prey away, when they dash forward to snap it up.

BELOW: 122 The classic fast-swimming predator of the reef, the jack, *Carangoides bajad*. Individuals or small groups patrol along the reef, rushing round coral bluffs to surprise unwary damselfish.

Quite a few of the species feed mainly at night, and they spend the day, usually in small groups, hanging inactively in mid-water just off the reef, or sheltering on the reef. This latter group includes *Lutjanus kasmira* and *Lutjanus fulviflamma*, which by day are characteristically found sheltering in surge channels, gullies and small caves near the wave-exposed crest of the reef; but at night these groups break up and the individuals hunt over the reef for nocturnally active worms and crabs.

GROUPERS AND THEIR ALLIES – SERRANIDAE Among the best known of coral-reef fishes, and the most important group of reef-based predators of other fish, are the groupers. These include a variety of species ranging from smaller ones a quarter to three quarters of a metre in length, which are commonly known as coral trout, to giant groupers up to two metres in length. There are also a number of much smaller fish on the reef, closely related to the coral trout and groupers, which are also predators.

All the groupers hunt their prey by using stealth and ambush. They lie in wait, partly hidden, until a suitable fish swims past and can be pounced upon, or on seeing a potential victim the grouper may stalk up to a suitable hiding space. Pouncing on the prey is aided by the fact that groupers have very large mouths, and bodies which are both broad and deep in relation to their overall length. A special arrangement of the jaws enables the mouth to open especially widely, rather in the fashion of a double-hinged travelling bag. The sudden expansion of mouth and throat, which takes place as the grouper leaps forward, creates a significant suction effect, so that the grouper can gulp in quite large prey all at one go.

The exact technique which the grouper uses to approach his prey varies with its size and species. The smaller red *Cephalopholis miniatus* shown in Plate 117 tend especially to lurk close to the roofs of coral overhangs and cliffs, jumping upwards at prey which may come down from above. The blue coral trout *Cephalopholis argus* wait resting, propped up on their pelvic fins, among coral heads, occasionally creeping stealthily forward towards some possible prey. The black hunch-backed coral trout *Aethaloperca rogaa* stalks down over the top of coral knolls and outcrops. The larger groupers,

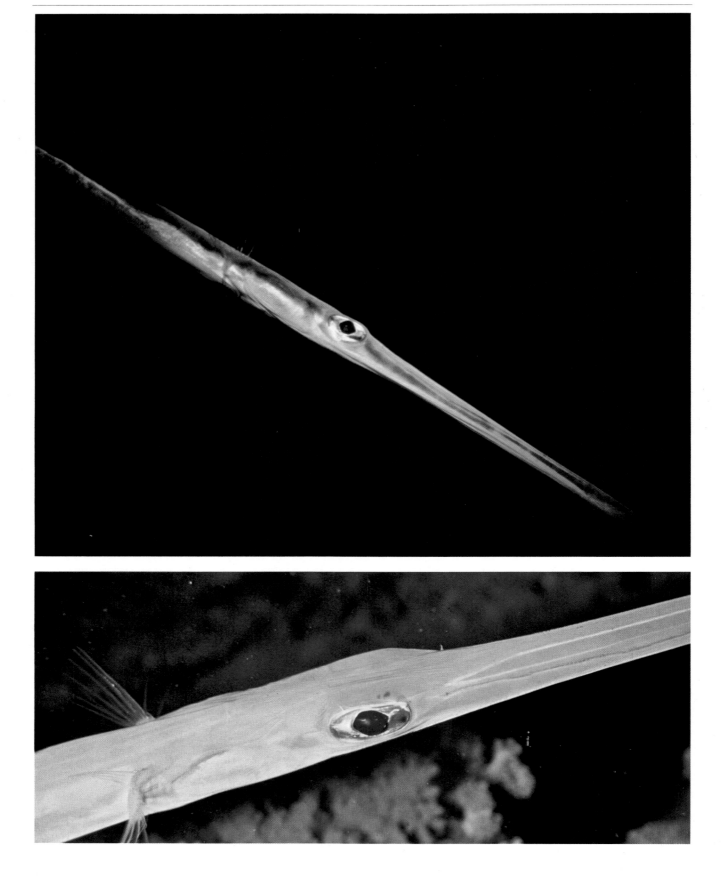

BOTTOM LEFT/TOP LEFT: 123/124 The cornetfish, *Fistularia petimba*, a cunning predator of smaller fishes. Narrow and very elongated, it approaches prey head-on, thus itself appearing small. The cornetfish is also an expert at colour change and camouflage.

BELOW: 125 The hawkfish or curlyfin, *Paracirrhites forsteri*, rests on small coral heads, waiting for hours to ambush an unobservant passer-by.

such as *Epiniphelus fuscoguttatus* or *Epiniphelus areolatus*, tend to wait resting on the bottom behind coral mounds close to which other fish are likely to pass. And the largest of the groupers, *Epiniphelus tauvina*, so named after its Arabic name *tauvina*, is reported to lurk in large caves with mouth wide open waiting for other fish to swim in, scarcely realising where cave ends and the groupers mouth begins. Because of their deep body and wide mouths these large groupers can take in prey almost as big as themselves; and some of the harbours of the Red Sea, according to local stories, are occupied by giant *tauvina* which can even take in the occasional sailor or swimmer at a single gulp!

Closely related to the groupers are two sub-families which, while being hardly as fearsome, well deserve to be mentioned; these are the species of *Anthias* (sometimes called jewelfish) and of *Pseudochromis*. The Anthiinae are the one exception to the observation that the swarms of tiny fish which swirl about the reef crest and face are all damselfishes; for often present in these schools are large numbers of the bright red *Anthias squamipinnis* (see Plates 158 to 162). Like *Chromis* species, the *Anthias* feed on the small animals of the plankton, especially on tiny crustacea. That the tiny *Anthias* are so closely related to the fearsome groupers is not really such a surprise since *Anthias* too are predators, hunting the animals of the zooplankton, the main difference being one of size. Something of the biology of *Anthias* is described in more detail in the next chapter.

The *Pseudochromis* also are small fish, five or so centimetres long, feeding on planktonic-like organisms; but they lurk among cover on the reef rather than swimming in mid-water near by. Best known and most conspicuous of the *Pseudochromis* is the brilliant violet *Pseudochromic fridmani* illustrated in Plates 119 and 120. This fish, which is unique to the Red Sea, is quite

BELOW/BOTTOM LEFT: 126/127 Another hawkfish, *Oxycirrhites typus*, camouflages beautifully on sea-fans and gorgonians where it waits to ambush prey.

BOTTOM RIGHT: 128 The squirrelfish, *Myripristis murdjan*; the large eyes and overall red coloration, which appears black by night, is typical of many nocturnally active species.

RIGHT: 129 The soldierfish, *Holocentrus spinifer*, waits by day close to the entrances of coral caves and overhangs which it appears to be guarding – hence its common name – but by night it emerges to hunt on the reef.

common beneath gentle overhangs and on cliff-like faces on the reef. The colour of the fish has a dazzling, almost luminescent, quality which seems to make it hard for the eye to focus on, and this effect is frequently heightened by contrast with the brilliant yellow, orange and red sponges which characteristically encrust its habitat.

As well as these two sub-families, there are several other not uncommon fish on the reef which are related to the groupers and which are predators. These include the goggle-eye (*Priancanthus hamrur*), which is mentioned again below, and also the longfins (family Plesiopidae) such as the White-spotted longfin, *Calloplesiops altivelis*, illustrated in Plate 121.

The groupers themselves are of course amongst the most important element in the catches of local fishermen who fish in coral-reef areas using hand lines. The flesh of the smaller species such as *Plectropomus maculatus* (known in Arabic as *nagil*) is particulary prized.

OTHER FISH-EATING PREDATORS As well as the groupers there are a number of other families, species of which live largely by catching other fish. And these fish show a great variety of strategies in the

LEFT: 130 Many nocturnal fish have luminescent parts to their bodies, enabling the school to maintain contact by night. These are hatchetfish, *Pempheris oualensis*, which by day are often found in dense schools hovering in gullies in the reef face.

BELOW/BOTTOM LEFT/BOTTOM RIGHT: 131/132/133 The goggle-eyed *Priacanthus hamrur*. A grouper-related nocturnally active species showing again the development of large eye and red coloration as an adaptation to this way of life.

way that they catch their prey.

Comparable to the groupers in their importance as predators of reef fish are the jacks (family Carangidae), especially the species *Caranx*. The jacks, however, are not totally based on the reef, but come in from surrounding waters in search of food. Their grey coloration, streamlined body form, and detailed fin shape, well shown in Plate 122, are characteristic of fast open-water swimmers. On reaching a reef the jacks, often in groups of two or three, scout along the reef face, dashing around points and outcrops on the reef in the hope of surprising small reef fish such as the shoaling *Chromis* or other species of pomacentrid. Sometimes a jack will swim along the reef close behind or alongside some larger species such as a Hump-headed wrasse or a Donkeyfish, using it as cover to approach a potential victim. The jacks will also hunt in larger groups, particularly when given the opportunity to tackle a large school of sardines or similar bait fishes such as antherinids. The jacks will charge the school from several different directions at once, swooping around and about, and trying to split off small groups or individual fish which can be much more readily caught (see the next chapter). The commonest

BELOW: 134 The commonest of the Red Sea pufferfishes *Arothron diadematus*. When provoked the pufferfishes swell up like balloons, making it more difficult for any predator to tackle them. The well-developed teeth are used to nip off the tips of the coral branches.

BOTTOM: 135 The white-spotted pufferfish *Arothron hispidus*, a charming and curious fish and a significant predator of the Crown-of-thorns starfish, *Acanthaster planci*.

BELOW: 136 The boxfish *Ostracion argus*. As it swims mainly with undulations of dorsal and ventral fins, the fish has less need to flex its body, which is boxed in for protection, leaving the fish apparently looking out like a miniaturised aquatic knight in armour.

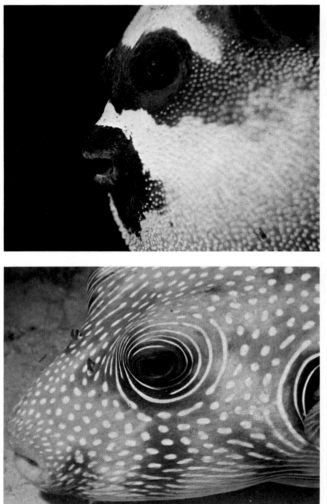

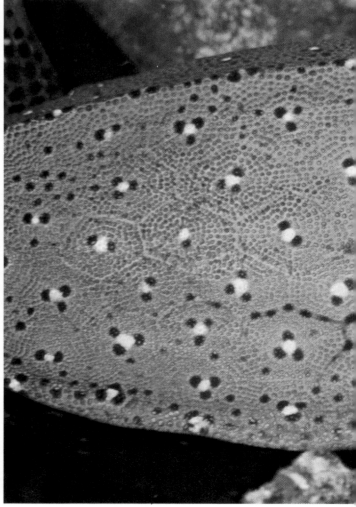

species of *Caranx* on Red Sea reefs are the blue and black-spotted *Carangoides bajad* and the yellow-spotted *Caranx fulvoguttatus*. The *Caranx* like the groupers are important local food fishes; they are known generally in Arabic as 'bayad'.

Another well-known group of semi open-water predators are the barracuda. There are a number of Red Sea species, but despite their fearsome reputation they have never been known to attack snorkellers or divers. In comparison with *Caranx*, barracuda use a rather different form of attack. They typically skulk in open water, wandering about a little way off the reef and keeping an eye open for possible situations which may

give the chance of a meal. Their coloration camouflages well against the background of the sea, and with their elongated and narrow body form they can turn in to face the reef in such a way that their apparent size is very small. However, this particular body form also gives them a tremendous power of acceleration, and at the right moment they can dash in to grab prey. Schooling barracuda can use a different technique to attack shoals of small open-water fish. Sometimes when a diver approaches such a school of barracuda they will form a rather impressive wall of fish swimming about him; the wall may be five or ten fish high, and the effect can, in fact, be a little unnerving. Barracuda are reported to

BOTTOM: 137 The tiny boxfish, *Ostracion cyanurus*, a particularly comical character as it manoeuvres among the corals.

form such a wall around schools of potential prey; gradually the circling wall contracts until the prey in panic breaks up to try to escape, when they can be picked off at leisure by the hungry barracuda.

Essentially the same elongated body form is adopted for the same sort of reasons by another predator, the cornetfish (*Fistularia petimba*), shown in Plates 123 and 124. However, whereas the barracuda approaches from open water, the cornetfish hunts across the reef, and in response to the varied form and coloration of the reef, is able to change its own colour through a great variety of patterns and shades. The cornetfish is also fond of aligning itself in disguise with similar elongated struc-

BELOW: 138 The tiny filefish *Oxymonacanthus halli*. Groups are usually found, as here, hovering among the branches of *Acropora* corals, and pecking at the polyps.

BOTTOM RIGHT/RIGHT: 139/140 Blennies are small reef fish, characteristically living in the smallest retreats, such as those left by boring bivalves, or created by sponges.

tures on the reef, and given the opportunity may often be found hovering gently alongside a boat's anchor line, waiting for smaller fish who fail to notice its presence.

Not all the fish-eating predators on the reef are found amongst the largest species; there are many small predators which eat even smaller fish. A good example of such a family would be the hawkfishes (Cirrhitidae). These are all from five to twenty centimetres in length and specialise in waiting, propped up on their pelvic fins, where particularly camouflaged against a suitable background, for smaller fish to pass by. The most noticeable of the hawkfishes on Red Sea reefs is *Paracirrhites forsteri* (see Plate 125), which tends to wait in ambush resting on a small coral head, such as a rounded lobe of *Porites*, or a small bush of the purple *Pocillopora*. The related *Cirrhitichthys oxycephalus* is particularly well camouflaged when lurking among stones and rubble on the reef top. But perhaps the most beautifully camouflaged of these hawkfishes is *Oxycirrhites typus* which, as shown in Plates 126 and 127, spends its time resting on the branches of gorgonians. The pattern of red lines on its side renders it particularly inconspicuous against the bright red fan-shaped gorgonians such as *Lophogorgia*.

The ultimate development of the technique of disguise and ambush is shown by the stonefish (*Synanceichthys verrucosa*) (see Plate 178), which looks like little more than a lump-shaped rock lying on the reef, and by its relatives the scorpionfish and the lionfish. These species are considered in detail in chapter 8.

NOCTURNAL FISHES We have already mentioned, in passing, a few species of reef fish which mostly feed at night, but there are several families which are almost completely nocturnal. The two most abundant of these are the squirrelfishes and soldierfishes (family Holocentridae) and the cardinalfishes (family Apogonidae).

The soldierfishes and squirrelfishes, names which are used more or less interchangeably, are medium-sized fishes of about fifteen to thirty centimetres in length. Almost all of them have one of two different colour patterns. Some, such as the scarlet soldierfish, *Holocentrus spinifer*, (see Plate 129) and the squirrelfish, *Myripristis murdjan* (see Plate 128) are more or less uniformly red in colour; others have a pattern of reddish brown and white longitudinal stripes. By day the squirrelfishes and soldierfishes are almost always seen resting close to the entrances in small coral overhangs and caves. In such locations they often appear to be almost guarding the entrance to such openings, and it is from this habit that their common name of soldierfishes arises. However, at night they leave these shelters to forage in the open reef. The largish eyes, which give rise to their other popular name of squirrelfishes, are an adaption to this nocturnal activity. The species of *Holocentrus* feed over the bottom on invertebrates such as shrimps, small crabs and polychaete worms; the *Myripristis* species however tend to feed more on planktonic animals. The red soldierfishes are often mistaken by inexperienced spearfishermen for red snappers. However, they are very poorly thought of as food, in contrast to the highly prized red snappers, and as often as not the spearfisherman only succeeds in badly damaging his spear against the back of the cave in which the soldierfish is sheltering.

Cardinalfishes are generally much smaller (five to ten centimetres in length) than the soldierfishes and are

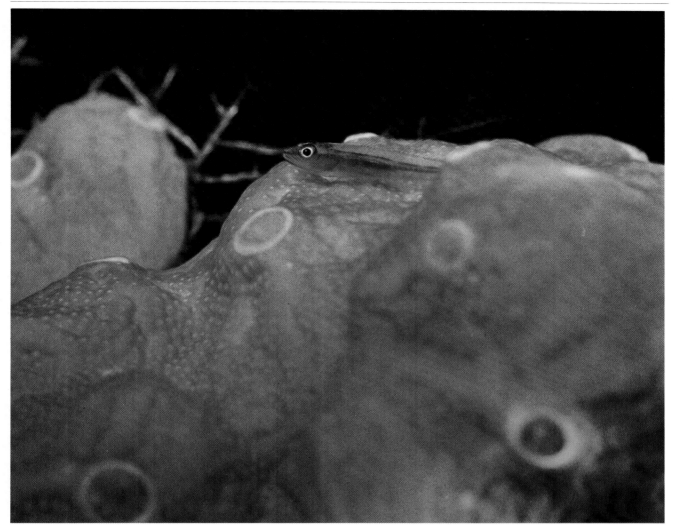

much less apparent by day, save that schools of them are not infrequently found sheltering within gullies and caves. Like the soldierfishes and squirrelfishes they are often either a brilliant red (hence the name) or have a pattern of longitudinal stripes; but some of the most common species are greyish and almost transparent, save for one or two dark blotches arranged regularly on the side of the body. Cardinalfishes feed mostly on small planktonic and semi-planktonic crustaceans, some foraging in mid-water, others nearer the sea bed.

The third group of nocturnal species which deserve mention are the goggle-eyes (family Priacanthidae) of which one species, *Priacanthus hamrur*, is not at all uncommon in the Red Sea, especially along the coast of Saudi Arabia. This species is well shown in Plates 131 to 133. It can be seen that like many of the other nocturnal species its most noticeable features are an overall red coloration and a large eye. The large eye is an obvious adaptation to night life, while it should also be noted that at night, under natural conditions, the red coloration

would appear black, thus rendering the fish inconspicuous. The goggle-eyes feed on small fish and cephalopods, such as cuttlefish, as well as on shrimps and other crustaceans.

TRIGGERFISHES, PUFFERFISHES AND BOX-FISHES – TETRADONTIFORMES

Not even a simple account of coral-reef fishes would be complete without some description of the range of species classified together in the order Tetradontiformes (from the Greek meaning with four teeth). This order includes fish of a great variety of size and form, but all of them have in common sharp teeth, powerful jaws and development of the dorsal and ventral fins for swimming. The use of these fins for swimming has had two consequences. Firstly, it means that the actual body need no longer be used for locomotion by being waggled from side to side as it is in the average fish; thus the body can be modified to help protect the fish from potential predators. Secondly, the undulating movements of the dorsal and ventral fins, which generate the movement, can more easily be thrown into reverse gear, and thus these fish can move backwards as well as forwards, with much more proficiency than can most other species. The particular significance of this is that they can lift up food and other objects by holding it in the mouth and backing away, or can enter narrow crevices or holes without running into the problem of how to get out again.

The most numerous family within this group are the triggerfishes (Balistidae), so called because of the single stout spine at the top of their back. This spine can be raised and lowered at will, and can be locked into an upright position when the fish is sheltering in some crevice, thus securely jamming it in place and making it very difficult for any predator to remove. The two most conspicuous Red Sea triggerfishes are *Rhinecanthus assasi*, the Red Sea form of the Picasso triggerfish – this species is more or less sandy grey in colour with a couple of blue lines passing through the eye, and is characteristic of more sandy areas – and the orange-lined *Balistapus undulatus*. These two species are twenty to thirty centimetres in size and mostly feed on invertebrates such as the smaller crabs and shrimps which are found hiding amongst the corals. Also common on Red Sea reefs are three or four larger species reaching fifty to sixty centimetres in length, including *Pseudobalistes*

flavimarginatus, Pseudobalistes fuscus and *Balistoides viridescens*. These species are able to cope with larger or more heavily armoured prey, and have developed a number of specialised techniques for finding and dealing with them. They can drag sea-urchins, such as the needle-spined *Diadema setosum*, out of their hiding-places and, picking them up, drop them upside-down so as to be able to attack their unprotected undersides. They can also deal with the notorious Crown-of-thorns starfish, *Acanthaster planci*, in much the same way. *Pseudobalistes flavimarginatus* also spends much time feeding in sandy and lagoon areas where it can dig quite sizeable pits in search for sand-dwelling shellfish and sea-urchins. This it does by positioning itself head down over a suitable site and blowing the sand away with jets of water directed by its mouth and pelvic fins; at the same time its dorsal and ventral fins are active to stop the fish from being shot backwards.

As well as eating large invertebrates, these larger triggerfishes can also take significant amounts of coral, generally biting off and swallowing whole tips of the branches of some of the bushy corals such as *Acropora* and *Pocillopora*. *Balistoides viridescens* in particular may thus combine two sorts of food in a single meal; on coming across a suitable branched coral it will break off and swallow the tips of some of the branches, and then break off the lower parts of the branches, throwing these aside but catching and eating the crabs and shrimps which were sheltering there.

The pufferfishes (family Tetrodontidae) have very similar feeding habits to those of the large triggerfishes, but they have of course a very different body form. They are in particular well known for their ability to take in large amounts of water, blowing themselves up like a balloon, and thus making themselves much more difficult for a potential predator to attack or swallow. In addition, pufferfishes contain within parts of their body a very powerful poison known as tetrodotoxin, and this of course makes them a not very advisable choice of food for predators. In consequence they are comparatively fearless and may even be caught with the unaided hands, and provoked into inflating themselves. Despite their poison pufferfishes are in fact a delicacy in Japan, but it is obviously vital that the liver and other poisonous parts are removed during preparation, and in fact a number of fatalities occur every year where not all of the poisonous tissues have been completely removed.

BELOW: 141 The yellow coral-goby *Gobiodon citrinus*. Pairs of these charming little fish are found among the branches of table-like or fan-like *Acroporas*.

The commonest of the Red Sea pufferfishes, and one that is slightly smaller than the others, is the black-eyed *Arothron diadematous*, shown in Plate 134. This species appears to feed largely on coral by nibbling at the tips of branches of bushy forms. The larger puffers such as the white-spotted *Arothron hispidus*, shown in Plate 135, as well as taking some coral, also tackle large invertebrates such as sea-squirts, sea-urchins and brittle-stars; in the Red Sea *Arothron hispidus* is also a significant predator of the Crown-of-thorns starfish which it tackles in a different manner from the trigger-fishes, by nibbling away at one or two arms until the unprotected side of the bases of the neighbouring arms are exposed. It can then chomp away at these, working its way in a circle around the whole starfish, eating the fleshy tissues of the base of the arms and the edge of the disc, and leaving the less edible tips of the arms scattered about in an irregular halo.

Very similar to the pufferfish is the porcupinefish *Diodon histrix*, but this species further protects itself with a coating of stubby spines which give rise to its common name. It takes much the same sort of food as do the larger pufferfishes, but does so almost entirely by night, when its rather large eyes are of value. By day they may be found sheltering beneath corals or hovering rather lethargically in mid-water not far off the reef.

An alternative way in which the body, no longer required for locomotion, can be used to protect the fish, is that used by the boxfishes (family Ostraciidae). They have developed a set of bony plates just beneath the skin which form an almost complete box, protecting the fish from many predators. The fins, tail and beak, further protected by small articulating plates, project out through the main box giving the boxfish the general appearance of a little man trying to row around in a rather awkward suit of armour. The main boxfish seen in the Red Sea is

BELOW: 142 The large batfish, *Platax orbicularis*. These attractive fish have great curiosity and will often approach very close to divers who take care not to frighten them.

RIGHT: 143 The flathead, *Platycephalus grandidieri*. To feed, the fish lies buried in the sand with little more than eyes showing and ready to pounce on passers-by.

the blue-spotted boxfish, *Ostracion argus*, shown in Plate 136; this is the Red Sea form of the better known *Ostracion tuberculatus*. It takes a variety of foods including shellfish, polychaete worms and algae.

Finally among the Tetrodontiformes we may mention the filefishes (family Aluteridae); these come in a considerable range of sizes and varieties of forms, but most of them look rather like very slim triggerfishes. They generally feed to a greater or lesser extent on corals, nibbling at the tips of branches in the fashion of *Arothron diadematous*. However, the smallest species, *Oxymonocanthus halli*, which is only five to eight centimetres long (see Plate 138), feeds by picking at individual coral polyps, and small groups of them may be found hovering head slightly downwards amongst the open branches of *Acropora* trees and similar coral.

OTHER FISHES Despite the ground covered in this chapter there remain of course many other families of fishes which are to be found on coral reefs in the Red

Sea. Most of these are represented by only one to two species, but in a few cases there are a great variety of species present. This is particularly true of two families of small fishes, the gobies and blennies. These are mostly narrow elongated fish not usually more than five to ten centimetres long living close to the substrate and spending much of their time hiding among the corals or in holes in the sand or rock (see Plates 139 and 140). Because of their small size and cryptic habits most of them are difficult for the snorkeller or diver to identify. One of the more readily identified species is the yellow coral-goby, *Gobiodon citrinus* (Plate 141), which is usually found perched among the branches of a table *Acropora*.

The great variety of species vary in their shape and form even beyond the range of the species already described. Two simple illustrations must suffice. As an example of a large fish flattened from side to side and swimming in open water, the Red Sea batfish *Platax orbicularis* is shown on Plate 142. These fish show a great deal of curiosity and, if not frightened, often approach very close to divers. Juveniles kept in aquaria readily become hand-tamed and make particular pets. By contrast the Flathead or Crocodile fish, *Platycephalus grandidieri*, is a specialised bottom liver, flattened from top to bottom. This species is a predator of smaller fishes, taking to extremes the technique we have already seen in the hawkfishes; for the flathead lies half buried in the sand, well camouflaged by its mottled sandy coloration, waiting for prey that may fail to notice it. Even the conspicuous shape of the eye is further camouflaged by a grey flap projecting down over the iris.

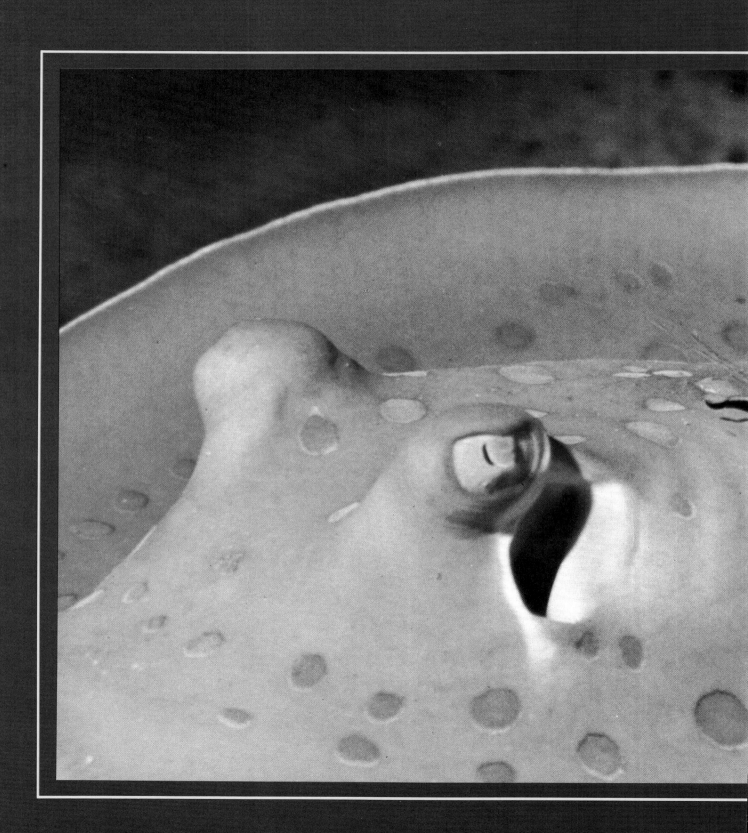

7 Private Lives

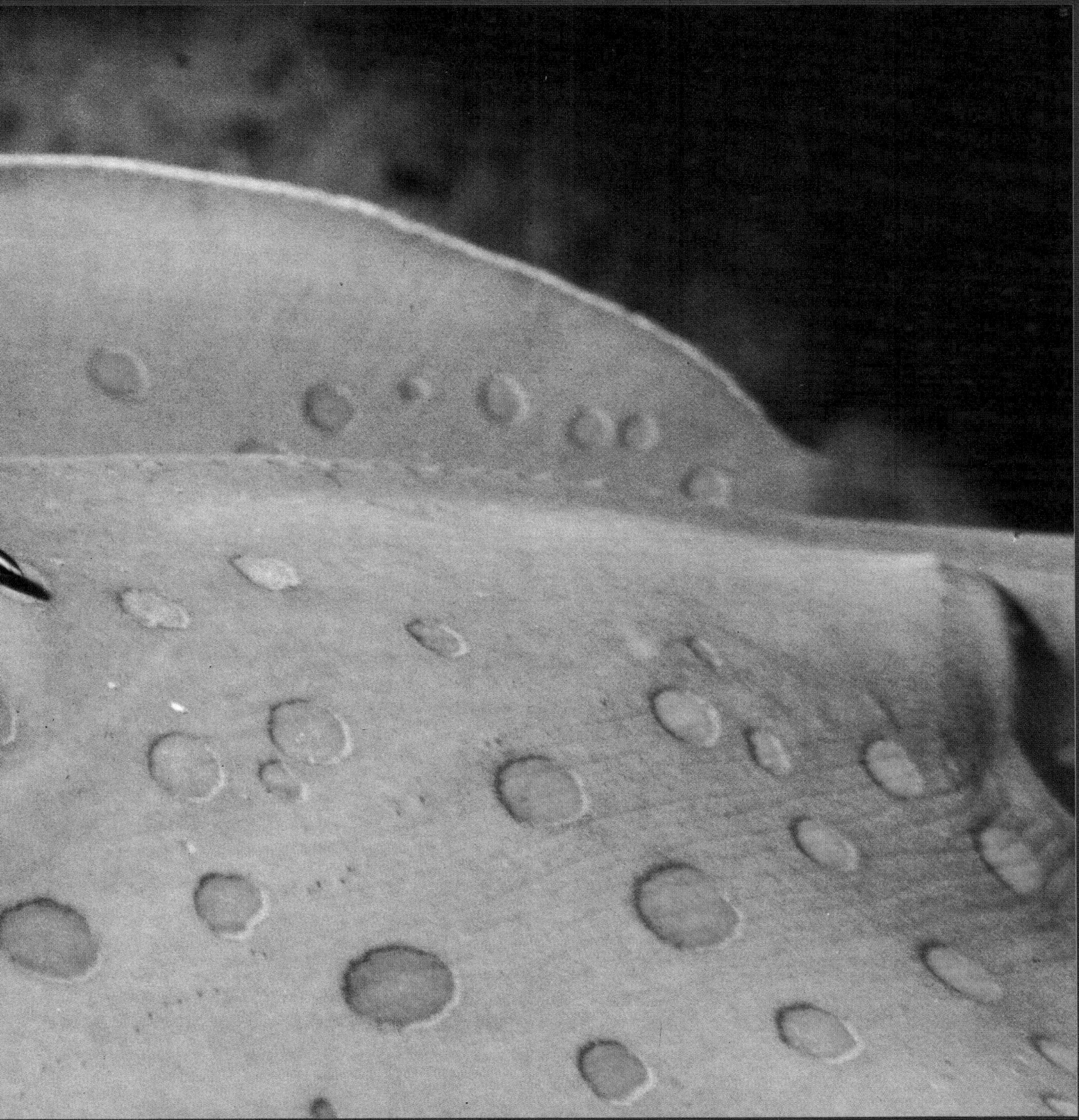

A theme of this book has been to point out how the many animals living together on a coral reef have become specialised in different ways to meet the problems of existence in this competitive society. But so far the examples of such adaptations have generally been briefly described and mainly related to the animal's morphology, that is its shape and its form. However, the behaviour of reef animals is also often highly modified to fit in with the particular mode of existence of a given species. Often this behaviour seems quite amazing and remarkable. Thus in this chapter we propose to describe in some detail some of these complex behaviours, such as may be shown especially by reef fishes in which such behaviour has been better studied, or may be more easily understood.

LIVING TOGETHER

A group of phenomena which regularly cause much fascination are those in which one type of animal is found living in close association with another animal of quite a different type. Such an arrangement is known technically as a *symbiosis* (from the Greek, meaning, quite simply, living together). Often one of the animals gains some advantage, such as a degree of protection, from living close to the other, while the second animal is hardly affected. In some cases the second animal is adversely affected, in which case the situation begins to approach one of parasitism. But the most attractive examples are those in which both animals of a pair gain some advantage from the association. Such symbioses are in fact not so uncommon in nature, for example the association between man and his domestic animals may be viewed in this light, since while man clearly benefits, the animals too are assured of a food supply and are able to continue breeding successfully. But such symbioses are especially common on the coral reef, and many of the text-book examples of such associations may be found on coral reefs in the Red Sea.

Perhaps the most amusing of these associations on Red Sea reefs is that between several species of goby and one or two species of alpheid shrimp (see Plates 145 and 146). Regularly in sandy lagoon areas one or a pair of these gobies, which are generally seven to fifteen centimetres long, may be found living in a small burrow together with one or a pair of these shrimps, which are up to ten or so centimetres long. The shrimps are almost blind but have well developed front claws with which they are able to excavate the burrow; often they place one claw in front of them and push a small pile of sand and pebbles out through the entrance and up on to the lagoon floor on either side. When busy in this way they resemble nothing so much as small animated bulldozers busily trundling back and forth. The shrimps, while thus busily engaged, would be very vulnerable to predation if it were not for the presence of the gobies, which however are quite unable to excavate such a burrow on their own. Accordingly, when a shrimp emerges from the protection of the burrow, the goby, which is normally to be found close at hand looking for food, adopts an on-guard position resting on pelvic fins about ten centimetres in front of the entrance. At any sign of the approach of potential predators, the goby warns the shrimp which scuttles back down the burrow, to be followed if necessary by the goby itself. Communications between the shrimp and goby seems to be largely tactile. The shrimp advises the goby that it is present by tapping around with its long antennae until it has touched the fish. The goby then adopts a comparatively immobile look-out posture, but, should danger threaten, it brushes its tail from side to side once or twice, contacting the shrimp and stimulating it to retreat. This partnership, and in particular the busy construction work of the shrimp, can be easily missed by the over-enthusiastic snorkeller or diver, for the warning system has often been put into effect before the visitor is close enough at hand to see what is going on. One needs to wait quietly a few metres away from the entrance to the burrow until the goby is convinced there is no immediate danger, and he allows his work partner to reappear.

In the Red Sea itself half a dozen or so different species of goby may be found living in these associations. These include species of *Cryptocentrus* (commonly with a series of pale and dark sandy coloured vertical bands arranged along the body), *Vanderhorstia* (basically sandy coloured, with a colourful mottling pattern) and an unusually small species of goby, *Lottilia graciliosa*, which is almost all black save for a distinctive white patch on the forehead. The commonest species of shrimp involved is *Alpheus djiboutensis*

The best known of the symbiotic associations to be found on the reef must be that between the colourful red and white banded clownfish (damselfishes of the genus *Amphiprion*) and the giant sea-anemones in which they

BELOW: 145/146 The goby *Cryptocentrus cyrptocentrus*, one of those which lives in a burrow constructed by an alpheid shrimp. The feelers of the shrimp maintain contact with the goby, a sudden movement of which warns the shrimp to retreat.

live. In the Red Sea the common clownfish is *Amphiprion bicinctus*, shown in Plates 154, 155–7, and this is most frequently found nestling amongst the tentacles of the huge anemone *Stoichactis gigas*. Commonly a pair of the clownfish are present, and these may also sometimes be accompanied by half a dozen or so rather smaller fish. Exactly how these clownfishes can live among the tentacles of the anemone which would normally sting to death and swallow fish of this size, and exactly what advantage, if any, the anemone gains from tolerating the fish, has been the subject of much speculation and research.

It seems fairly clear that there is a considerable advantage for the clownfish in living with the anemone. The clownfish forages for food, both drifting particles and items on the sea bed within a metre or so of its home; but when danger threatens the fish retreats back into the folds of the anemone, and any predator which pursues it there risks being badly stung or killed by the anemone. In line with this threat to any potential attacker, the conspicuous and gay coloration of the clownfish is in fact a classic warning pattern. These warning patterns are widespread throughout nature and consist of vertical striping of yellow or red together with white or black. It seems to have been advantageous throughout the animal kingdom that those species which possess hidden defences such as poison, toxic spines or stings should warn potential predators of the fact by developing a standard coloration; this makes it much easier for such predators to be aware or learn that these one or two different patterns indicate that an animal is to be avoided. But of course in the case of the clownfish its warning coloration warns not of some

weapon possessed by the fish, but of the powerful stinging action of the anemone.

It is suggested that the anemone may also gain some advantage. In aquaria, at least, clownfishes will often bring back food items which they have found near by and drop them on to the anemone, not presumably with the specific intention of feeding it, but much as many fish will retrieve food to their shelter to be able to eat at leisure and out of danger. Nevertheless the anemone certainly gets some food this way. Also clownfish have been seen cleaning their anemone, removing and fanning away dirt and sediment which the anemone has difficulty removing itself, and which may cause it harm. Whether the anemones gain significant advantage from either of these two habits in the wild has not clearly been established. In addition it has been suggested that the anemones benefit from the activity of the fishes in continually swimming around within their tentacles and wafting them to and fro. Larger invertebrates of this type often have a problem in promoting sufficient respiration, gaining sufficient oxygen from the environment and ridding themselves of carbon dioxide, for they have no specialised respiratory and circulatory organs such as lungs and vascular system; thus the largest anemones tend to be found only on those parts of the reef where maintained wave action or strong currents bring a good supply of fresh oxygen. The clownfishes, however, by their general activity, and by their apparent bathing among the tentacles, may well increase the water flow across the anemone and increase the rate of gas exchange.

Most interest however has centred on the way in which the clownfish itself is able to tolerate living within

BELOW/BOTTOM: 147/148 The cleaner wrasse *Labroides dimidiatus* feeds by cleaning dead tissue and ectoparasites from the bodies and mouths of other fish. The host fish benefit from this service and even predators such as the moray eel, *Gynnothorax javanicus*, and the coral trout *Cephalopholis miniatus* happily tolerate their attentions.

BELOW: 149 The false cleaner *Runula aspidontus* is a species of sabre-toothed blenny which uses its resemblance to the cleaner wrasse to approach victims from which it nips bits of fins and flesh.

the anemone. It was the eminent Egyptian authority on the marine life of the Red Sea, H.A.F. Gohar, who first pointed out that while one clownfish might be living very happily within an anemone, another of the same species of clownfish, taken from a different species of anemone, or kept for a time on its own, could readily be killed when forced on to or into the first anemone. Such a new clownfish must first approach a different anemone with great caution. It at first touches the anemone but very briefly with head or fin, backing away for a pause before trying again. Only over a period of some hours, or even a couple of days, does the clownfish come to immerse itself totally within the anemone. This process whereby the fish accustoms itself to the anemone, or vice versa, has become known as *acclimation*.

Various ideas have been put forward to explain what was happening during this time. It was suggested that in fact the anemones were not actually able to harm fish of the size of the clownfish, or that the fish accustomed the anemone to its presence by some aspect of its swimming behaviour hypnotising its host, as it were, into not harming it. However, it now seems clear that the key feature of this phenomenon is the production in the slimy mucus coat covering the clownfish of a chemical which inhibits the discharge of the stinging cells of the anemone. To further describe how this effect might work, it is first necessary to explain that the anemone itself is faced with a similar problem in that it needs to prevent its tentacles stinging each other or other parts of its body. Since the anemone has no centralised nervous system it has to do this by means of chemical recognition. The mucus secreted over the surface of the anemone contains a compound which enables the different parts of the animal to recognise itself, and prevents the stinging cells from being activated. Clearly if a fish could contain or mimic this particular component within its own mucus it could enter an anemone without being stung.

The importance of the mucus coat on the fish can most simply be seen if a fish should be slightly injured, for example by having a few scales removed or by receiving a small cut; the injured part of the fish is no longer covered with the mucus, and thus gets badly stung even though the rest of the fish remains unharmed. Often a clownfish is slightly injured in this way when caught for an aquarium, and the stinging of one or more parts of its body, where the mucus coat has been scraped

away by the catching net, is apparent in the way that the tentacles of the anemone appear to stick to these points. Thus a newly caught clownfish should not be forced into close contact even with its own anemone, but must be allowed to recover and reacclimate.

The significance of the fish's mucus coat can be more precisely demonstrated experimentally. If a small piece of meat from another type of fish is presented to the anemone this is immediately stung and grasped by the tentacles, even if the piece of meat is covered in skin and presented skin-side first. However, if a piece of flesh from an anemone fish is placed skin-side down on its own anemone this is not stung or taken, unless the tentacles come into contact with the bare flesh. If a small piece of plastic sponge is coated in the mucus from another fish and lowered into the anemone it is immediately stung and grasped, whereas if the sponge is coated in mucus from a clownfish living in that type of anemone, the anemone fails to respond.

In fact a compound has now been detected chemically in the clownfish mucus which is present only after the acclimation, and which is probably the one responsible for this effect. Exactly how the active component gets into the mucus of the clownfish is not yet established. It may be that the clownfish is able, during the acclimation process, to gradually coat itself with mucus produced by the anemone; once it has entered the anemone, fresh anemone mucus is continually being rubbed over its skin. Or it may be that the clownfish is able to generate the active mucus itself, perhaps by some immunological type of process. It has also been suggested that since the fish often begins acclimation by nibbling at the tentacles, and swallowing amounts of mucus and stinging cells, it may be able to absorb the key component and secrete it again in its own skin.

This ability of the clownfishes to associate with anemones is in fact not a totally isolated one. Most other damselfishes show a greater or lesser degree of attachment to particular hiding-places on the reef, and often corals are present around these hiding places and must thus be tolerated. In particular, species of the genus *Dascyllus* live among the branches of various bushy shaped corals. These corals are, of course, like anemones, members of the phylum Coelenterata, and like them they have stinging cells, albeit with a less powerful action.

In the Red Sea, besides the clownfish *Amphiprion*

bicinctus, a species of damselfish, the Domino damselfish
Dascyllus trimaculatus, is also often found in association
with *Stoichactis* anemones. This species is easily recognisable, being black save for two or three conspicuous
white spots on both flanks. The young are often found
living among the tentacles of the anemone, in the
manner of, and often in the company of, clownfish,
while the adults often wander further away and may
even occur quite apart from any protecting anemone.

HOW FISH KEEP CLEAN

It has been known for over a hundred years that some
fish obtain their food by cleaning other fish. In fact, not
only fish but other types of organisms, especially
shrimps, may perform this function, and it seems that at
least one or two animal species may be found carrying
out this activity in most sizeable bodies of salt or fresh
water. Some of these species are obligate cleaners, that is
that cleaning is the only way in which they can acquire
food; others show this behaviour in a facultative fashion,
feeding in this way when it is the most profitable thing to
do, but turning to other sources of food as necessary.

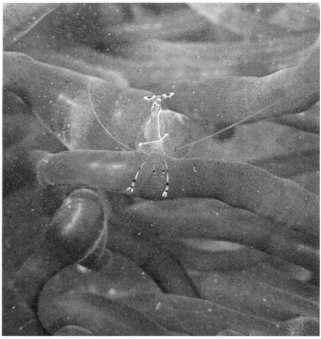

LEFT: 150 The banded coral shrimp *Stenopus hispidus*, one of the largest and most commonly seen of coral-reef shrimps. It also acts as a cleaner to both fish and other crustaceans, waving its long white antennae as a signal of invitation.

BOTTOM LEFT: 151 A large anemone harbouring a cleaner shrimp (*Periclimenes sp.*)

BELOW TOP: 152 A shrimp, a probably undescribed species of *Periclimenes*, cleans a pennant fish *Heniochus intermedius*. This shrimp is one of the commonest cleaners on many Red Sea reefs.

BELOW BOTTOM: 153 The cleaner shrimp will even clean the hand of the patient diver, but the shrimp never ventures far off the anemone or corals where it shelters.

Almost the best known of these cleaner fishes, *Labroides dimidiatus*, is the principal one to be found on Red Sea reefs, and it is widely known as the Cleaner wrasse. It is well illustrated at work in Plates 147 and 148.

The Cleaner wrasse has been especially well studied. They occur as individuals or pairs at conspicuous points on the reef, commonly along the reef edge, and here they are visited by numerous fish from round about. The client fish poses motionless while the Cleaner wrasse works over its body removing bacteria, ecto-parasites, bits of mucus, and dead bits of fins and skin. The Cleaner wrasse may also enter the mouth and throat of the client, sometimes through the gill slits to remove parasites and bits of food that may be lodged there. Many fish arrive regularly for this treatment, and some may even come a considerable distance; thus cleaning stations on large knolls a little way off the reef may be visited by large groupers and Manta rays.

The client fishes recognise the Cleaner wrasses at least in part by their conspicuous coloration which, as can be seen from the photographs, consists of three blue-black longitudinal stripes separated by two stripes of a lighter blue, which in the juvenile have an almost neon-like quality. The Cleaner or Neon goby (*Elacatinus oceanops*) of the Caribbean has a very similar coloration, and it has been suggested that this to some extent constitutes a standard signal in some ways comparable with the standard warning colorations mentioned above. However, many of the species that clean have a great variety of colour patterning so that it is clear that this mark has not become standardised to the same extent. In any case client fishes also recognise the cleaner by its distinctive behaviour, and they also seem to learn the whereabouts of the particular cleaning stations where the Cleaner wrasse are active. If a particular site is kept free of cleaners, client fish will still continue to arrive for some days; and sites are known which have been active as cleaning stations for many years.

Interaction between the cleaner and a client may be initiated by either individual. The cleaner will either swim directly towards a potential customer and begin to try to inspect it, apparently moving over the fins and body, or it may show a specialised cleaner dance by which other fish may recognise its intention. This dance, sometimes known as *nod swimming*, involves the fish in adopting a slightly head down posture and swimming along an undulating course in a rather jerky fashion.

Just as the Cleaner wrasse tries to gain itself a potential customer, other client fish may try to solicit the attention of the wrasse. This they do by adopting a characteristic pose, one which is also assumed while the cleaner is at work. The exact position varies somewhat with the species, but all involve the fish in poising motionless, generally with mouth open and all fins extended. Some fish, especially the parrotfishes, pose thus in a characteristic head up position, almost, as it were, standing on their tails; some other fish, for example the species of *Cheilinus*, tend to adopt a head down position. On the other hand many species, such as gaterins, unicornfishes and damselfishes, tend to remain quite level in the water. Yet other fish such as rays may be cleaned while they are resting on the bottom, but the poses adopted by the other species may in general be

BELOW: 154 Clearly at home, the clownfish, *Amphiprion bicinctus*, shelters among the tentacles of a large anemone. The guest species produce a mucus inhibiting the powerful stinging cells of the anemone, which may still injure would-be predators of those animals. In return the shrimp may clean the anemone, and the fish bring food.

BOTTOM/BELOW/RIGHT: 155/156/157 Studies of the clownfish *Amphiprion bicinctus*. The yellow and white banding is a typical warning coloration (as on a wasp or bee) advising would-be predators not of the clownfish's weapons but of the anemone's powerful sting.

INSET RIGHT/BELOW TOP/BELOW CENTRE/BELOW BOTTOM/RIGHT:
158/159/160/161/162 The private life of the jewelfish *Anthias squamipinnis*.
After a planktonic larval life the young fish, still mostly transparent, settles at
a suitable site where others are present. Growing, it passes through a juvenile
stage to develop into a mature female (161). The mature male (159) with
dorsal crest and elongated tail always develops by sex change from a large
female, which passes within several days through an intermediate stage (158).
In display the males develop a brilliant violet coloration (162).

recognised by their apparently free-floating nature.
Indeed it is probable that these poses originated as the
positions which each fish's body naturally adopts when
the fish itself can no longer manoeuvre and retains its
stability. Whether a head down position or a head up
position results depends on whether the centre of
gravity of the fish, tending to pull the fish down, is in
front of or behind the air bladder within the fish, which
is responsible for holding it up.

The Cleaner wrasse seems to much prefer serving
certain types of fish, such as the parrotfishes and various
predators, and may have to chase after them to get them
to pose. On the other hand, other fish may tend to be
neglected by the cleaners and may have to spend much
time posing in order to obtain service; even then they
may be left in the middle of treatment for a preferred
individual. Probably the wrasse's preferences have to do
with the numbers of parasites and the amount of food
remains that it can expect to find on the client.

Labroides, while it is inspecting its host, maintains
tactile communication by continually vibrating its ventral fin against the other fish or prodding it with its
mouth. Thus the client knows the whereabouts of the
cleaner on its body and can extend a fin, open its mouth
or gills, or hold still as necessary. Should the client want
to breathe more deeply while the cleaner is within its
mouth, it may briefly half shut its jaws, thus warning the
cleaner. Or should the client have had enough attention
and wish to leave, it may shrug or jerk its body thus
allowing the cleaner to move away.

It has been suggested that at times the presence of
cleaners may be essential to maintain the health of the
surrounding fish population. On the other hand, as an
experiment, the cleaners have also been removed from
an area of reef with little apparent adverse effect upon
the local fishes. Of course it may be only from time to
time, when an outbreak of parasites is threatening, that
their role becomes a really critical one. By contrast it is
certain that at other times the activity of cleaners may
tend to be slightly harmful, in that if the cleaner obtains
insufficient parasites and dead tissue from its cleaning
activities, it will begin to bite and consume quite healthy
skin and fins. It seems that in the normal course of
events many fish will quite happily put up with a small
amount of parasitism of this sort, since they may not
easily be able to tell, for example, when parasites are
being removed, or a new wound created; also it is

apparent that the client fish find that the sensations generated by the attentions of the cleaner provide a comparatively pleasant experience, and they will continue to seek service from a cleaner even when cleaning is not strictly necessary. On the other hand some fish, especially those kept in close proximity with a cleaner in an aquarium, may become distinctly 'sore' from its activities, and will avoid its attentions, or chase it away if it attempts to clean.

No mention of the behaviour of Cleaner wrasses would be complete without some mention of a rather interesting twist to the tale. Among the blennies to be found on the coral reef are one group, the sabre-toothed blennies, which feed almost entirely by attacking rather larger passing fish and nipping small pieces out of their skin or fins. These blennies, like others of the same family, often spend much of their time in the shelter of small holes in the coral, especially the neat tube-like holes extending into live corals made by boring shellfish or tubeworms which are no longer there. Thus it is in fact not an infrequent experience for the diver or snorkeller swimming along a reef to feel a sudden sharp little jab on the leg, and on turning round to see nothing save an innocent little blenny peeping out of such a hole.

One species of blenny in particular, *Runula* (or *Azalea*) *aspidontus*, which is quite common on Red Sea reefs, has capitalised on the presence of the Cleaner wrasse. As shown in Plate 149, it has developed a coloration almost identical to the wrasse and is very similar in shape and size, and is thus known as the Cleaner mimic blenny. It even has a form of nod swimming, although on careful observation it can be told apart since, while wrasse swim mainly by using their pectoral fins, blennies swim by wriggling move-ments of their body and tail. Nevertheless the mimicry is sufficiently effective to make the blenny appear to be soliciting as a cleaner, and other fish may allow it to approach, or prospective clients may actually approach the mimic. But the blenny, instead of cleaning, makes a rapid dash at the other fish, tearing off and consuming a chunk of fin or skin. Needless to say the other fish does not retain its cleaning pose but, after perhaps briefly attempting to chase the blenny away, quickly moves off. While this sabre-toothed blenny may be able to attack some other fish by posing as a cleaner, it also attacks, as do the other sabre-toothed blennies, fish which have failed to notice its presence.

It is interesting to note that in some areas of the Indo-Pacific different colour varieties of Cleaner wrasse are present, and here the colour of the mimic changes to match that of the model, thus confirming that the resemblance between blenny and cleaner is no mere coincidence. Finally, with regard to the mimic, the interesting point may be made that such a strategy, like many other examples of mimicry, can only work provided the mimic is rather less common than the species which it is copying; for if the Cleaner mimic blenny were too common, fish would associate this particular coloration with this irritating predator rather than with the process of cleaning, and the signal would no longer confer any protective benefit.

Besides the Cleaner wrasse several other species of fish in the Red Sea may occasionally be seen to pick at items on the body of larger fish. In particular the juveniles of several other wrasse, such as the Common green wrasse, *Thalassoma ruppelli* and the small *Larabicus* (or *Labrichthys*) *quadrilineatus* tend to do this, and it is interesting from this point of view that the juvenile *Larabicus* have a very similar coloration to that of the young Cleaner wrasse.

A number of species of shrimp are also active cleaners of fish. These are often to be found especially in the vicinity of cleaning stations, and they attract the attention of potential clients by waiting around the entrances to coral crevices and waving their antennae. The fish when being cleaned pose as for the cleaner fish, but close to the coral refuge of the shrimp; the shrimp stimulates the fish by movement of its antennae. Amongst the shrimps to be found acting as cleaners in the Red Sea are the conspicuously red and white banded *Stenopus hispidus* (see Plate 150), and a smaller species of *Periclimenes*. This latter species, which is often found protected among sea-anemones (see Plate 151), is transparent save for a series of conspicuous white dots on the body and appendages. It is nicely shown tending to several different customers in Plates 152 and 153.

SEX AND SOCIETY

Fish and animal species become adapted to the needs of their particular environment, not only in their form, feeding behaviour and relationship with other species, but also in their detailed reproductive and social behaviour. The general way in which such aspects of the life of fishes can vary can be seen by surveying the range of different social arrangements which may link male with female. Thus some coral-reef fish live in mono-gamous pairs, a single male and single female remaining in close company with each other, often within their own territory. Such is the case with most butterflyfishes, and the rabbitfish *Siganus stellatus*. In other species a single male will occupy the territory within which he maintains several females which together are known technically, for obvious reasons, as a harem. Such an arrangement is quite common among the wrasses (for example, the Sling-jaw wrasse *Epibulus insidiator*, and several species of *Cheilinus*) and the parrotfishes (for example the large and colourful *Cetoscarus bicolor* and *Scarus gibbus*). The Cleaner wrasse has a variety of this arrangement in that the male *Labroides dimidiatus* holds a large territory within which are a number of females; but whereas the females of a harem generally wander throughout the male's territory, and often do so in a group, in this case each female occupies her own sub-territory, each based on her own cleaning station. The male will wander around visiting his females and may feed at any of these cleaning stations.

Many fishes, however, may have no permanent territory and no permanent bonding between particular males and particular females. In some of these species, when it is time for reproduction, numbers of males and females will come together and spawn in a group, releasing clouds of eggs and male gametes into the water so that fertilisation can occur. Similarly the green damselfish *Chromis* spawn together in a group, generally on a dead *Acropora* table or similar surface; the females in a milling group deposit their eggs on the surface, and the males hovering around fertilise them. However, in yet other species which have no permanent territories or pair-bondings, spawning may still take place pair-wise between individual males and females. In some of these species, for example the Common green wrasse, *Thalassoma ruppelli* and the Elephant wrasse *Gomphosus caeruleus*, the males establish small temporary territories just over the period of spawning and solely for the purpose of attracting females. Thus most of the day the Common green wrasse wanders around individually over the reef feeding; but in the early afternoon large numbers of males, which are slightly larger and more colourful, establish a string of small territories, each only a metre or two across, along the crest of the leeward side of the reef where spawning occurs. The females, which are

much more numerous than the males, are attracted to the territory of their choice and there, after a few preliminary displays, each female spawns individually with the territory-holding male. Male and female swimming side by side or one above the other rush upwards for several metres towards the surface of the sea; at the top of this movement a cloud of gametes is released and both fish then return down to the reef. The female only spawns once on each particular occasion, but the male will spawn consecutively with a series of females who happen to be attracted to his territory. Naturally there is a great deal of chasing and aggression between males over the few hours of spawning as they compete to hold the parts of the reef to which most females may be attracted.

In some families, however, including the wrasses (Labridae), parrotfishes (Scaridae), damselfishes (Pomacentridae) and groupers (Serranidae), this whole picture is further complicated by the fact that most of the male fishes develop in the first place by sex change from female fishes. That is, a fish which manages to survive to full size begins life as a female; it continues growing and may breed as a female for some years until, when it is larger than most other females, it will change sex to become a male; as a male it will continue growing and may, if lucky, again breed for several years. Such an arrangement is known biologically as *protogynous hermaphroditism* (protogynous simply meaning female first).

One of the species in which such a sequence of events was first demonstrated was the little red jewelfish *Anthias squamipinnis*. The stages through which an individual passes are clearly shown in Plates 158 to 162. If the young fish survive the hazards of their larval period they arrive at suitable areas on the reef face and crest where both cover and food may be available; at this stage they are still transparent save for their red eyes and yellow internal organs (see Plate 158). As they grow they develop the characteristic red skin pigmentation and the attractive blue stripe through the eye; at maturity (Plate 159) they develop into females and behave accordingly. When they are large enough and the opportunity arises the female may begin to develop into a male and, as shown in Plate 161, the fins begin to lengthen and a long spine to develop at the front of the dorsal fin; at the same time the internal organs change from those characteristic of a female to those characteristic of a male. The fully

INSET TOP RIGHT/RIGHT/INSET LEFT/INSET BOTTOM RIGHT: 163/164/165/166
Schooling fish dazzle the predator: it is almost impossible to follow and home
in on a particular fish in the middle of a rapidly manoeuvring school.
Predators must somehow isolate individuals to one side. Many juveniles
congregate – there is safety in numbers.

developed male, shown in Plates 160 and 162, has a distinctly darker red coloration, more extensive violet markings, with violet spots on the pectoral fins, and longer fins with, in particular, a long crest at the beginning of the dorsal fin and elegant extensions to the top and bottom of the tail fin.

In *Anthias*, and in many of the other species which have this system of protogynous hermaphroditism, the exact time at which a female can change into a male is controlled by the social behaviour of other males. Thus a small school of *Anthias* may only have a single male present, or a larger school may have a number of males present, but, on average, it is only when an existing male dies or is otherwise lost from the group that a large or dominant female can change sex to replace it. This can easily be demonstrated in the aquarium. If half a dozen females and a single male are placed together in a tank, and then after some time the male is removed, the most dominant, usually the largest, female will then change sex, often, so far as external appearances are concerned, within the space of only a few days. In those species of wrasse and parrotfish which have harems the change from female to male is normally controlled in a similar way by the presence or absence of the male. Thus in the Cleaner wrasse, *Labroides dimidiatus*, when a male dies or disappears the females from his harem compete to establish the most dominant individual, and she then changes sex to become the new harem-owning male. The females from a group rapidly become aware when the male has been lost, since there is an abrupt cessation of the regular visit of the male to the different feeding stations, where he exhibited dominance and sexual behaviour towards the female. In those other species in which there is no clearly organised social structure, the change of female into male probably depends as much on the size and age of the individual as on the male/female proportion of individuals already present in the population.

In a few species, among which the Common green wrasse, *Thalassoma ruppelli*, is a good example, there is an added rather fascinating complication. In this wrasse there are actually two types of male. There is the 'usual' type of male, which is developed by sex change from a female, and in addition there are a minority of males which are born as such, but which retain the appearance and coloration of females, and do not always develop, even with increased size, the brighter and more gaudy coloration typical of the main group of males. This peculiar way in which the second group of males retains the appearance of females is in fact part of a cunning little strategy enabling them to survive and reproduce more successfully. As was explained above, the main group of males, during the period of reproduction, each establish small territories on the reef crest at sites where females may come to spawn; these males furiously drive other males who may be competing for these same females out of their territory. But these other males, who although born as such retain the dress of females, are able by virtue of this disguise to enter the territories of the more dominant males, and to gain access to and spawn with some of the females who are waiting there. This situation has attracted a great deal of attention among biologists, since although different species do, as already described, show considerable differences in their social and reproductive behaviour, in this case we have two different varieties of the same species which adopt different behaviour and are apparently competing with each other. By studying the factors which favour either of the two alternative strategies it may be possible to learn a great deal more about the processes which determine the behaviour of different species.

GOING TO SCHOOL

Finally in this chapter we will consider one of the most important features that has to be determined for a species or population of fishes – whether the individuals should live and feed independently, or whether it is more advantageous for them to group together in schools of various sizes. Biologists have recently been particularly interested in discovering what factors determine the most appropriate arrangement for any particular species, and it has become increasingly clear that there are in fact quite a large number of factors which affect the eventual outcome; the behaviour eventually shown by the fish reflects a balance between a variety of opposing forces.

To begin with one ought to emphasise that there is at least one considerable disadvantage to schooling. If for a particular fish the appropriate food supply is comparatively evenly distributed over the reef, then a school of that species will very quickly exhaust it in one part of the reef. They will have to move on, perhaps eventually covering a considerable area. Even if the fish have the time to go far enough together in a single day to

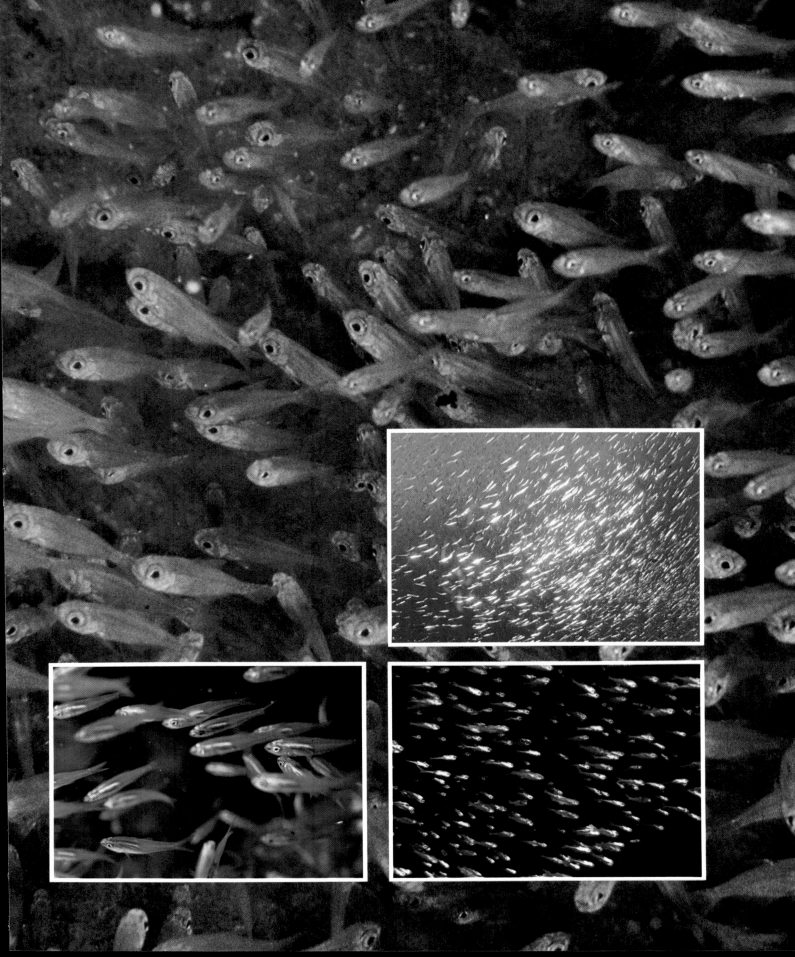

get a sufficient supply of food, it is still rather wasteful of energy, since the fish will actually have to eat more to cover the extra energy required to swim the longer distance. On these grounds it would be much better if each fish kept to its own area of reef which was just big enough to meet its own food requirements. Explained very simply, one could say that territorial behaviour was the eventual outcome of this line of thought, since territorial behaviour ensures that each individual fish keeps to its own area in just this way.

Against this and any other reasons favouring a solitary existence there are, it has become apparent, quite a few reasons for living in the company of individuals of one's own species. The first group of reasons has to do with the advantage that can thus be gained over potential predators which might threaten one's existence. In the first place many eyes are much better at keeping a lookout for the approach of a predator than are just a single pair. Thus among the schools of *Chromis* swarming along the reef edge, if a single individual spots a jack rushing in towards them it rapidly dives for cover on the reef; this diving movement is detected by its neighbours who likewise drop down, and thus a wave of contraction spreads through the school as they all dive for cover among the rocks and coral. This effect can be stimulated by a diver who finds

a suitable school hovering around a point in the reef. If from one side of the point the diver makes a threatening movement with his hand, visible to only part of the school situated on that side of the point, the resulting rush for cover can be seen to spread to the other half of the school who were unable to see the original threat.

A second effect which helps to reduce the threat of predation is a purely mathematical one. If a predator sets out over a reef to capture an individual of a particular prey species, the chance of the predator finding such an individual will be greatly reduced if the population of the prey species on the reef gets together in a single school. If all of the prey individuals were to wander around on their own, the predator would very likely come across one on whatever part of the reef he happened to search. With the prey fish in a single school, the predator may have to search for a long time before discovering the exact whereabouts of that school on the reef. In a similar way, should the predator be territorial and a number of them be present on the same reef, it is actually better for all of the prey fish to crowd into one of these territories rather than be distributed across the reef, since in that way only a single predator can eat its fill whereas otherwise quite a large number of predators might be able to do so. Thus, for example, the school of nocturnal cardinalfishes (*Apogon*) and hatchet-

LEFT: 167 A school of fusiliers, *Caesio lunaris*, a typical feeder on plankton in the water just off the reef face. Schooling also helps in finding food; should one fish in a scattered shoal come across a dense patch of plankton, the others will notice and gather about to feed.

fishes (*Pempheris*) may reduce the rate at which they are taken by coral trout of the different species of *Cephalopholis* by remaining within particular territories of these predators.

The third and most easily appreciated anti-predator advantage of schooling (see Plates 163 to 166) lies in the problem this causes the predator in trying to pick out and grasp individual prey fishes. This effect is one which has often been suggested by biologists working on such fish, but which has been much more difficult to establish scientifically. Indeed, at first thought, one would imagine that once a predator such as a jack (*Caranx*) has found, for example, a school of sardines, all that would be necessary would be for the jack to charge the school, when it could hardly help but hit a target. However, when jacks do rush individually into the middle of a sardine school the school immediately swerves to either side leaving an empty void around the predator. Moreover the jack has the problem that it is insufficient simply to hit a sardine with any part of its body. It has to grab and hold a sardine firmly in its mouth. When a jack is attacking an isolated sardine this is not too great a problem in that the jack can follow the movement of the sardine and estimate exactly where it should grab in order to intercept its meal. However, it is almost impossible to follow visually in a frightened sardine school any individual for long enough to be able to estimate its course of movement and swim to intercept it. Any sardine that catches the eye is immediately lost again as other sardines swim in front of it. This can easily be seen if one attempts oneself to follow visually an individual fish in a shoal of sardines or a similar small species which one is harassing under water.

Some evidence for this sort of effect comes from the observation that oddly coloured or marked individuals within fish schools are much more liable to predation than are normal school mates; for example, fish which have been tagged as part of some scientific study tend to get taken by predators much more readily than they otherwise would. This is partly because it is much easier to follow the movement of such a conspicuously marked individual within a shoal. Although it may frequently be obscured by other fish passing in front of it, the same individual can repeatedly be recognised and thus its swimming course be followed, and an intercepting attack initiated. It is in response to the problem of picking out individual prey from a school of this sort that some jacks and barracuda have developed specialised group behaviour aimed at breaking up the school and splitting off individuals as described in the previous chapter.

Besides the benefits of schooling which assist the individuals of a species to avoid predation, there are others which are effective by increasing the efficiency with which the fish is able to feed. We have just mentioned that predators, by themselves forming groups, may be more able to attack successfully schools of a prey species. More generally if the food of a species is unevenly distributed and occurs in large amounts just here and there, then the presence of individuals in the school searching for food may make it much more likely that each individual will eventually get fed. Thus when a group of the grey swallow-tailed fusiliers, *Caesio lunaris* (see Plate 167), are searching for a suitable swarm of plankton, if one fish on the edge of the school discovers such a swarm, as it starts to feed all the other fish are attracted to it. In such a case the fish which first discovers the food loses comparatively little by having the other fish arrive, since the food is present in large excess; rather, by also having the opportunity to feed when other members of the school discover the source of food, each individual benefits from being a member of the school.

In view of the variety of effects which may influence the desirability of fish living together in groups or schools, it is hardly surprising that in practice such a great variety of conditions are found among reef fish, some living individually, some in pairs, some in small groups and others in large schools. The exact social behaviour shown by a fish will depend on what status, considering these different mechanisms, is most advantageous to it.

There are many people who, despite the attractions of the reef, hesitate to visit one themselves, because of the dangers they may encounter; and there are probably as many who have visited the reef but are still a bit wary and uncertain about exactly what risks they may be running. In fact the dangers of swimming on coral reefs are often much exaggerated in the public mind, an attitude engendered at least in part by a certain school of divers, who, of course, like to imply that the risks they have taken are perhaps somewhat greater than they really may have been. But in encouraging the visitor to the Red Sea to experience the area's coral reefs at first hand, a major contribution can be made by indicating how few in fact are the risks involved. At the same time there are some dangers, and it is of course important that the diver should know what these are. Thus it seems appropriate to devote a chapter to these dangers, both real and imagined.

SHARK!

There is no danger with which the newcomer to the reef is more concerned than with that of the presence of sharks. Snorkellers may cluster, fearful, in the shallowest water – divers may feel themselves compelled to come weighed down with diving-knives and spear-guns. No other predator has attracted so much general public attention in recent years as the shark. Everyone is familiar with the fact that famous bathing beaches in Australia and California must be protected by shark nets. Interest was further stimulated by Cousteau's TV programmes and Peter Gimble's awesome film *Blue Water, White Death*. Finally, of course, with *Jaws*, public fear, and locally even hysteria, reached its peak. With this in mind it is curious to learn that in the last century it was generally believed in Europe that sharks were harmless, there being little possibility that they might harm anyone, while as late as 1916 a large sum of money was offered to anyone who could prove that sharks actually did attack human beings.

Sharks may of course attack and kill people, but the average visitor to a Red Sea reef will be comparatively lucky if he sees a shark, and certainly lucky if he gets a photograph of one. Even when a shark does appear, the common problem is not to get away from it, but to get anywhere near it! The truth of the matter is that there is a wide variety of different species of shark of which comparatively few would normally present a danger to the diver, but some others may do so if they are provoked in one way or another. The sharks which actually occur on the reef in inshore areas of the Red Sea are nearly always smaller than man, usually flee as soon as they see him, and will only attack if physically provoked, or tempted with food. In the vicinity of deep-water reefs, however, some larger species of shark do occur which even though they do not normally come close to the shallow parts of the reef, can certainly be found by diving and/or attracting the sharks with food. Even then these larger sharks will not usually attack anything as large as a diver.

An essential point is, of course, that the diver or snorkeller is in a very different position to the ordinary swimmer or the bather on shore. Not only can the snorkeller or diver see any shark that may come by, but the shark can see the whole of the diver. By contrast all the shark may see of a bather could be the lower parts of the legs, each looking like a separate animal, and just about the right size for a meal!

There are three species of shark commonly seen on Red Sea reefs, the Reef whitetip (*Triaenodon obesus*), the Blacktip (*Carcharhinus melanopterus*), and the Grey reef shark (*Carcharhinus amblyrhynchos*). The first and third grow to about 1.7 metres, the second to about 1.4 metres, although like all fish they tend to look a little bigger than this under water. The Blacktip reef shark is readily identifiable by the clear black tip to its dorsal fin, and the dark ends to its pectoral fins; it is the shark which is most frequently seen in really shallow water or right on top of the reef. The Whitetip is markedly the commonest of the three, and can be distinguished from the two other important sharks with a white-tipped dorsal fin by its very long slender appearance. The reef sharks are essentially predators of small and medium-sized fish such as damselfish, wrasse, parrotfishes and snappers. These they may take by racing along the reef and surprising potential prey by their speed; but the Whitetip at least may also be adept at prising their way into coral crevices at night in order to capture sleeping parrotfishes, etc. Octopuses and crustaceans may also be caught, while it is assumed that dead prey items are also taken. Whitetip sharks especially are often found resting in caves or crevices on the reef by day, and the same individual or group appears to return to the same hiding-place over long periods. The sharks may be photographed in this situation, but it is unwise to tease or provoke them.

Moving to reefs in deeper water several larger species of shark may be seen. Perhaps the commonest is the Silvertip or Oceanic whitetip shark (*Carcharhinus albimarginatus*). This grows up to 2.5 metres in length, and is a deeper bodied shark than the Reef whitetip, from which it is also distinguishable by the conspicuous white trailing edge to the dark pectoral fins. Of the others the most likely to be seen are the Tiger shark (*Galeocerdi cuvieri*) and the long-finned shark (*Carcharhinus longimanus*). The latter grows up to 4 metres in length, and has peculiarly long rounded fins which are whitish at the ends. The Tiger shark, named from the series of dark vertical bars on its upper flank, reaches only about 3 metres, but is very deep bodied, and of the sharks which might possibly be met with it is the one that is perhaps likely to make an unprovoked or unstimulated attack. This behaviour is very possibly related to the fact that other sharks apparently form a significant part of its diet.

Other large sharks are very occasionally reported from deep water, such as Mako sharks (*Isurus* species); and the Great white shark is also said to occur in the Red Sea. This of course is the largest of the predatory sharks, growing up to 10 metres in length, and is the species featured in *Blue Water, White Death* and in *Jaws*. For the making of the first film, however, no Great white could be found in the region, and the species is mostly recorded in cooler waters, principally those south-west of Australia. The Great white shark is the one species which seems to attack divers without warning; apparently seals form a major part of their diet, and as has been observed before, a diver in a wet suit looks not that different from a rather slow seal!

Two other somewhat atypical forms of shark also deserve mention. Hammerhead sharks (*Sphyrna* species) are not uncommon; they may be seen, sometimes several together, near the sea bed in the region of some outer reefs; they may also be found in sandy areas and will

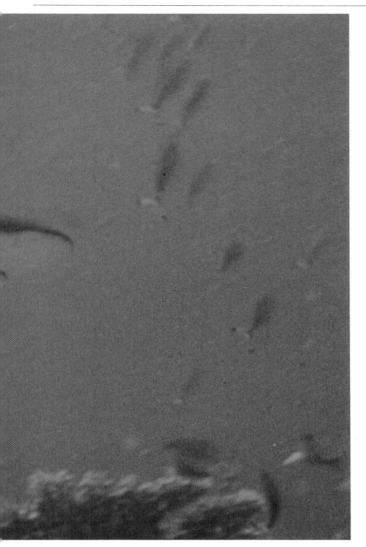

LEFT/BOTTOM LEFT: 171/172 Rarely do sharks spontaneously attack anything as large as a snorkeller or diver. But sharks are stimulated by sounds of a struggle, or the smell of blood in the water. Spearfishing produces both – sharks are attracted to and attack a speared grouper.

enter the backwaters of creeks. And also, perhaps more frequently recorded from the Red Sea than other areas, is the largest of all the sharks, the Whale shark *Rhincodon typus*. This grows up to lengths of 15 metres, but is completely harmless, feeding, like the basking sharks and also incidentally like the largest of the whales, on plankton. The Whale shark is humpbacked and flat-bellied, dark grey with an irregular pattern of white blotches. The diver who sees one is fortunate indeed; yet rare as they are they seem more frequent in the Red Sea than Great whites – so if you see a really huge shark, why not swim towards it?

FEEDING BEHAVIOUR A better understanding of the risks that might be involved in dealing with sharks can be gained from a consideration of their feeding behaviour. Four different senses may be used by a predatory shark in tracking and taking prey: hearing and vibratory sense, smell, vision and taste.

Sharks like most fish are able to detect sound and vibration under water by means of their lateral line, the slightly paler line that runs along the middle of the flank of almost all fishes, and along which are arranged numerous sensitive cells. Sharks can sense disturbance in the water over long distances. Even a human diver may hear under water when a large ship is dropping anchor a kilometre or more away. In response to a notable splash a nearby shark may come to investigate, but if there is nothing to excite him, will swim away again. However, sharks are particularly attracted by somewhat higher-frequency vibrations of the type which might emanate from the death struggle of an injured fish. This type of vibration they can detect at distances of up to 300 metres or more, and this will naturally stimulate their feeding behaviour in the expectation that a dead or injured fish will be available. Consequently sharks may be attracted in particular by spearfishing, because speared fish, jacks or groupers, regularly struggle for a while on the end of the spear. At the same time the sounds and vibrations produced by bathers enjoying themselves, or by noisy or panicky swimmers, have much the same character, and so will also serve to attract the attention of sharks. Probably effective for the same reason is a method of attraction used by shark fishermen in Polynesia (described by James Hornell in his book *Fishing in Many Waters*). The fishermen use a pair of coconut shells as a rattle, shaking them vigorously

RIGHT/INSET RIGHT: 173/174 The Lionfish or Chickenfish *Pterois volitans* has
poison glands associated with spines in both dorsal and ventral fins. They
sometimes threaten or dart at intruders, turning dorsal side on, so one should
not approach too close by. Nevertheless these are fascinating fish, with
outstretched pectoral fins, driving smaller prey into some corner where they
can be snapped up.

together, although here it is apparently believed that the
sound is mistaken by the sharks for the excited cries of
seabirds, feeding on a shoal of fishes.

The shark's sense of smell is atuned especially to the
scent of blood, and when blood is carried downstream in
the current sharks may be attracted from a considerable
distance. The sense of smell is also used at close
quarters, when the shark is searching for injured prey
among rocks, or deciding what to attack. In particular,
however, the scent of blood seems to have a powerful
releasing effect in stimulating instinctive attack behaviour.
Animals which carry the scent of blood, for example
spearfishermen, are attacked even though they may be
large and clearly uninjured. And if large amounts of
blood are released into the water this may stimulate,
especially when numbers of sharks are about, the
famous feeding-frenzy. The sharks race and dash
around, snapping at almost anything that moves, including each other, and a shark thus killed adds more
blood to the water, and thus to the frenzy.

Visual stimuli will influence or guide the shark as it
comes in to inspect an object and perhaps attack. Sharks
will rarely attack something as large as a diver without
making several close passes to get a better look, unless
the smell of blood is already in the water. Much effort
has gone into investigating what visual characteristics
might influence a shark to attack or not to attack once its
attention has been drawn to a diver or a surface
swimmer, for example a sailor from a foundered ship, or
airman from a ditched plane. The evidence is rather
confused. On the one hand, the high rate of shark attack
upon ditched airmen in tropical waters has been
attributed to the conspicuous coloration of their clothes
and lifevests, designed so that they may easily be spotted
by rescuers. On the other, some trials have shown that,
given a choice, sharks will mostly prefer to attack a dark
object rather than a light one. Two separate effects may
occur; conspicuous colours may more readily attract
their attention, whereas once an object has been seen,
duller objects may be attacked with less hesitation. One
or two divers have preferred to rely on this second effect,
painting white bands on their wet suits, as an anti-shark
device, trying to avoid being mistaken for a seal or
imitating the warning colorations of, for example, some
species of sea-snakes.

In the light of the above discussion, it is easier to
appreciate the procedures which should be followed in

BELOW: 175 Another species of Lionfish, *Pterois radiata*, distinguishable by the fine white lines and pointed spines, equally well equipped with venom glands.

RIGHT/BOTTOM RIGHT: 176/177 The scorpionfish or false stonefish, *Scorpaenopsis gibbosa*, rests well-camouflaged on the rocky surface of the reef. With its large mouth it pounces on small fish which pass too close.

order to avoid attracting the attention of sharks. Too much splashing should be avoided in areas where sharks are likely to be present; this applies especially when one is swimming in open water. If it is necessary to swim a significant distance over deep water, possibly in emergency after the loss or breakdown of a boat, it would be advisable to use as silent and as regular a stroke as possible.

Above all however it is spearfishing which may attract sharks to the reef and encourage them to attack. The vibrations of the struggling fish as they are speared from time to time, and in particular the blood carried away in the water, will serve to alert any shark present over quite a large area. It is for this reason as much as for reasons of conservation that spearfishing should be banned in any area regularly used by others for recreational diving and snorkelling. The blood in the water and around or on the spearfishermen will stimulate otherwise safe species to attack; of particular significance

are a number of reports of even the Common reef whitetip (*Triaenodon obesus*) attacking or trying to attack spearfishermen, although in no case did this result in really serious injury. If it is essential to spear fish, for example for food, it is strongly advised that each fish be removed from the water as soon as it is caught – in particular do not hang them from your belt which is asking for trouble. It is for such reasons too that the carrying of spear-guns, claimed as a protection against sharks, is to be strongly discouraged. It is a rare man who can resist just the occasional pot shot at some potential supper!

While most visitors to the reef will be quite happy to accept that they will see few if any sharks, some divers are interested in attracting them. This may be for photography, for the excitement, or perhaps just to experience the extraordinary grace with which these creatures swim. The same principles can be applied as when trying to avoid them; the best method of attraction

TOM BLACKERBY

is to spear and cut up several large fish, place the pieces out as bait, and then take partial cover on the reef. The results can be quite variable, and on inshore reefs quite frequently no sharks may appear. To attract and see larger sharks it is necessary to dive on one of a limited number of offshore reefs where there is deep water, the sort of reefs on which sizeable shoals of other large fish also tend to gather.

Our own experiences, mainly with the Oceanic whitetip (*Carcharhinus albimarginatus*) illustrate various points. The sharks may often circle before paying attention to or perhaps locating the bait. If the bait is fresh but partially hidden they may have difficulty locating it, perhaps because the blood is so widely dispersed in the water, whereas later on a newly arriving shark may be able to track down and locate the bait immediately. At an even later stage, if no sharks arrive in the first half hour or so, sharks which pass by later may fail to be lured by even a clearly exposed bait, presumably because there is no longer any sound or scent to draw their attention to it. The only occasion on which one of us was threatened was when his wetsuit had become smeared with blood from the speared fish; the shark ignored the fish but approached closer and closer to the diver and had to be fended off with pushes and kicks.

Having thus reinforced the average reader's awareness of sharks by daring to discuss them, one should perhaps emphasise again how negligible is the risk of shark attack to the normal visitor to the reefs. On fewer than one in a hundred excursions does one see a decent-sized shark (unless one goes to look for them) and the risk of being molested by one is even less. In fact we know of no record of a diver or snorkeller having been seriously injured by a shark in the Red Sea.

POISONOUS FISHES

A group of fishes of which the visitor to the reef should be more aware than of sharks are the few species of poisonous fish. A surprising amount of misinformation seems to have developed around the topic. The poisonous species with which we need to be concerned are the lionfish, the scorpionfish, the stonefish, and the catfish *Plotosus*.

The commonest of these species in the Red Sea is the lionfish or chickenfish, *Pterois volitans*, illustrated in Plates 173 and 174. This species has a multiplicity of common names, also being known as the zebrafish, turkeyfish, featherfish, firefish or butterfly cod. It is, as can be seen, a very unusual and attractive fish. The danger lies in the venom which is carried in a fleshy integument at the base of each of the thirteen dorsal spines. This arrangement is essentially a defensive one designed to injure large predators who may otherwise try to snap up the fish, which is a slow-moving species and otherwise comparatively easily caught. Thus the chief risk is that a visitor to the reef may be attracted by a lionfish and think that he can catch one with his bare hands, and thus suffer multiple spine wounds. However, the lionfish may also take offensive action against either predators or humans which are bothering it or appear to be about to do so. They rush briefly forward, at the same time twisting over, so as to try to jab the predator with the dorsal spines. Particularly in the Gulf of Aqaba, where lionfish are especially common, they seem to be inclined to show this aggressive behaviour, and several

divers have been slightly injured in this way. But such behaviour is not generally observed in the central Red Sea. Why this difference should occur is not known; it may be a genetically determined regional difference, or it may be that in the Gulf of Aqaba, where much more diving has so far taken place, the lionfish have learnt from experience that divers are likely to pester them.

The injection of lionfish venom causes effects lasting for up to seventy-two hours. There is nausea, weakness and fever, there may be periods of semi-consciousness and the victim may have difficulty in breathing. But the main problem is the intense pain which the poison apparently causes, and many of the observed symptoms may in fact be secondary effects of this pain. After up to seventy-two hours the patient gradually recovers. Apparently even light contact with the dorsal spines may cause superficial pain and itching lasting for about thirty minutes, so care needs to be exercised when closing in for a photograph.

Lionfish are however an extremely interesting species, both as regards their form and their behaviour. They are cunning predators of smaller fish. On the one hand, when waiting still in mid-water, the frilled shape and irregular banding of the lionfish may lead to their being mistaken for floating pieces of seaweed; small fishes may fail to notice the danger, or may even try to seek shelter within the apparent fronds of the algae. On the other hand, the lionfish can extend its wide pectoral fins well out from its side and use them like a pair of arms, or two nets, to shoo one or more small fish into a corner on the reef and capture them. Both form and coloration also serve to protect the fish. Any similarity to a strand of algae or other material floating in the water may result in predators failing to notice the fish. But once the lionfish has been seen, the red and white bandings also constitute, as explained in the last chapter, a standard form of warning coloration, in this case advising the potential predator of the spines and poison glands.

There is a second species of lionfish which, though not so common, is still fairly frequently seen in the Red Sea; this is *Pterois radiata*, which is illustrated in Plate 175. This species lacks the feathered appearance of *Pterois volitans*, but has similar spines and poison glands, and generally similar behaviour.

Lionfishes scarcely represent a danger to the snorkeller or diver, once forewarned not to chase them. But a

BELOW: 178 The stonefish, centre left of the picture (with arched mouth and eye swellings to the right) brilliantly disguised as a mud-covered rock on a sandy slope. The poison in the glands associated with the dorsal spines is considered the most potent produced by any fish. Such large cryptic stonefishes and scorpionfishes are the most significant animal danger to humans on the reef, and one should look very carefully before placing a hand on any stone, especially in areas of sand and rubble.

cousin, the stonefish (*Synanceichthys verrucosa*) probably represents the danger on the reef with which the visitor should be most concerned. As mentioned in chapter 6 the stonefish is a predator which has taken the strategy of disguise and ambush to its ultimate limit. As can be seen from Plate 178, it is a bottom-dwelling fish which has developed an extraordinary resemblance to an encrusted stone. The mimicry is perfect down to the finest detail, the skin being covered with numerous filamentous-like projections which look completely like an untidy growth of green algae. Snorkellers searching for shells have even been known to try and turn over a stonefish, and been taken aback on discovering that it was alive! In order to resemble a stone the stonefish has largely sacrificed its mobility and can only move very clumsily. But by virtue of a surprisingly large mouth it can gulp in unsuspecting smaller prey, which may even have come specifically to take cover beside this welcoming rock. Being such a sluggish mover the stonefish is clearly in need of other means of protection and its dorsal, anal and pelvic fins are equipped with spines and poison glands, thirteen on the dorsal fin, three on the anal, and two on each pelvic fin. Moreover, the toxin is considered to be the most poisonous in any fish, and if received in sufficient quantity can prove lethal, if medical treatment is not given within a very short time. The effects of the

toxin are broadly similar to those of lionfish toxin, except that the effects are more severe, the pain excruciating and local tissue destruction occurs around the wound.

The venom is apparently an unstable protein, the breakdown of which may be promoted by heat and by potassium permanganate, external application of both of which are recommended for treatment of such a wound. An antiserum, of uncertain effectiveness, may also be obtained for injection from specialist suppliers, and it would certainly be sensible for diving expeditions to include phials of this in their medical kit. But the most important defence against the stonefish is to prevent injury. The great risk is that of treading on one accidentally when wading in shallow water near the top of the reef; this zone, with its numerous algal-covered rocks and stones, is the habitat which they prefer. It is to guard against this risk in particular that, as emphasised in the next chapter, tennis shoes, sneakers or other thick-soled foot-cover should always be worn when wading on the reef, while, when diving, slipper-type flippers or thick-soled diving boots should always be used. It is also helpful when wading to shuffle one's feet along the bottom since this will avoid treading on a stonefish, while, as the fish are unaggressive they will not injure an individual who kicks rather than steps on

them. Finally, care should be taken when snorkelling in shallow water not to rest one's hand on any algal-covered stone of a particular size without just glancing at it, to check that it is not a stonefish.

Besides the stonefish, there are on coral reefs a variety of species of closely related scorpionfishes (see Plates 176 and 177). These are mostly of rather smaller size, and may be well camouflaged against a variety of backgrounds. The largest of the Red Sea scorpionfishes is the false stonefish, *Scorpaenopsis gibbosa*; it resembles the true stonefish in that it too has skin appendages resembling bits of algae, and has the general appearance of a weed-covered rock. But the resemblance is less complete and the animal is more readily discernible as a fish. It is more upright in stance, has brilliant orange undersides to the pectoral fins which are exposed when the fish swims, and is much more mobile than the true stonefish; it can jump forwards for up to a metre to snap up prey, or swim rapidly over distances of several metres. Scorpionfishes also have thirteen dorsal spines each with an associated poison gland, but the toxin is not as powerful as that of the stonefish.

Only one other poisonous fish, quite unrelated to the scorpionfishes and stonefish, is likely to be met with on Red Sea reefs. This is the plotosid catfish, *Plotosus anguillaris*, illustrated in Plate 179, which shows a school of juveniles. Such schools are sometimes found milling closely together under large boulders, or may occasionally be seen forming dense spherical schools in open water. As the fish grow the yellow stripes become less distinctive, and the shoals break up, the adults being found individually on sandy inshore bottoms. The poisonous feature of these catfish is a pair of venom glands associated with the single dorsal spine and each of the pectoral spines.

RAYS AND EELS

Rays and eels are two other groups of fish which have often been thought of as being in some way dangerous. In fact the danger associated with either group is pretty minimal.

Rays are of course closely allied to sharks, but are characteristically dorsoventrally flattened with enlarged pectoral fins fused with the body. A diagnostic character is the opening of the gill slits onto the ventral surface, water being drawn in during respiration through a tube, the spiracle, on the dorsal surface, and then expelled through the gills. There are perhaps five species which might attract attention.

By far the commonest on Red Sea reefs is the Blue-spotted lagoon ray (*Taeniura lymma*) shown in Plates 180 and 181. This is an extremely interesting fish which digs in the lagoon for molluscs and echinoids and, as described in the last chapter, when feeding is typically surrounded by a variety of wrasse and other fish waiting for whatever else the ray may turn up. The lagoon ray belongs to the family Dasyatidae, the stingrays, as do several other species to be found in the Red Sea. Of these the most conspicuous is perhaps *Dasyatus favus*, which is large and kite-shaped, a metre and a half wide, and has a long tail approximately one and a half times the length of the disc. It is most frequently seen where there is a deep lagoon behind the fringing reef.

The stingrays are so called because of one or more very sharp large spines located underneath the tail towards its base. Although these rays are unaggressive and no danger to the swimmer or snorkeller, it is possible when wading in shallow water to tread on, or close by, a resting ray, which may then slash at the intruder with its tail. The spine may be driven deeply into the heel or lower leg, causing immediate and intense pain, which apparently increases to a peak within ninety minutes, and lasts, if untreated, for from six to forty-eight hours.

There has been much discussion as to whether any venom is associated with the spines of stingrays, some authors claiming that the spine is coated with a venomous mucus or by a venom-producing layer of tissue. This uncertainty may have been resolved if the report is correct that about 30 per cent of stingrays have lost their venomous capability through damage to the tissue about the spine. Apparently the appropriate treatment for a wound caused by a stingray is to carefully wash the wound, removing any foreign tissue or material; then to keep the wounded area in as hot a salt solution as the patient can stand for one to one and a half hours – this apparently neutralises the venom.

Another not uncommon species of ray is the graceful Spotted eagle ray (*Aetobatus narinari*) (see Plate 182). This species has a distinct head projecting in front of the wings, is dark above with evenly spaced whitish spots, and including its long tail reaches lengths of over three

metres. It feeds on bivalves, and is most commonly seen in large lagoons. Like the stingrays it has a spine at the base of its tail.

Very different in shape and with quite a different method of defence is the Electric ray, *Torpedo fusco-maculata*. This species lacks the grace of the other rays, having a rounded disc and a shortish thick tail. The Electric ray generally lives in shallow water, often buried in mud or sand, where it feeds on a variety of prey. The electric organs are situated below the skin on either side of the head, and may be used both in capturing prey, and as a defence mechanism. The rays have been recorded as briefly delivering more than 200 volts and 2,000 watts; despite this, however, large sharks may apparently feed on them.

Finally among the rays must be mentioned the largest of them all, the superbly graceful Manta ray (*Manta birostris*). With wings as much as seven metres across they seem to fly through the sea with slow but elegant beats and effortless beauty. Individuals may weigh as much as two tons, but they are quite harmless to divers, although they very occasionally manage to overturn small boats by trying to scrape their backs on the underside. The Manta feeds on plankton directed into the mouth by a pair of elongated lobes which project forward from the head, one on either side, and which constitute a diagnostic feature. Most usually Mantas are seen in the open water from a boat, especially when as they sometimes do in courtship, they leap out of the water in spectacular fashion, hitting the sea again with a thunderous splash. But they may also come into the reef when, being of a curious nature, they will sometimes come right up to a diver, provided he remains fairly still.

Leaving the rays, we turn to the eels, the type typical of coral reefs being, of course, the moray eels (family Muraenidae). There are in fact many different species of moray eel, some of which are quite conspicuously coloured with white, red or yellow. But the one species normally seen is the brown moray eel, *Gymnothorax javanicus*, which grows to a metre or more in length. The morays are predators, living in holes and crevices in the reef, and specialised at winding their way through dense coral growth, perhaps to take resting fish, or to lunge from openings at passers-by.

Because of their ugly snake-like appearance morays are often feared as being aggressive. The impression

LEFT/INSET LEFT: 180/181 The blue-spotted lagoon ray or sting ray, *Taeniura lymma*. This interesting fish is quite unaggressive. The sting is a protective barb under the tail which can slash your foot or ankle if you happen to tread on one while wading in shallow water, yet another reason for always wearing flippers or gym shoes when paddling.

BELOW: 182 Close-up of the large eagle ray, *Aetobatus narinari*, digging in the lagoon sand for shellfish. These rays are breathtaking to meet under water, but quite harmless. They fly through the water with extraordinary grace.

may be enhanced because of their habit, when peering out of the home crevice, of rhythmically opening and closing the mouth, baring as it were their numerous pointed teeth. This behaviour however is used by the fish to maintain a respiratory current in through the mouth and out over the gills, and morays will not attack a diver except when provoked, or when mistaking a flipper prodded into a hole for a rather smaller fish. If a speared fish is exposed in front of a moray's hole the eel will of course strike and with a powerful bite try to grab the bait. But some divers have successfully trained individual morays to emerge and eat out of the hand, gently taking pieces from the food which is offered.

However, divers or snorkellers have very occasionally been nastily bitten by a moray when thoughtlessly sticking a hand or leg into a hole that happened to be the eel's home. The best advice is to avoid doing this!

THE REAL THINGS TO WATCH FOR

Although the various fishes just discussed are undoubtedly the most impressive threats to be found on the reef, they are not the things most likely to cause wounds or injury to the visitor, and, the stonefish apart, they need hardly concern him.

The most likely source of small wounds is undoubtedly the coral itself. The snorkeller or diver unfamiliar with the reef can easily knock against corals, especially when trying to manoeuvre against current or wave action. The thing for the beginner to remember when approaching or near a reef crest where noticeable waves are coming in, is to maintain a body angle with the head pointing away from the reef, so that a bit of flippering can get you out of trouble. If you face head on to the reef and are not too experienced, a wave may sweep you onto the coral before you have time to back

away. The other thing is to appreciate that branched or fragile corals can not be held on to, or stood on; they easily graze the hand, or give way under the weight of the foot so that the ankle may get unpleasantly scraped. Such coral wounds are usually very minor, but seem to develop infections fairly easily, perhaps as a result of bacteria that were present on the coral. Thus it is sensible always to treat such injuries with a suitable antiseptic. While an experienced reef diver may rarely get hurt, it is difficult for the beginner to avoid at least some scratches, and it may be a good idea to wear a stout pair of gloves for the first week or two.

Sea-urchins are another possible source of occasional minor injury. The common black needle-spined urchin (*Diadema setosum*) (see chapter 4) does not have any specific poison associated with its spines, but these are sharp and the thin film of tissue overlying the spine may have a general toxic effect. These urchins are often densely crowded in shallow water near the shore, so one needs to take care when wading in, and to wear well-soled shoes or flippers. The less common urchin, *Echinothrix diadema* (see chapter 4), is however equipped with a specific toxin which is contained within the hollow smaller spines and which thus escapes when the spines break off inside a wound. This urchin, which is reddish and has slightly shorter spines than *Diadema setosum*, occurs in small numbers mainly on offshore reefs, but by day it seems to hide very effectively within crevices, etc., and thus is not so often seen. At night however *Echinothrix* emerges and is in the habit of feeding on top of rocks or mounds, and more in the open than does *Diadema*, just in the sort of place a diver might well rest during a night dive. Thus they are probably the biggest problem associated with night diving on Red Sea coral reefs, and well worth keeping an eye open for if one intends to try this fascinating experience.

The two other main points are that fire corals need to be recognised, and avoided (see chapter 3), and as mentioned in chapter 5, great care should be taken when handling cone shells; they should not be carried close to the skin.

AND DANGERS THAT DO NOT OCCUR Finally it is worth mentioning that the three most venomous animals to be met with on coral reefs in other parts of the world are unknown in the Red Sea. Neither the Sea wasp (box jellyfish) nor the Blue-ringed octopus occur. And there is no definite record of a sea-snake from the Red Sea, although some small moray eels do look superficially very like them.

SNORKELLING AND DIVING ON CORAL REEFS

The first part of this chapter is included in the hope that this book may have encouraged at least some readers who have not previously visited a coral reef to get out and have a look at one for themselves. These may be snorkellers or divers with some experience of cold water diving, but who have not yet had the opportunity to dive in the tropics. Or there may be people visiting or working in the Red Sea area who have not previously been involved in sub-aqua activities, but who, on learning that they are on the threshold of one of the wonders of the natural world, may be encouraged to take the plunge.

For the first group we include a few comments based on our own experience, useful tips on coral-reef diving that may save inconvenience or frustration, and also odd warnings regarding possibly unappreciated danger-points. For the second group we offer some advice on how to set about snorkelling on the reef, and how to take up SCUBA diving. However, this chapter does not set out to be a diving manual for beginners or to give detailed instruction in such topics as dive planning, dive signals and emergency procedures under water. Rather it is intended to underline the need for proper education and training *BEFORE* one starts to dive.

SNORKELLING FOR BEGINNERS Snorkelling involves swimming on the surface of the sea, equipped with a dive mask, snorkel and fins. In addition, with the aid of a single deep breath it is possible to 'duck dive' and swim underwater to depths of ten metres or more, or for up to half a minute or so.

The first points are those to consider when choosing the equipment. The mask, sometimes called the goggles or dive-mask, should fit comfortably and easily on the face and cover the nose as well. You can test the fit as follows: place the mask in position but leave the strap hanging loose; then while breathing in very gently through the nose, let go of the mask; if the mask fits, the suction effect thus created should hold it onto the face until you breathe out again through your nose, but if there is a leak, air quickly seeps in and the mask falls off earlier. This is particularly important if you have either a rather broad or a rather narrow face, in which case some masks may not fit. Check that the rubber flange that fits up against your face is in good condition. It is

also a good idea to check that the glass is 'tempered' – that is of the sort which does not splinter into small pieces should it get broken or cracked.

Basically the snorkel should be of the simplest and hence cheapest type available. The type with a ping-pong ball at the top is considered dangerous, and so too is the type which comes already attached to a larger mask covering the mouth. For an adult the length of the snorkel should not be more than 35 cm from mouthpiece to top, since if it is longer the diver will have difficulty breathing in against the greater hydrostatic pressure. Also the diameter of the snorkel should be a minimum of 18 mm, otherwise the resistance to airflow is too great. But the total volume of the snorkel should not be more than a fifth of a litre, otherwise there is too much 'dead space', and carbon dioxide tends to accumulate in the lungs.

The best flipper for the ordinary snorkeller (or diver) in a coral reef area is the type with a complete sole and heel, like a slipper. This is because of the likelihood of occasionally treading on sharp corals, sea-urchins, or other animals or objects that might otherwise injure the bottom of the heel. Alternatively if the type with a heel strap is used, they should be worn over tennis shoes or sneakers or some other protection for the bottom of the foot. Flippers should fit easily on the foot, again rather like a slipper, especially because in warm salty water the foot tends to swell slightly and a previously well-fitting flipper becomes very uncomfortably tight. In fact you probably need a size of flipper that is a size bigger than the size of shoe you wear. Finally the flipper should be flexible, but not too flexible or else when you try to swim, the flipper will bend and you get nowhere.

Once in the water the main worry for the first-time snorkeller is usually how to prevent water getting down the snorkel. This however is really the wrong philosophy; the great thing is to learn as quickly as possible to master the art of 'clearing your snorkel' – that is of blowing back out of the top any water that gets in. This in fact requires a powerful explosive blowing action. The best thing is to practise this art while standing in shallow water; tip your head over to let a little water in, and then try to blow it back out. If you really cannot manage this, you can, when swimming, lift your head up out of the water as necessary and, taking the mouthpiece out of your mouth, drain the water from the bottom. But it's much more of an effort in the long run!

Various problems may also arise with the mask. The commonest cause of leaks into a beginner's well-fitting mask are odd strands of hair hanging down over the forehead and trapped under the edge of the mask. Water is drawn in by capillary action around even a single hair trapped in this way; so make sure the hair on your forehead and cheeks is pushed back well out of the way as you put on your mask. If you are having problems with the mask misting up, do as most divers do and rub a little spit, or a spot of detergent, round the inside of the mask before putting it on. And occasionally people get into discomfort by breathing in slightly through the nose with the mask on; this creates a slight suction effect within the mask which tends to do funny things to your eyes!

If you try duck-diving the important thing to know about is 'clearing your ears'. As you go down the pressure of the depth of water outside your ears builds up against the outside of your eardrums. The pressure on the inside remains as it was at the surface, unless you open a valve which connects the inside of your throat to your ear drums (via the eustachian tube). This valve may open automatically if you swallow, or should do so if you hold your nose and try to blow out gently against this blockage. If you do not clear your ears the pressure difference increases with increasing depth, so that below two to four metres or so the ears become increasingly painful. If you clear your ears you should hear a squeaking or popping noise as the pressures are equalised, and any pain should go. Do not try to go deeper without clearing your ears – your ear drums may burst and the resulting pain and dizziness may lead to drowning. If, despite repeated gentle attempts, you still fail to clear, you should seek advice from a qualified doctor.

Some final points to watch when snorkel diving. It is natural to take one or two *deep* breaths, just before duck-diving, but do not take more than this. Taking a series of rapid deep breaths (a practice known as 'overbreathing') just before diving does make it possible to hold the breath for longer, but it may suppress the need to breathe for so long that you actually black out first. In fact, it is also sensible not to continue snorkel diving at any time when you feel more than moderately out of breath or exhausted – again this may occasionally result in sudden loss of consciousness. And lastly, when snorkel diving, it is important to *look up* as you *come up* – otherwise its very easy to hit your head against the bottom of your boat, or the propeller – or on a coral reef to bang into a coral overhang.

SCUBA DIVING FOR BEGINNERS Diving with an aqualung or an air bottle is nowadays generally known as scuba diving and the equipment is known as SCUBA gear, SCUBA standing for 'self contained underwater breathing apparatus'. Basic SCUBA gear, in addition to the snorkelling equipment, normally consists of a dive tank and harness, a regulator, a weight belt, a wet suit and a lifejacket. The dive tank is a steel or aluminium bottle filled with normal air to a pressure of 200 or 300 bars (3,200 or 4,500 psi). The regulator or demand valve supplies air to the mouthpiece, reducing the pressure from that in the tank to that of the surrounding water. The harness to hold the tank and the weight belt are fitted with fast-release clips so that they can be immediately dropped in an emergency. And the wet suit is made of neoprene rubber; in colder waters it helps to keep the diver warm, and in reef areas may help to protect against cuts and grazes from the coral.

The most vital point to be made here however is that before one enters the undersea world using SCUBA gear it is absolutely essential to receive the necessary training. It is extremely dangerous to borrow or purchase a set of equipment and set off for the ocean floor prior to obtaining proper instruction. It may seem easy enough to breath from the bottle, but there are a series of ways in which failure to follow very particular and *not obvious* procedures may lead to a fatal accident.

Training can be obtained at special diving schools, on special courses, or through a diving club. There are diving schools or diving organisations in several towns in Saudi Arabia, including in particular Jeddah, and also in most of the other large coastal towns in other countries bordering the Red Sea. There are also many such schools throughout Europe and America, and each country also has its own national diving organisation (such as the British Sub-Aqua Club in the United Kingdom), which in turn run numerous diving clubs and branches. In the USA there are a series of organisations co-ordinating diving and training: PADI, YMCA, NAUI, NASDS, SSI, and LA County. The main international diving organisation to which the national diving associations of over fifty countries are affiliated is CMAS, which has its headquarters in Paris.

A typical training course for the use of SCUBA gear

LEFT BELOW: 186 Checking gear and preparing to descend. When diving or snorkelling near the reef in a current, face the current and use the flippers as necessary to maintain position. One can rest or put one's hand on the rounded corals, but not the branched corals which may break, scratch or even sting.

might include fifteen to twenty hours of theoretical studies (on topics such as diving medicine, diving calculations, dive-tables, dive planning and safety) and twenty to thirty hours of practical training, at first in a pool and then in the sea. After passing a theoretical exam and a practical test, the student receives a certificate, and increasingly in many countries such a certificate is required by law before a person is allowed to pursue this sport further.

COMMENTS ON CORAL-REEF DIVING FOR EXPERIENCED DIVERS

● The one factor which has led to several diving fatalities in the Red Sea is the tendency of divers coming recently from colder waters to assume, because of the much brighter lighting at depth, that they are much nearer the surface than they actually are. A Red Sea reef can be brighter at 40 metres than parts of the North Sea at 4 metres. It's very easy to stay at or drift down to depths of 30–40 metres, while thinking that you are only at 10–20 metres: moreover, things on the reef are often so interesting that you may not notice time passing. Consequently you can run out of air, or run into decompression troubles, when you weren't even looking at your depth gauge. So keep an eye on both your watch and your depth gauge. Use a tank with a reserve supply so that this can get you back to the surface, should you run out in this way. And always have a spare full tank available so that in an emergency you can go back down to decompress. The warmer waters make this alternative possible, provided you are conscious and otherwise in a good state; and there are few if any decompression chambers around the Red Sea.

● When snorkelling, the interest of the reef and the comparative ease of getting down to fifteen metres or more in a warm well-lit sea under a hot sun may encourage even experienced divers to become too exhausted or hyperventilate – be careful!

● The coral environment provides plenty of points for lines and cords to become ensnared and entangled. Check that no items which might become entangled (e.g. transect lines, speargun lines, etc.) are attached to you except in a way where they can be immediately released in an emergency – especially when snorkelling.

● If you are taking or using a small boat make sure you

BELOW: 187 A pair of divers swim over a particularly beautiful coral formation in shallow water. For safety, it is always necessary to keep close to your diving partner.

use anchors suitable for coral-reef areas. There must be a length of chain between the anchor and the rope, so that the rope doesn't fray against the corals. It is best to put down a spare anchor, on a slack line, and when you get in swim down to the anchors and check that they are securely placed, among solid rocks or corals. There is nothing more alarming when coming up from a dive on an offshore reef to find that your boat has drifted away to the horizon. On the other hand, do try to avoid damage to fragile corals when dropping anchor – this is a major cause of coral destruction on the best dive sites.

● When using any boat in remote or hot tropical seas, check yourself that the sensible emergency supplies are on board. There may not be a local coastguard to come and look for you. Such supplies might include engine spares and tools, fishing gear, a sail or oars, a medical kit of course, and especially lots of spare drinking water.

Also let someone else know beforehand where and when you are going, so that the alarm can be raised should you not return.

● In general wet suits are not essential in the Red Sea during the summer. In fact you should take an old shirt and loose jeans to wear in the water during most of the first week or so in order to prevent sunburn. This can happen very easily and quickly when snorkelling. Wet suit tops may be useful during November to May and the complete suit during January to March, especially in the Gulf of Aqaba where the water is not quite so warm as in the central Red Sea. A wet suit top can be most missed when one is just snorkelling at those times of year; especially in the northern Red Sea there is a strong north-easterly breeze which can have an uncomfortable chilling effect. If you're a keen photographer, wet suit bottoms may still prove valuable so that you can wedge

your knees among the rocks and corals, to hold still, without grazing or cutting your legs, but if you intend to do this it is best to attach protective patches over the parts of the trousers which may otherwise become badly damaged.

● Extra care of equipment may be needed under the hot salty conditions of the Red Sea, otherwise things tend to rust, corrode or perish with surprising speed. Face mask and flippers should not be left in the sun, especially if still salty from the sea, or within a month or two they begin to perish. But there is no need to waste valuable fresh water in washing them, provided they are kept in the shade. Regulators of course need thorough rinsing in fresh water. Dive tanks are best made of aluminium for tropical use. Steel tanks can rust more quickly than under temperate conditions, and they need more frequent testing – every year or two – and testing

facilities are rare in the Red Sea area. The date of the last test should be stamped on the neck of the bottle. Also aluminium cylinders are lighter for air transport. Cameras also should not be left in the direct sunlight which can raise the temperature, especially of metal objects, far in excess of that of the surrounding air. And do of course check all your gear works and that you have the vital spares before you board the plane for that long-awaited Red Sea holiday. Too often a newly purchased underwater flash-gun has never been tried out under water at home, and faulty or broken components cannot be replaced abroad.

● A final point about footwear. In coral-reef areas the bottom of the foot and heel must be protected against standing on sharp corals, sea-urchins or stonefish. Moreover, in order to dive from the shoreline in tropical waters one often has to walk out across the fringing reef. In the area north of Jeddah, for example, the distance out to the reef edge is an average hundred metres or so. Use either the slipper type of flipper, or a larger heel-strap type flipper combined with tennis shoes, sneakers or stout-bottomed dive boots. With the latter combination the flippers can be carried out to the reef edge and put on there. With slipper type flippers it may be necessary to risk leaving sneakers, tied or weighed down, at a conspicuous spot on the reef edge – although a few people have developed a sort of frog walking technique, wearing flippers, to a fine art! Also, because the skin tends to swell slightly in warm salty water, do not bring flippers that are tight fitting. A comfortable slack fitting is required; most people find that it is best to use the same flippers *without* wetsuit boots in the Red Sea that they would use at home *with* wetsuit boots.

UNDERWATER PHOTOGRAPHY

In the second part of this chapter we offer a brief introduction to underwater photography, together with a few useful tips, which may be of help to the visitor to the Red Sea area who might be stimulated to try his hand. Underwater photography has of course much in common with landscape and nature photography. But there are three important differences: first, one needs to master the techniques of scuba diving or snorkelling safely; second, because of the water and especially because of the increased pressure at depth, one needs

RIGHT: 189 Looking under a coral overhang – many of the most interesting
animals on the reef are partly hidden in such places. A school of *Anthias* swim
nearby; the foreground corals are *Acropora humilis* (pink, centre right) and
Acropora haimei (pale blue, bottom centre).

specially designed or housed cameras; and third, because of the filtering of the sunlight by the water, with increasing depth natural colours are not visible, and so it is best to be equipped with a special underwater flash unit or strobe.

CAMERAS When one selects an underwater camera, two options can be considered. One can purchase a special amphibious camera, which means a camera built to withstand water in its normal housing. Or alternatively one can place a regular camera in a sealed underwater housing. Among the amphibious cameras (or amphicameras) there are several low-cost and simple alternatives, but the only one worth considering is the slightly more costly Nikonos. Five models of Nikonos exist. The older ones are the Calypso, the Calypso-Nikkon, the Nikonos II and the Nikonos III; the present model is called the Nikonos IV. Among the major differences between the earlier models and the present Nikonos IV is the automatic exposure feature.

The Nikonos is a small, light and very sturdy camera; and the fact that the camera is watersealed gives it the additional advantage that it can be used in sandstorms, dusty areas, rain, snow or even be sterilized for use in a hospital operating theatre. The camera has a reliable mechanism and is easy to operate under water. The lenses, made by Nikon of Japan, are of very high quality. It is not however a mirror reflex camera so that distance has to be measured or estimated separately. The camera has all the normal controls but these have to be set manually. There are four standard lenses for the camera: the superior Underwater Nikkor 15mm, 1:2.8, with a special viewfinder; the Underwater Nikkor 28 mm, 1:3.5; the W-Nikkor 35 mm, 1:2.5; and the Nikkor 80 mm, 1:4; the first two lenses are for underwater use only, but the last two can be used both under water and on land. There are several other lenses available for the Nikonos camera which are made by other manufacturers at competitive prices.

The Nikonos can also be used to take close-up photographs. Several of the pictures in this book were taken with extension rings (or tubes) enabling the Nikonos to be used for 'macro-photography'. Alternatively Nikon manufactures a close-up attachment which is an optical lens that is slipped on in front of the ordinary 28 mm or 35 mm lens. This can be done very simply under water, offering the photographer the opportunity of obtaining a variety of perspectives. With the same camera the extension rings used for macro-photography cannot however be positioned or removed under water. Since the focusing point is so close to the camera lens and the depth of field so narrow, a focusing frame is often attached to the front of the camera when extension rings are being used. Because it is small, light and ultra reliable, the Nikonos has proved very popular with diving scientists who may well have to carry other equipment as well.

UNDERWATER HOUSINGS The alternative to using an amphibious camera is to use a standard land camera mounted in an underwater housing. If a person is technically skilled and has access to tools and materials, building one's own housing is feasible and cheap. However, for reliability and durability a factory-made housing may be best, especially if an expensive camera is at risk. In selecting a camera for use with a housing, one which has an interchangeable viewfinder and can be equipped with an 'action finder' or 'speed finder' is preferable. This is because the projected image in the viewfinder is then larger, whereas it is very difficult to peer into the normal little hole of the standard prism viewfinder, as built into most mirror reflex cameras, once the camera is inside its housing and you have your face mask on.

Most normal or single lens reflex (SLR) cameras of course use 35 mm film; but top-quality professional standard pictures can be obtained much more readily using 6×6 cm film in an appropriately larger camera. However, two factors militate against this system; one is the cost of this kind of camera, the other is their size which makes them bulky to handle under water.

In fact, of all the cameras available, two 35 mm SLR cameras are the most used by underwater photographers. These are the Nikon F 2 and the Canon F 1, which are preferred because of their size, quality and the extensive range of accessories offered. Many underwater housings are factory-made for these two cameras. Here two only can be mentioned. Ikelite in the USA manufactures a very reasonable housing made of high quality plexiglass (perspex) (1979 cost approx. $200 US); and Oceanic Products of California manufacture a moulded aluminium housing of very high quality. All pictures taken with a Nikon for this book were taken using the Oceanic housing. It is very reliable and can withstand rough

treatment under extreme conditions. The cost, however, is greater, and was in 1979 around $600 US. Both Ikelite and Oceanic offer the option of interchangeable front ports. This is an important feature, for when using a wide-angle lens one needs to have a spherically corrected dome port, while for macro-photography with a 55 mm or 105 mm macro-lens one needs a flat port on the housing.

Some lenses are superior to others or offer special opportunities for underwater photography. The Micro-Nikkor 55 mm, 1:3.5, and the Micro-Nikkor 105 mm, 1:4, are recommended for taking portraits; and the Fisheye-Nikkor 16 mm, 1:3.5, and the Nikkor 18 mm, 1:4, or any other good quality wide-angle lens are valuable for pictures of underwater scenery because of their great depth of field and wide view.

However there is one further option for the occasional snorkeller or diver who would merely like to take a few 'snaps' for himself or to show friends. A large range of plexiglass (perspex) underwater housings are made, for example by Ikelite. A variety of simple cameras, including automatics and semi-automatics, can thus be housed, particularly if it is not intended to take them to any great depth – the results can be very adequate, and should the housing leak, it is not an expensive camera that is being written off.

UNDERWATER FLASH UNITS Good photographs can be taken using sunlight in very shallow water, especially in the Red Sea. But at depth, or even in shallow water, one must use a flash-unit if one wants to bring back to the picture the range of bright colours that may exist; for under water the warm colours (reds, yellows) are filtered away, and most subjects tend to appear blue/green.

Until recent years flash-bulbs were used under water. Underwater electronic flash units were at first very unreliable, whereas Nikon, for example, produced an easily used flash-bulb unit for use with the Nikonos. Now electronic flash units are much more reliable. There are two alternative approaches. Ikelite for example manufacture a variety of different plexiglass housings to contain most standard flash attachments. One advantage of a standard housing is that should the housing get flooded it is easy to repair or exchange the ruined unit. Alternatively Oceanic Products, among others, manufacture several strobe units, specially built for use under water. They are reliable and of good quality and there are several models at a range of prices.

Of the different connectors between an underwater camera housing and underwater flash unit, the EO type seems to be the most reliable. It has to be emphasised that the connector between camera and flash-gun is a

BELOW: 190 A diver using a Nikon camera in a custom-built underwater housing. But patience is also part of the photographer's equipment; only by waiting could the moment be captured when a school of fish swam in front of the other photographer.

BOTTOM: 191 A diver equipped with a Nikonos and electronic flash. In fact in this instance the flash-gun in view is triggered by a 'slave' sensor unit, attached to the Nikonos. The sensor detects the light from the flash-gun of the second camera with which this picture was taken, so that the subject appears to be caught in the act of taking a flash photograph.

RIGHT: 192 A diver's sea and sky. For most of the time the Red Sea is warm and calm, especially in early morning. As the sun heats the air over the desert causing it to rise, an onshore wind gets up by midday.

very sensitive part, and very often the source of malfunction. Special care and attention to the connector is necessary.

TECHNIQUE IN UNDERWATER PHOTO-GRAPHY When one sets out as a beginner in underwater photography there is always the illusion and the hope that one will get 'the picture' direct on the first dive. In fact it takes some practice to get good quality pictures. There are often three stages to be gone through when one starts. First, one has to learn how to handle the equipment correctly under water: how the camera functions and where the controls are: and how to aim the beam of the flash so that it illuminates the subject effectively. Second may follow a so-called 'blurry picture' period. One must solve the problem of focusing and getting the correct exposure settings. Finally, when the pictures are technically satisfactory, one has to work to find and approach suitable subjects, to get effective photographs of them, and to master the skills of composition. The best and hardest way to learn is through one's own mistakes. It is costly, but very effective.

To aim the flash it is easiest to proceed as follows: slightly loosen the adjustment bolts or screws and then turn the camera and flash attachment around so that it faces you. Hold it on a straight arm and look right into the lens. Now without turning the head, lift the eyes and check that the flashbeam aims right into your eyes, or adjust it until it does so. The flash and lens are now set for a distance of around 50–60 cm. From here it is fairly easy to either extend or shorten the angle of the flash-unit to suit the distance of different subjects.

Learning how to focus and set the right aperture is often best achieved if you sit still on the bottom and work patiently with the equipment. When you start to dive what you most enjoy is the freedom of floating and swimming freely in the water. Now, with camera equipment, you must however sit down and be still. You can either add some extra weight to your weight belt, and/or search out a good coral 'hump' and sit down with your knees around it, gripping the coral head to stay still. Now you can look carefully over the camera and check the different settings. A buoyancy vest or lifejacket can be used to offset the effect of the extra weights during other parts of the dive. It is also easier if you consistently use the same kind of film so that you get to know its characteristics.

Choice of lens is of course important; for example a macro-lens is often best for portraits. For these it is also important to try to isolate the subject, by contrasting it with its natural surroundings or another species. With a very powerful strobe you can use a small aperture opening, which cuts out the natural light and gives a dark contrasting background. The picture then almost appears to have been taken at night and this can be very effective. For pictures of underwater scenery a very wide-angle lens or fisheye lens is best. Now you should not use a powerful strobe, but a flash which has just sufficient light output, to give a 'fill in' effect, while keeping the natural blue colours of the water and the existing light. Beyond this, different photographers are of course striving for different kinds of pictures; thus it is difficult to give more detailed advice. But it cannot be overstressed that mistakes, practice and criticism are the best teachers in underwater photography.

A final comment should be made about the care of underwater photographic equipment. Every time the camera has been underwater, especially in the hot salty conditions of the Red Sea, it should be thoroughly and carefully rinsed off with fresh water and then cleaned. The main 'O' rings should be inspected at every use and they should be regularly cleaned with tissue paper and regreased with silicon grease. Take special care with the connectors between the flash unit and camera. Also take special care of the equipment while on the move in boats or cars; unless adequately padded or even held, the jarring or banging of a choppy sea or a desert road can easily cause distressing damage.

LEFT: 193 Returning to the shore after a day's diving.

Bibliography

The following is a short list of books and biological articles which may be of interest to the general reader wishing to pursue further some of the topics raised in this book. The list does not pretend to be exhaustive, but mainly contains a selection of references which we have found to be particularly useful or well written.

On the biology of coral reefs: for the general reader

BENNETT, I. (1971), *The Great Barrier Reef*, Lansdown, Melbourne.
CAMPBELL, A.C. (1976), *The Coral Seas*, Orbis, London.
EIBLE-EIBESFELD, I. (1965), *Land of a Thousand Atolls*, McGibbon & Kee, London.
FAULKNER, D. (1974), *This Living Reef*, Quadrangle and The New York Times Book Co, New York.
FAULKNER, D. (1976), *Dwellers in the Sea*, Reader's Digest Press, New York.
FRICKE, H.W. (1973), *The Coral Seas*, Putnams, New York; Thames & Hudson, London.
RIEFENSTAHL, L. (1978), *Coral Gardens*, Collins, London.

Books containing specialised scientific articles on many aspects of coral reef biology

JONES, O.A. and ENDEAN, R. (eds) (1973–77), *Biology and Geology of Coral Reefs*, (4 volumes), Academic Press, New York, San Francisco, London.
Proceedings of the 2nd International Symposium on Coral Reefs (1974) (2 volumes), Great Barrier Reef Committee, Brisbane, Australia.
Proceedings of the 3rd International Symposium on Coral Reefs (1977) (2 volumes), Rosenstiel School of Marine and Atmospheric Science, Miami, Florida.

The identification of Red Sea fishes

There are as yet no books which deal with the fish of the Red Sea, although Dr Jack Randall, the leading authority on tropical marine fish, is completing work on such a volume. Until his book is published the two most useful books are probably those given below in which descriptions can be found of most of the fish mentioned in this book.

CARCASSON, R.H. (1977), *A Field Guide to the Coral Reef Fishes of the Indian and West Pacific Oceans*, Collins, London.
SMITH, J.B.L. and M.L. (1969), *Fishes of the Seychelles*, J.B.L. Smith Institute of Icthyology, Rhodes University, Grahamstown, South Africa.

The identification of Red Sea Corals

The situation with coral identification for the amateur is even more difficult. There are as yet no standard books dealing with the identification of corals in any part of the Indo-Pacific area, let alone the Red Sea. This situation reflects the problems still surrounding the identification of many of the corals. However, the enthusiast would probably find the following two scientific works moderately approachable.

VERON, J.E.N., PICHON, M. and WYSMAN-BEST, M, (1977), *Scleratinia of Eastern Australia*, Part II, Australian Institute of Marine Science Monograph, vol. 3, Australian Government Publishing Service, Canberra.
VERON, J.E.N. and PICHON, M. (1976), *Scleratinia of Eastern Australia*, Part I, Australian Institute of Marine Science Monograph, vol. 1, Australian Government Publishing Service, Canberra.

The identification of other invertebrates

Again there are no books dealing specifically with Red Sea species, but the following books will enable many specimens to be put approximately in their right place.

GEORGE, D. and J. (1979), *Marine Life. An Illustrated Encyclopaedia of Invertebrates in the Sea*, Harrap, London
DANCE, S.P. (1974), *The Encyclopaedia of Shells*, Blandford Press, London.
OLIVER, A.P.H. (1975), *The Hamlyn Guide to Shells of the World*, Hamlyn, London.
CLARK, A.M. and ROWE, F.W. (1971), *Monograph of Shallow Water Indo-West Pacific Echinoderms*, British Museum of Natural History, London.

Ecology and behaviour

The following references may be of interest in giving more detail concerning a variety of the aspects of the behaviour and ecology of reef fish discussed in chapters 6 and 7.

HIATT, R.W. and STRASBURG, D.W. (1960), 'Ecological relationships of the fish fauna on coral reefs of the Marshall Islands', *Ecological Monographs*, vol. 30, pp. 65–127.
HOBSON, E.S. (1974), 'Feeding relationships of teleostean fishes on coral reefs in Kona, Hawaii', *Fishery Bulletin*, vol. 72, pp. 915–1031.
ORMOND, R.F.G. (1980), 'Occurrence and feeding behaviour of Red Sea coral reef fish', in *Proceedings of the Symposium on the Coastal and Marine Environment of the Red Sea, Gulf of Aden and Tropical West Indian Ocean*, University of Khartoum Press, Khartoum, Sudan.
EHRLICH, P. (1975), 'The population biology of coral reef fishes', *Annual Review of Ecology and Systematics*, vol. 6, pp. 211–47.
ALLEN, G.R. (1972), *The Anemone Fishes*, T.F.H. Publications, New York.
MARISCAL, R.N. (1972), 'Behaviour of symbiotic fishes and sea anemones', in *The Behaviour of Marine Animals*, edited by Winn, H.E. and Olla, B.L., Plenum, New York, vol. 2. pp. 327–360.
LOSEY, G.S. (1971), 'Communications between fishes in cleaning symbiosis', in *Aspects of the Biology of Symbiosis*, edited by Cheng, T.C., University Park Press, Baltimore, Maryland, pp. 45–76.
LOSEY, G.S. (1978), 'The symbiotic behaviour of fishes', in *The Behaviour of Fish and Other Aquatic Animals*, edited by Mostofsky, D.I., Academic Press, New York, pp. 1–31.
POTTS, G.W. (1973), 'The ethology of *Labroides dimidiatus* (Cuv. and Val.) (Labridae; Pisces)', *Journal of Animal Behaviour*, vol. 21, pp. 250–91.
WICKLER, W. (1968), *Mimicry in Plants and Animals*, Weidenfeld & Nicolson, London.
FISHELSON, L. (1970), 'Progynous sex reversal in the fish *Anthias squamipinnis* (Teleostei, Anthiidae) regulated by the presence or absence of a male fish', *Nature*, vol. 227, pp. 90–1.
ROBERTSON, D.R. (1972), 'The social control of sex reversal in a coral reef fish,' *Science*, vol. 177, pp. 1007–9.

General advice related to diving and photography

The British Sub-Aqua Club Diving Manual (1977), 10th edition, British Sub-Aqua Club, 70 Brompton Road, London.
COUSTEAU, J.Y. and P. (1970), *The Shark*, Cassell, London.
CHURCH, J. and C. (n.d.), *Beginning Underwater Photography*, Church, J. and C., P.O. Box 80, Gilroy, California.

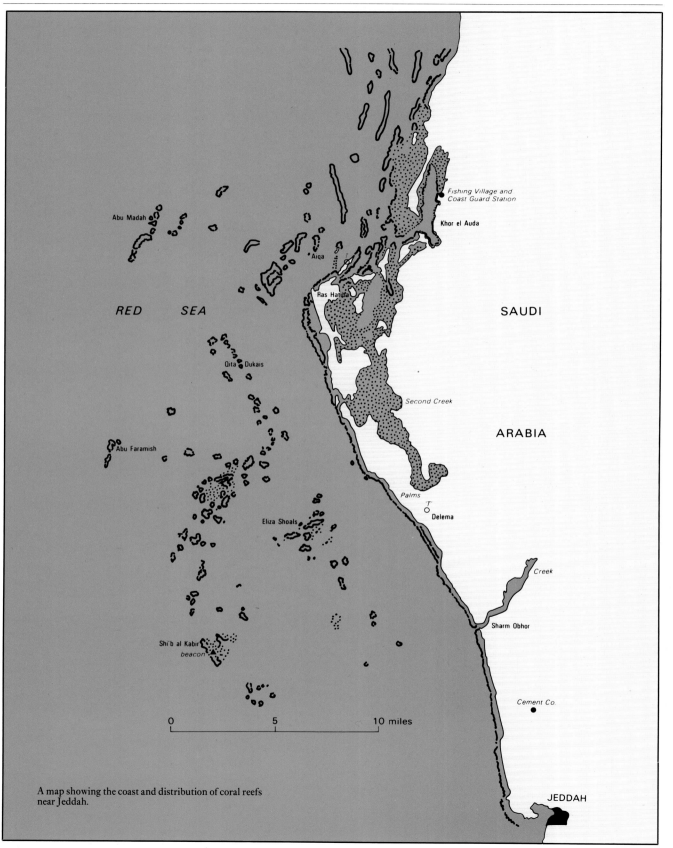

A map showing the coast and distribution of coral reefs
near Jeddah.

Appendix

Technical details to illustrations

Date is followed by location, co-diver(s), type of camera, lens, strobe, aperture and film.

Cover picture: 4th May 1979, L-Reef, Allan Falk, Nikonos II, UW-Nikkor 15mm 1:2.8, Oceanic 2000, f5.6 Kodachrome.

Titlepage picture: 23 February 1979, 6-mile Reef, Tore Dahm, Nikonos II, UW-Nikkor 15mm 1:2.8, Oceanic 2000, f5.6, Ektachrome E6.

1 26 September 1976, the bay at Jaar-Rajis, Nikkormat EL, Nikkor 35mm 1:1.4, no strobe, camera set on automatic, Ektachrome E4.

2 15 January 1978, Jeddah, Nikon EL2, Nikkor ED 300mm 1:4.5, no strobe, camera on automatic, Kodachrome.

3 20 May 1977, Eliza Shoals, Victoria Fontain and Doreen Sharabati, Nikon F, Fishcheye-Nikkor 16mm 1:3.5, Rollei E36RE, f8, Kodachrome.

4 20 April 1976, south of Al-Wajh, Nikkormat El, Nikkor 35mm 1:1.4, no strobe, camera set on automatic, Ektachrome E4.

5 May 1977, south of Jeddah Port, Nikkormat El, Nikkor 135mm 1:2, no strobe, camera set on automatic, Ektachrome E4.

6 20 January 1978, Chicken Wreck, Doreen Sharabati, Nikon F, Fisheye-Nikkor 16mm 1:3.5, Rollei E36RE, f8, Kodachrome.

7 14 April 1978, L-Reef, Tom Blackberby and Doreen Sharabati, Nikon F, Micro-Nikkor 55mm 1:3.5 Rollei E36RE, f11, Kodachrome.

8 20 January 1978, Chicken Wreck, Doreen Sharabati, Nikon F, Fisheye-Nikkor 16mm 1:3.5, Rollei E36RE, f8, Kodachrome.

9 28 February 1975, east of Tower Shi'b al Kabir, Brynn Bruijn, Nikon F, Nikkor 35mm 1:2, Rollei E36RE, f8, Ektachrome.

10 20 May 1977, Eliza Shoals, Victoria Fontain and Doreen Sharabati, Nikon F, Fisheye-Nikkor 16mm 1:3.5, Rollei E36RE, f8, Kodachrome.

11 23 February 1979, 6-mile Reef, Tore Dahm, Nikonos III, UW-Nikkor 15mm 1:2.8, Oceanic 2000, f5.6, Ektachrome E6.

12 13 May 1977, north of Rabigh, Ulf af Klinteberg, Jim and Dolores Ciardelli, Nikon F, Fisheye-Nikkor 16mm 1:3.5, Rollei E36RE, f11, Kodachrome.

13 10 June 1977, Hagens Beach, May Loring, Nikon F, Fisheye-Nikkor 16mm 1:3.5, Rollei E36RE, f8, Kodachrome.

14 21 January 1977, Doug Island, Tom Blackerby and Mike Totten, Nikon F, Fisheye-Nikkor 16mm 1:3.5, twin-mounted Oceanic 2000, f8, Kodachrome.

15 2 May 1978, Sharm Obhor, from a helicopter, Nikon EL2, Nikkor 18mm 1:4, no strobe, camera on automatic, Kodachrome.

16 13 May 1979, Sharm Obhor, Nikon FE, Micro-Nikkor 55mm 1:3.5, no strobe, camera set on automatic, Ektachrome E6.

17 13 May 1979, Abu Madah, aerial photography, Nikon EL2, Micro-Nikkor 55mm 1:3.5, camera on automatic Kodachrome.

18 5 May 1978, Abu Faramish, Issam, Doreen and Nora Sharabati, Nikonos III, W-Nikkor 35mm 1:2.5, with double extension tubes 2:1, Oceanic 2003, f22, Kodachrome.

19 15 September 1978, Stephanos Reef, Issam Sharabati, Nikon F, Micro-Nikkor 105mm 1:4, Rollei E36RE and Oceanic 2000 slave, f8, Kodachrome.

20 19 March 1979, northern Be, Tore Dahm, Nikon F, Micro-Nikkor 55mm 1:3.5, Rollei E36RE, f8, Kodachrome.

21 20 May 1977, Eliza Shoals, Victoria Fontain and Doreen Sharabati, Nikonos III, W-Nikkor 35mm 1:2.5 with one extension tube 1:1, Oceanic 2003, f22, Kodachrome.

22 28 February 1977, northern Be, Tom Blackerby, Bob Richardson and Allan Falk, Nikon F, Micro-Nikkor 105mm 1:4, Rollei E36RE, and Oceanic 2003, f22, Ektachrome E6.

23 23 May 1977, northern Be, Tom Blackerby, Ulf af Klinteberg and Bob Richardson, Nikon F, Micro-Nikkor 55mm 1:3.5, Rollei E36RE, f8, Kodachrome.

24 23 May 1977, northern Be, Tom Blackerby, Ulf at Klinteberg, Bob Richardson, Nikon F, Micro-Nikkor 55mm 1:3.5, Rollei E36RE, f8, Kodachrome.

25 10 June 1977, Hagens Beach, May Loring, Nikonos III, W-Nikkor 35mm 1:2.5, with double extension tubes 2:1, Oceanic 2003, f22, Kodachrome.

26 21 May 1976, mouth of Sharm Obhor, Colonel Williams, Nikon F, Micro-Nikkor 55mm 1:3.5, Rollei E36RE, f11, Ektachrome E4.

27 18 February 1979, 6-mile Reef, Tore Dahm, Nikonos III, W-Nikkor 35mm 1:2.5, with double extension tubes 2:1, twin-mounted Nesse-strobes, f16, Kodachrome.

28 20 May 1977, Eliza Shoals, Victoria Fontain and Doreen Sharabati, Nikonos III, W-Nikkor 35mm 1:2.5, with one extension tube 1:1, Oceanic 2003, f22, Kodachrome II.

29 20 May 1977, Eliza Shoals, Victoria Fontain and Doreen Sharabati, Nikonos III, W-Nikkor 35mm 1:2.5, with one extension tube 1:1, Oceanic 2003, f22 Kodachrome II.

30 11 February 1977, "Aiqa" Island, Doreen Sharabati, Nikon F, Fisheye-Nikkor 16mm 1:3.5, Oceanic 2003, f11, Ektachrome E4.

31 27 May 1977, south of Rabigh, Mike Totten, Nikonos III, W-Nikkor 35mm 1:2.5, with one extension tube 1:1, Oceanic 2003, f22, Kodachrome.

32 16 February 1979, 7-mile Reef, Glenn Posey, Bob Rhodes and Joe Prine, Nikonos II, UW-Nikkor 15mm 1:3.5, Oceanic 2000, f5.6, Ektachrome E6.

33 14 April 1978, L-reef, Tom Blackerby and Doreen Sharabati, Nikon F, Micro-Nikkor 55mm 1:3.5, Rollei E36RE, f11, Kodachrome.

34 19 November 1976, Hagens Beach, Tom Blackerby, Nikonos III, W-Nikkor 35mm 1:2.5, with double extension tubes 2:1, Oceanic 2003, f22, Ektachrome E4.

35 7 March 1975, southern tip of Shi'b al Kabir, Didi Bennett, Nikon F, Nikkor 35mm 1:2, Rollei E36RE, f11 Ektachrome E4.

36 3 June 1977, Doug Island, May Loring and Ulf af Klinteberg, Nikonos III, W-Nikkor 35mm 1:2.5, with one extension tube 1:1, Oceanic 2003, f22, Kodachrome.

37 27 May 1977, south of Rabigh, Mike Totten, Nikonos III, W-Nikkor 35mm 1:2.5, with one extension tube 1:1, Oceanic 2003, f22, Kodachrome.

38 15 July 1977, northern Be, May Loring, Nikonos II, W-Nikkor 35mm 1:2.5, with double extension tubes 2:1, Oceanic 2003, f22, Kodachrome.

39 13 May 1977, north of Rabigh, Ulf af Klinteberg, Jim and Dolores Ciardelli, Nikonos III, W-Nikkor 35mm 1:2.5, with one extension tube 1:1, Oceanic 2003, f22, Kodachrome II.

40 1 December 1976, south of Rabigh, Tom Blackerby, Bob and Rene Richardson, Nikonos III, W-Nikkor 35mm 1:2.5, with double extension tubes 2:1, Oceanic 2003, f22, Ektachrome E4.

41 13 March 1978, Hagens Beach, Dennis Bell and Shannon Barrett, Nikonos III, W-Nikkor 35mm 1:2.5, with double extension tubes 2:1, Oceanic 2003, f22, Kodachrome.

42 5 May 1978, Abu Faramish, Issam and Nora Sharabati, Nikonos III, W-Nikkor 35mm 1:2.5, with double extension tubes 2:1, Oceanic 2003, f22, Kodachrome.

43 23 February 1979, 6-mile Reef, Tore Dahm, Nikonos III, W-Nikkor 35mm 1:2.5, with double extension tubes 2:1, twin-mounted Nesse strobes, f16, Kodachrome.

44 17 April 1978, northern Be, Ulf af Klinteberg, Nikon F, Micro-Nikkor 55mm 1:3.5, Rollei E36RE, f11, Kodachrome.

45 3 June 1977, Doug Island, May Loring and Ulf af Klinteberg, Nikonos III, W-Nikkor 35mm 1:2.5, with one extension tube 1:1. Oceanic 2003, f22, Kodachrome.

46 15 July 1977, northern Be, May Loring, Nikonos II, W-Nikkor 35mm 1:2.5, with double extension tubes 2:1, Oceanic 2003, f22, Kodachrome.

47 22 October 1976, south of Rabigh, Bob and Rene Richardson, Jim and Dolores Ciardelli, Nikon F, Nikkor 35mm 1:2, Oceanic 2003 and Oceanic 2000 slave, f22, Kodachrome.

48 16 March 1979, southern tip of Shi'b al Kabir, Isam Sharabati and Tore Dahm, Nikonos II, UW-Nikkor 15mm 1:3.5, Oceanic 2000, f56, Kodachrome (Photography by Issam A. Sharabati).

49 17 February 1975, Kay's cabin in Obhor, Brynn Bruijn, Nikon F, Nikkor 105mm 1:2.5, with Nikon close-up lens No. 0, Rollei E36RE, f11, Kodachrome.

50 16 March 1979, southern tip of Shi'b al Kabir, Issam Sharabati and Tore Dahm, Nikonos II, UW-Nikkor 15mm 1:3.5, Oceanic 2000, f56, Kodachrome.

51 28 February 1975, southern tip of Shi'b al Kabir, Brynn Bruijn and Didi Bennett, Nikon F, Nikkor 35mm 1:2, Rollei E36RE, f11, Ektachrome E4.

52 4 February 1977, south of Rabigh, Bill Vaughan, Nikon F, Fisheye-Nikkor 16mm 1:3.5, no strobe, f16, Ektachrome.

53 28 March 1975, north of 29 Palm-trees, Peter and Brynn Bruijn and Kaj Granholm, Nikon F, Nikkor 35mm 1:2 with Nikon extension rings E1, E2 and E3, Rollei E36RE, f16, Ektachrome.

54 13 May 1977, north of Rabigh, Sue, Jim and Dolores Ciardelli and Ulf af Klinteberg, Nikon F, Fisheye-Nikkor 16mm 1:3.5, Rollei E36RE, f11, Kodachrome.

55 24 April 1978, northern Be, Ulf af Klinteberg, Nikon F, Micro-Nikkor 105mm 1:4, Rollei E36RE, f11, Kodachrome.

56 10 May 1976, jetty at Raytheon, Victoria Fontain, Nikon F, Micro-Nikkor 55mm 1:3.5, Rollei E36RE, f11, Ektachrome, E4.

57 23 March 1979, Abu Faramish, Issam Sharabati, Woody Pridgen, Hagen Schmid and Tore Dahm, Nikonos II, UW-Nikkor 15mm 1:2.8, Oceanic 2000, f5.6, Kodachrome.

58 30 March 1979, Rudder Reef, Goffie, Nikonos II, UW-Nikkor 15mm 1:2.8, Oceanic 2000, f5.6 Kodachrome.

59 17 April 1978, northern Be, Ulf af Klinteberg, Nikon F, Micro-Nikkor 55mm 1:3.5, Rollei E36RE, f11, Kodachrome.

60 2 March 1979, mouth of Sharm Obhor, Tore Dahm, Nikon F, Micro-Nikkor 105mm 1:4, Rollei E36RE and Oceanic 2000 slave, f8, Kodachrome.

61 7 February 1975, north of Sharm Obhor, Brynn Bruijn, Terry and Didi Bennett, Nikon F, Nikkor 35mm 1:2 Rollei E36RE, f16, Ektachrome E4.

62 19 March 1979, northern Be, Tore Dahm, Nikon F, Micro-Nikkor 55mm 1:3.5, Rollei E36RE and Oceanic 2000 slave, f8, Kodachrome.

63 9 December 1976, family cabins at Sharm Obhor, Tom Blackerby, Bob and Rene Richardson, Nikon F, Micro-Nikkor 55mm 1:3.5, Oceanic 2003 and Oceanic 2000 slave, f11, Ektachrome E6.

64 30 November 1976, south of Rabigh, Tom Blackerby, Bob and Rene Richardson, Nikon F, Micro-Nikkor 55mm 1:3.5, Oceanic 2003, f8, Ektachrome E4.

65 25 April 1975, north of Sharm Obhor, Keith Rooney, Nikon F, Nikkor 105mm 1:2.5 with Nikon close-up lenses No. 0+No. 1, Rollei E36RE, f11, Ektachrome E4.

66 9 December 1976, family cabins at Sharm Obhor, Tom Blackerby, Bob and Rene Richardson, Nikon F, Micro-Nikkor 55mm 1:3.5, Oceanic 2003 and Oceanic 2000 slave, f11, Ektachrome E6.

67 28 January 1975, family cabins at Sharm Obhor, Jim Hinz, Brynn Bruijn and Doug Vaughn, Nikon F, Nikkor 105mm 1:2.5 with Nikon close-up lenses No. 0+No. 1, Rollei E36RE, f11, Ektachrome E4.

68 17 April 1978, northern Be, Ulf af Klinteberg, Nikon F, Micro-Nikkor 55mm 1:3.5, Rollei E36RE, f11, Kodachrome.

69 26 September 1976, the bay at Jaar-Rajis, Nikkormat EL, Nikkor 35mm 1:1.4, no strobe, camera set on automatic, Ektachrome E4.

70 3 November 1978, northern Be, Bette Lord, Nikon F, Micro-Nikkor 55mm 1:3.5, Rollei E36RE and Oceanic 2000 slave, f8, Ektachrome E4.

71 28 February 1977, northern Be, Tom Blackerby, Bob Richardson and Allan Falk, Nikon F, Micro-Nikkor 105mm 1:4, Rollei E36RE, and Oceanic 2003, f8, Ektachrome E4.

72 1 November 1979, Abu Madah, Goffie, Nikon F, Micro-Nikkor 55mm 1:3.5, Rollei E36RE and Oceanic 2000 slave, f8, Ektachrome E6.

73 27 February 1975, mouth of Sharm Obhor, Raymond Naccachian, Bengt Johansson and Brynn Bruijn, Nikon F, Nikkor 105mm 1:2.5 with Nikon close-up No. 0, Rollei E36RE, f11, Ektachrome E4.

74 3 February 1975, family cabins at Sharm Obhor, Brynn Bruijn, Nikon F, Nikkor 105 1:2.5 with Nikon close-up lenses No. 0+No. 1, Rollei E36RE, f11, Ektachrome E4.

75 17 October 1975, mouth of Sharm Obhor, Rick Powers, Nikon F, Nikkor 105mm 1:2.5, with Nikon close-up lenses No. 0+No. 1, Rollei E36RE, f16, Ektachrome E4.

76 18 March 1977, mouth of Sharm Obhor, Ulf af Klinteberg, Nikon F, Micro-Nikkor 105mm 1:4, Oceanic 2003, f8, Ektachrome E4.

77 4 February 1979, northern Be, Marie-France de la Taste, Nikon F, Micro-Nikkor 55mm 1:3.5, Rollei E36RE and Oceanic 2000 slave, f8, Kodachrome.

78 8 May 1978, northern Be, Ulf af Klinteberg, Tom Blackerby and Göran Widström, Nikon F, Micro-Nikkor 55mm 1:3.5, Rollei E36RE, f11, Kodachrome.

79 7 February 1975, north of Sharm Obhor, Brynn Bruijn, Terry and Didi Bennett, Nikon F, Nikkor 35mm 1:2, Rollei E36RE, f16, Ektachrome E4.

80 3 May 1975, northern Be, Kaj Granholm, Brynn Bruijn, Chad Henderson and Allan Falk, Nikon F, Nikkor 105mm 1:2.5 with Nikon close-up lens No. 1, Rollei E36RE, f8, Ektachrome E4.

81 10 October 1975, mouth of Sharm Obhor, Rich Powers, Nikon F, Nikkor 105mm 1:2.5 with Nikon close-up lenses No. 0+No. 1, Rollei E36RE, f11 Ektachrome E4.

82 29 April 1977, Hagens Beach, Sue Ciardelli, Nikon F, Micro-Nikkor 105mm 1:4, Rollei E36RE, f11, Kodachrome.

83 30 May 1975, Hagens Beach, Bud Reichel, Nikon F, Micro-Nikkor 55mm 1:3.5, Rollei E36RE, f11, Ektachrome E4.

84 27 January 1978, L-Reef, Issam Sharabati and Hagen Schmid, Nikonos III, W-Nikkor 35mm 1:2.5 with double extension tubes 2:1, Oceanic 2003, f22, Kodachrome.

85 22 April 1978, L-Reef, Tom Blackerby, Issam and Doreen Sharabati, Nikon F, Micro-Nikkor 105mm 1:4,Rollei E36RE, f11, Kodachrome.

86 10 June 1977, Hagens Beach, May Loring, Nikonos III, W-Nikkor 35mm 1:2.5, with double extension tubes 2:1, Oceanic 2003, f22, Kodachrome.

87 11 November 1975, mouth of Sharm Obhor, Peter Bruijn, Nikon F, Nikkor 105mm 1:2.5, with Nikon close-up lens No. 2, Rollei E36RE, f11, Ektachrome E4.

88 6 November 1979, Stephanos Reef, Karl Gerlof, Nikon F, Micro-Nikkor 105mm 1:4, Rollei E36RE and Oceanic 2000 slave, f11, Ektachrome E6.

89 15 October 1976, south of Jeddah Port, John White and Jerry Valek, Nikon F, Nikkor 35mm 1:2, Rollei E36RE, f16, Ektachrome E4.

90 22 October 1976, south of Rabigh, Bob and Rene Richardson Jim and Dolores Ciardelli, Nikon F, Nikkor 35mm 1:2, Oceanic 2003 and Oceanic 2000 slave, f22, Kodachrome.

91 1 December 1976, south of Rabigh, Tom Blackerby, Bob and Rene Richardson, Nikon F, Micro-Nikkor 55mm 1:3.5, Oceanic 2003, f8, Ektachrome E4.

92 12 November 1978, Hagens Beach, Bette Lord, Nikonos II, UW-Nikkor 15mm 1:2.8, Oceanic 2003, f11, Kodachrome.

93 6 April 1979, Abu Faramish, Sue Stiles and Issam Sharabati, Nikon F, Micro-Nikkor 55mm 1:3.5, Rollei E36RE, f8, Kodachrome.

94 23 February 1979, 6-mile Reef, Tore Dahm, Nikonos II, UW-Nikkor 15mm 1:2.8, Oceanic 2000, f5.6, Ektachrome E6.

95 4 April 1975, northern Be, Brynn Bruijn and Didi Bennett, Nikon F, Nikkor 105mm 1:2.5 with Nikon close-up lens No. 0, Rollei E36RE, f11, Ektachrome E4.

96 6 May 1977, 65km south of Jeddah, Sue Ciardelli and Tom Blackerby, Nikon F, Micro-Nikkor 105mm 1:4, Rollei E36RE, f11, Kodachrome.

97 24 November 1978, southern tip of Shi'b al Kabir, Marie-France de la Taste, Nikon F, Micro-Nikkor 55mm 1:3.5, Rollei E36RE and Oceanic 2000 slave, f8, Ektachrome E6.

98 6 June 1975, south of Sharm Obhor, Terry Bennett and Bruce Smith, Nikon F, Nikkor 105mm 1:2.5, Rollei E36RE, f11, Ektachrome E4.

99 3 May 1975, northern Be, Kaj Granholm, Brynn Bruijn, Chad Henderson and Allan Falk, Nikon F, Nikkor 105mm 1:2.5 with Nikon close-up lens No. 1, Rollei E36RE, f8 Ektachrome E4.

100 16 March 1977, northern Be, Ulf af Klinteberg, Nikon F, Micro-Nikkor 105mm 1:4, Oceanic 2003, f11, Ektachrome E6.

101 23 February 1979, 6-mile Reef, Tore Dahm, Nikon F, Micro-Nikkor 105mm 1:4, Rollei E36RE and Oceanic 2000 slave, f8, Kodachrome.

102 26 November 1976, Hagens Beach, Tom Blackerby and Bob Richardson, Nikon F, Micro-Nikkor 55mm 1:3.5, Oceanic 2003, f8, Ektachrome E6.

103 21 October 1979, 8km north of Jeddah, Issam Sharabati, Nikon F, Micro-Nikkor 105mm 1:4, Rollei E36RE and Oceanic 2000 slave, f11, Ektachrome E6.

104 23 February 1979, 6-mile Reef, Tore Dahm, Nikonos II, UW-Nikkor 15mm 1:2.8, Oceanic 2000, f5.6, Ektachrome E6.

105 23 February 1979, 6-mile Reef, Tore Dahm, Nikon F, Micro-Nikkor 105mm 1:4, Rollei E36RE and Oceanic 2000 slave, f8, Kodachrome.

106 4January 1980, south end Shi'b al Kabir, Karl Gerlof, Douglas Sturkey, Nikon F, Micro-Nikkor 105mm 1:4, Rollei E36RE and Oceanic 2003, f8, Kodachrome.

107 20 June 1975, mouth of Sharm Obhor, Colonel Williams and Colonel Art Emmerson, Nikon F, Fisheye-Nikkor 16mm 1:3.5, Rollei E36RE, f11, Ektachrome E4.

108 20 December 1974, mouth of Sharm Obhor, Magnus Hagelstam, Nikon F, Nikkor 105mm 1:2.5 with Nikon close-up lenses No. 0+No. 1, Rollei E36RE, f11, Ektachrome E4.

109 2 May 1975, Three Palmtrees, Allan Falk, Nikon F, Nikkor 105mm 1:2.5 with Nikon close-up lens No. 1, Rollei E36RE, f11, Ektachrome E4.

110 2 May 1975, Three Palmtrees, Allan Falk, Nikon F, Nikkor 105mm 1:2.5 with Nikon close-up lens No. 1, Rollei E36RE, f11, Ektachrome E4.

111 22 September 1978, L-Reef, Issam and Doreen Sharabati, Nikon F, Micro-Nikkor 105mm 1:4, Rollei E36RE and Oceanic 2000 slave, f8 Kodachrome.

112 4 April 1975, northern Be, Brynn Bruijn and Didi Bennett, Nikon F, Nikkor 105mm 1:2.5 with Nikon close-up lens No. 0, Rollei E36RE, f11, Ektachrome E4.

113 21 October 1979, 8km north of Jeddah, Issam Sharabati, Nikon F, Micro-Nikkor 105mm 1:4, Rollei E36RE and Oceanic 2000 slave, f11 Ektachrome E6.

114 30 November 1976, south of Rabigh, Tom Blackerby, Bob and Rene Richardson, Nikon F, Micro-Nikkor 55mm 1:3.5, Oceanic 2003, f8, Ektachrome E4.

115 6 May 1977, 65km south of Jeddah, Sue Ciardelli and Tom Blackerby, Nikon F, Micro-Nikkor 105mm 1:4, Rollei E36RE, f11, Kodachrome.

116 7 May 1976, Hagens Beach, Goffie, Nikon F, Micro-Nikkor 55mm 1:3.5, Rollei E36RE, f11 Ektachrome E4.

117 15 September 1978, Stephanos Reef, Issam Sharabati, Nikon F, Micro-Nikkor 105mm 1:4, Rollei E36RE and Oceanic 2000 slave, f8, Kodachrome.

118 2 May 1975, Three Palmtrees, Allan Falk, Nikon F, Nikkor 105mm 1:2.5 with Nikon close-up lens No. 1, Rollei E36RE, f11, Ektachrome E4.

119 11 March 1977, south of Shi'b al Kabir, Goffie, Nikon F, Micro-Nikkor 105mm 1:4, Rollei E36RE, f11, Ektachrome E6.

120 29 August 1975, Ras Hatiba, Chad Henderson, Nikon F, Nikkor 105mm 1:2.5 with Nikon close-up lenses No. 0+No. 1 Rollei E36RE, f11, Ektachrome E4.

121 8 April 1977, Hagens Beach, Jim Ciardelli, Nikon F, Micro-Nikkor 105mm 1:4, Rollei E36RE, f11, Ektachrome E6.

122 5 May 1978, Abu Faramish, Issam, Doreen and Nora Sharabati, Nikon F, Micro-Nikkor 105mm 1:4, Rollei E36RE, f8, Kodachrome.

123 4 February 1979, northern Be, Marie-France de la Taste, Nikon F, Micro-Nikkor 55mm 1:3.5, Rollei E36RE and Oceanic 2000 slave, f8, Kodachrome.

124 3 December 1978, northern Be, Marie-France de la Taste, Nikonos II, UW-Nikkor 15mm 1:2.8, Oceanic 2000, f5.6, Ektachrome E6.

125 18 January 1980, east of Shi'b al Kabir, Doreen and Issam Sharabati, Nikon F, Micro- Nikkor 105mm 1:4, Rollei E36RE, f8, Kodachrome.

126 24 November 1978, southern tip of Shi'b al Kabir, Marie-France de la Taste, Nikon F, Micro Nikkor 55mm 1:3.5, Rollei E36RE and Oceanic 2000 slave, f8, Ektachrome E6.

127 18 March 1977, mouth of Sharm Obhor, Ulf af Klinteberg, Nikon F, Micro-Nikkor 105mm 1:4, Oceanic 2003, f8, Ektachrome E4.

128 19 March 1979, northern Be, Tore Dahm, Nikon F, Micro-Nikkor 55mm 1:3.5, Rollei E36RE and Oceanic 2000 slave, f8, Kodachrome.

129 15 September 1978, Stephanos Reef, Issam Sharabati, Nikon F, Micro-Nikkor 105mm 1:4, Rollei E36RE and Oceanic 2000 slave, f8, Kodachrome.

130 28 October 1978, Hagens Beach, May Loring, Nikon F, Micro-Nikkor 105mm 1:4, Oceanic 2002, f8, Kodachrome.

131 17 April 1975, Three Palmtrees, Allan Falk, Nikon F, Nikkor 105mm 1:2.5 with Nikon close-up lenses No. 0+No. 1, Rollei E36RE, f11, Ektachrome E4.

132 14 April 1978, L-Reef, Tom Blackerby and Doreen Sharabati, Nikon F, Micro-Nikkor 55mm 1:3.5, Rollei E36RE, f11, Kodachrome.

133 14 April 1978, L-Reef, Tom Blackerby and Doreen Sharabati, Nikon F, Micro-Nikkor 55mm 1:3.5, Rollei E36RE, f11, Kodachrome.

134 10 February 1975, mouth of Sharm Obhor, Jerry Hooper, Jim Hinz, Lynne Smith and Brynn Bruijn, Nikon F, Nikkor 105mm 1:2.5 with Nikon close-up lens No. 0, Rollei E36RE, f11, Ektachrome E4.

135 24 February 1975, family cabins at Sharm Obhor, Brynn Bruijn, Jim Hinz, Lynne Smith and Jerry Hooper, Nikon F, Nikkor 105mm, 1:2.5 with Nikon close-up lens No. 0, Rollei E36RE, f11, Ektachrome E4.

136 10 February 1975, mouth of Sharm Obhor, Jerry Hooper, Jim Hinz, Lynne Smith and Brynn Bruijn, Nikon F, Nikkor 105mm 1:2.5 with Nikon close-up lens No. 0, Rollei E36RE, f11, Ektachrome E4.

137 4 February 1979, northern Be, Marie-France de la Taste, Nikon F, Micro-Nikkor 55mm 1:3.5, Rollei E36RE and Oceanic 2000 slave, f8, Kodachrome.

138 15 March 1977, Shi'b al Kabir, Issam, Doreen and Nora Sharabati, Nikon F, Micro-Nikkor 105mm 1:4, Oceanic 2003, f8, Kodachrome.

139 22 April 1977, Hagens Beach, Tom Blackerby and Scott, Nikon F, Micro-Nikkor 105mm 1:4, Rollei E36RE, f11, Kodachrome II.

140 4 May 1979, L-Reef, Allan Falk, Nikon F, Micro-Nikkor 55mm 1:3.5, Rollei E36RE and Oceanic 2000 slave, f8, Kodachrome.

141 10 January 1978, Hagens Beach, May Loring, Nikon F, Micro-Nikkor 105mm 1:4, Oceanic 2002, f8, Kodachrome.

142 5 May 1978, Abu Faramish, Issam, Doreen and Nora Sharabati, Nikon F, Micro-Nikkor 105mm, 1:4, Rollei E36RE, f8, Kodachrome.

143 6 January 1978, Hagens Beach, May Loring, Nikon F, Micro-Nikkor 105mm 1:4, Oceanic 2002, f11, Kodachrome.

144 17 April 1975, Three Palmtrees, Allan Falk, Nikon F, Nikkor 105mm 1:2.5 with Nikon close-up lenses No. 0+No. 1, Rollei E36RE, f11, Ektachrome E4.

145 9 October 1975, outside COE at Sharm Obhor, Goffie, Nikon F, Nikkor 105mm 1:2.5 with Nikon close-up lenses No. 0+No. 1, Rollei E36RE, f11, Ektachrome E4.

146 9 October 1975, outside COE at Sharm Obhor, Goffie, Nikon F, Nikkor 105mm 1:2.5 with Nikon close-up lenses No. 0+No. 1, Rollei E36RE, f11 Ektachrome E4.

147 9 October 1975, Outside COE at Sharm Obhor, Goffie, Nikon F, Nikkor 105mm 1:2.5 with Nikon close-up lenses No. 0+No. 1, Rollei E36RE, f11, Ektachrome E4.

148 6 February 1975, jetty at Raytheon Compound, Brynn Bruijn and Terry Bennett, Nikon F, Nikkor 105mm 1:2.5 with Nikon close-up lens No. 0, Rollei E36RE, f11, Ektachrome E4.

149 18 February 1979, 6-mile Reef, Tore Dahm, Nikon F, Micro-Nikkor 105mm 1:4, Rollei E36RE and Oceanic 2000 slave, f8, Kodachrome.

150 12 April 1977, northern Be, Allan Falk, Nikon F, Micro-Nikkor 105mm 1:4, Rollei E36RE and Oceanic 2000 slave, f8, Ektachrome E6.

151 17 October 1975, Outside COE at Sharm Obhor, Colonel Art Emmerson and Rick Powers, Nikon F, Nikkor 105mm 1:2.5 with Nikon close-up lenses No. 0+No. 1, Rollei E36RE, f11, Ektachrome E4.

152 11 September 1975, outside COE at Sharm Obhr, Chad Henderson, Nikon F, Nikkor 105mm 1:2.5 with Nikon close-up lenses No. 0+No. 1, Rollei E36RE, f11, Ektachrome E4.

153 27 May 1977, south of Rabigh, Mike Totten, Nikonos III, W-Nikkor 35mm 1:2.8 with one extension tube 1:1, Oceanic 2003, f22, Kodachrome.

154 13 May 1977, north of Rabigh, Sue, Jim and Dolores Ciardelli and Ulf af Klinteberg, Nikon F, Fisheye-Nikkor 16mm 1:3.5, Rollei E36RE, f11, Kodachrome.

Index

190

RED SEA CORAL REEFS

Cheilinus, 108, 143, 149
C. fasciatus, 34, 106, 108
C. undulatus, 86, 106
Chelonia mydas, 37
chickenfish, 160, 164
Chicoreus ramosus, 89, 90
chitons, 82
Chlamys, 93
Chromis, 114, 149, 152
C. caeruleus, 29
C. ternatensis, 29
Chromodoris, 92
C. annulata, 84
C. quadricolor, 84, 91
Cirrhipathes anguina, 57, 58
Cirrhitichthys oxycephalus, 130
Cirrhitidae, 130
Cirripedia, 78–9
clams, 94, 96
Clanculus pharaonis, 83, 84
Cleaner goby, 143
Cleaner mimic blenny, 148
Cleaner wrasse, 143, 146–8, 149, 150
Cliona, 101
Clionidae, 101
clownfish, 114, 138–9, 139–42, 144
coelenterates, 141
classification of, 61
Coenobita scavola, 77
cones, 89, 90
Constantinople, 15
Conus spp., 90
C. geographicus, 90
C. textile, 90
copepods, 78
coral goby, 133, 135
coral shrimp, 143
coral trout, 118, 121, 140, 153
Corallum rubrum, 57, 58
corals
Acropora, 33, 53, 72; A. corymbosa, 46
ahermatypic, 43
Anthias, 29
Antipatharia, 57–8
Antipathes, 57
Balanophyllia, 43, 45
Cirrhipathes anguina, 57, 58
Corallum rubrum, 57, 58
Cyphastrea, 54
Dendronephthya, 50, 56–7
Echinopora, 54
Favia, 48, 54
Faviidae, 53, 54
Favites, 48, 54; F. virens, 47
fire, 25, 58–61
Fungia, 45; F. fungites, 43
Galaxea fascicularis, 47, 54
Goniastrea, 33, 48, 54
Goniopora, 40, 53; G. planulata, 54
Gorgonacea, 57
Gorgoniidae, 57
hermatypic, 43, 52
Heteroxenia, 56
Hydnophora, 54
Litophyton, 57
Lobophyllia, 54–5; L. corymbosa, 54
Lobophyton, 57
Lophogorgia, 57
Millepora, 34, 58–61; M. dichotoma, 25, 48, 61; M. platyphylla, 33, 61
Milleporina, 58–61

Montipora, 33, 34, 54
Mycedium, 54; M. elephantotus, 54
Nephthiidae, 56–7
Nephthya, 56–7
Oxypora, 54; O. lacerta, 34, 54
Pachyseris, 54; P. speciosa, 54
Pavona decussata, 54
Platygyra, 31, 47, 48, 54
Plerogyra sinuosa, 55
Pocillopora, 34, 53, 71, 72, 74; P. danae, 20, 33, 53, 72, 110
Podobacia, 54; P. crustacea, 34, 54
Porites, 29, 31, 33, 53, 54, 86
Sarcophyton, 49, 57; S. glaucum, 29
Scleractinia, 43
Seriatopora, 31, 53, 74; S. histrix, 53
Sinularia, 57
soft (Alcyonacea), 55–7
Stylophora, 31, 34, 53, 71, 74; S. pistillata, 26, 53
Symphyllia nobilis, 54
Tubipora musica, 33
Turbinaria, 54; T. mesentarina, 47, 54
Xenia, 20, 49, 56, 162
Xeniidae, 56
cornetfish, 123, 129
cowries, 21, 84, 87–9
coxcomb oyster, 94
crabs, 72–7
Calliactis polypus, 74
Coenobita scavola, 77
Dardanus, 74, 77
Geograpsus crinipes, 74–7
Grapsidae, 74
Hapalocarcinidae, 74
Hapalocarcinus marsupialis, 74
Lupa pelagica, 74
Lybia leptocheilus, 72
Ocypodidae, 77
Pagurus asper, 74
Petrolisthes, 74
Pilumnus incanus, 72
Portunidae, 74
Quadrella, 72
Tetralia, 72
Thalamita, 74
Trapezia, 72, 74
Triactis producta, 72
Xanthiidae, 72
crinoids, 65, 71, 72
crocodile fish, 135
Crown-of-thorns starfish, 67–8, 77, 89, 128, 132
crustaceans, 71–9
Cryptocentrus spp., 138
Ctenophores, 61
cumacean shrimps, 78
cup coral, 43
curlyfin, 123
cuttlefish, 97
Cymatidae, 89
Cymatium pileare, 89
Cyphastrea, 54
Cypraea spp., 189
C. exusta, 83
C. pantherina, 87–9
Cypraeidae, 21, 84

Daedalus reef, 30
daisy coral, 54
damselfishes, 114–17, 138–9, 142, 149

Amphiprion bicinctus, 114
Chromis caeruleus, 29, 114;
C. dimidiatus, 114; C. ternatensis, 29, 114
Dascyllus aruanus, 26
Stegastes nigricans, 114
Dardanus, 74, 77
Dascyllus spp., 141
D. aruanus, 26, 117
D. trimaculatus, 142
Dasyatidae, 167
Dasyatus favus, 167
date-mussels, 94–6
Dendronephthya, 50, 56–7
Dendropoma maximum, 86–7
Diadema setosum, 68, 69, 78, 132, 171
Diodon histrix, 133
Discodoris, 92
Discovery deep, 12
dog whelks, 89
domino damselfish, 142
Donax spp., 93
donkeyfish, 110
Dosinia, 93
Drupa spp., 89
dugong, 37
Dunganab Bay, 29, 30, 94
dye shells, 89, 90

Eagle ray, 167, 169
echinoderms, 64–71
echinoids, 65, 68–70; for individual species see under sea urchins
Echinometra mathei, 69
echinopora, 54
Echinostrephus molaris, 69, 87
Echinothrix diadema, 70 171
eels, 167–9
El Akhawein reef, 30
Electric ray, 167
Elephant wrasse, 108, 149
Eliza Shoals, 30
Elysia grandiflora, 91–2
emperor-breams, 120–1
Engina mendicaria, 89
Epibulus insidiator, 108, 149
Epinephelus areolatus, 118, 121–3
E. fuscogutatus, 121–3
E. tauvina, 123
Eretmochelys imbricata, 37
Etelis spp., 120
Euborlasia quinquestriata, 98
Eurythoe complanata, 98

fan shells, 93
fanworms, 89, 91, 98–100
Fasciolaria trapezium, 89
Fasciolaridae, 89
Favia, 48, 54
Faviidae, 33, 48, 53, 54
Favites, 48, 54
F. species, 47
feather-stars, 65, 67, 71, 72
featherfish, 164
filefish, 130, 134
fire corals, 25, 48, 58–61
firefish, 164
Fistularia petimba, 123, 129–30
flask shells, 94
flathead, 134, 135
flatworms, 89, 97
Foraminifera, 103
Foul Bay, 29

Fromia ghardaqana, 67
Fungia, 45
F. echinata, 45
F. fungites, 43
Fungiacava eilatensis, 96
fusiliers, 153
Fusus polygonoides, 89, 90

Gafrarium pectinatum, 93
Galaxea fascicularis, 47, 54
Galeocerdi cuvieri, 158
gall-crabs, 74
gaping clams, 94
Gari spp., 93
Gastrochaenidae, 94
gastropods, 82–92
Gaterin gaterinus, 34, 118
Gena varia, 83
Geograpsus crinipes, 74–7
Gezeirat Zabargad, 30
ghost crabs, 77
giant clams, 96
gobies, 135, 138, 143
Gobiodon citrinus, 133, 135
goggle-eye, 126, 127, 131–2
Gomophia aegyptica, 67
Gomphosus caeruleus, 108, 149
Goniastrea, 33, 48, 54; G. retiformis, 25
Goniopora, 40, 53; G. planulata, 54
Gonodactylus, 78
Gorgonacea, 57
gorgonians, 53, 55
Gorgoniidae, 57
Grapsidae, 74
Great white shark, 158
green turtle, 37
Grey reef shark, 156
groupers, 118, 121–6, 149
Gymnothorax javanicus, 140, 167

Halichoeres centriquadratus, 106, 107
Halimeda, 64
Halodule univervis, 36
Halophila ovalis, 36
H. stipulacea, 36
Hammerhead sharks, 158
Hapalocarcinidae, 74
harps, 89
Harpa armoureta, 89
hatchetfishes, 127, 152–3
hawkfishes, 123, 124, 130
hawksbill turtle, 37
Heniochus intermedius, 31, 113, 143
hermatypic corals, 52
hermit crabs, 74, 77
Hermodice carunculata, 98
Heterocentrotus mamillatus, 69, 70
Heteroxenia, 56
Hexabranchus sanguineus, 92
Hexacorallia, 61
Hodeida, 29
Hoekia monticulariae, 79
Holocentridae, 130
Holocentrus spp., 130
H. spinifer, 124, 130
Holothuria atra, 70
holothuroids, 65, 70–1; for individual species see under sea-cucumbers
horn shells, 84–6
humbugs, 117
Hump-headed wrasse, 86, 87, 106, 108
Hydnophora, 54
Hydrozoa, 61